How to Live With—and Without—
ANGER

How to Live
With—and Without—
ANGER

ALBERT ELLIS, Ph.D.

READER'S DIGEST PRESS
Distributed by
Thomas Y. Crowell Company
New York   1977

Manufactured in the United States of America

LIBRARY OF CONGRESS CATALOGING IN PUBLICATION DATA

Ellis, Albert, 1913–
    How to live with—and without—anger.

    Bibliography: p.
    Includes index.
    1. Anger.   2. Rational-emotive psychotherapy.
I. Title.
BF575.A5E44   1977   158'.1   77-1251
ISBN 0-88349-127-3

10 9 8 7 6 5 4 3 2 1

OTHER BOOKS BY ALBERT ELLIS

Growth Through Reason (with Ben N. Ard, Jr., John M. Gullo, Paul A. Hauck, Maxie C. Maultsby, Jr., and H. Jon Geis)

Executive Leadership: A Rational Approach

Sex and Sex Education: A Bibliography (with Flora C. Seruya and Susan Losher)

Murder and Assassination (with John M. Gullo)

How to Master Your Fear of Flying

The Civilized Couple's Guide to Extramarital Adventure

The Sensuous Person: Critique and Corrections

Humanistic Psychotherapy: The Rational-Emotive Approach

A New Guide to Rational Living (with Robert A. Harper)

Sex and the Liberated Man

How to Stop Procrastinating and Start Living

Rational-Emotive Therapy: Handbook of Theory and Practice (with Russell Grieger)

MONOGRAPHS BY ALBERT ELLIS

An Introduction to the Principles of Scientific Psychoanalysis

New Approaches to Psychotherapy Techniques

What is Psychotherapy?

The Place of Value
in the Practice of Psychotherapy

FOR JANET
with love

Acknowledgments

Just about all published books, these days, result from collaborations between the author and several other important contributors. So with this one. Although I take full responsibility for all its ideas, it would never have achieved its present form without the diligent work and rewriting skill of Byron L. Bowyer. Nor would it have gone through press so beautifully, and with such unusual dispatch, without the continual valuable suggestions and sage advice of Susanne W. Howard, my editor at Reader's Digest Press. Finally, Robert H. Moore, a staff member of the Florida branch of the Institute for Rational Living at Clearwater, has once again helped me put this book into consistent E-prime. I want to thank all these collaborators for their far-beyond-the-call-of-duty aid and encouragement.

Introduction

Why another book on anger? Although numerous books exist today which tell us how to deal with anger, none of them seems to work effectively and efficiently in all situations. Generally these books support one of two positions. Some advise you to assume a passive, nonresistant attitude when others treat you unfairly. Such an attitude may give people the impression that you very much control yourself and the situation, but it hardly will help you achieve anything beyond this type of meaningless self-flattery. And many people may assume that your passivity and acceptance of their unfair treatment toward you means you have no objection to their treating you shabbily or unfairly. Therefore, they will have no reason to change their attitude and may continue to mistreat you. Your passivity will give others a green light, so to speak, to deal with you as they may please.

On the other hand, a multitude of books advise you to openly and freely give vent to and to express fully your feelings of anger and rage. They fail to point out that when you do this to others, it will help to make them angry with you and they will respond with resentment. You can easily see that both of the above-mentioned approaches have many weak points and that neither of them succeeds in presenting an effective solution to the problems of anger.

The solution? Epictetus, a remarkably wise Stoic philosopher, pointed out some two thousand years ago that you *choose* to overreact to the obnoxious behavior of others while you could more wisely choose to react in a very different manner. Rational-Emotive Therapy (RET) has found that by following the age-old wisdom of the philosophers and by combining it with the most modern methods of psychotherapy, anyone can learn to reduce or eliminate self-defeating, angry reactions and to live successfully with feelings of this nature, which he or she may still experience.

Can you do this by yourself? Yes, you definitely can—as Dr. Robert Harper and I particularly show in a previous book, *A New Guide to Rational Living.* Here I will explain exactly how you create your own *philosophy of anger* by consciously and unconsciously subscribing to absolutistic, command-oriented thinking and exactly how, by changing the thoughts, feelings, and behaviors which underlie and accompany your rage, you can greatly reduce that rage. Through careful attention to the RET theory, you can learn effectively to deal with your anger in a remarkably short period of time.

We find a unique theory of language known as E-prime central to Rational-Emotive Therapy. E-prime stems from the work of D. David Bourland, Jr., a follower of the noted general semanticist Alfred Korzybski. In the linguistic formula (E-prime = E-e), E represents all the words of the standard English language, while e represents all the forms of the verb "to be," such as "is," "was," "am," "has been," "being," etc. The theory shows that when we use any form of the verb "to be" as a primary predicate, we tend to overgeneralize and thus distort the actual meaning of the statement or thought. For instance, in the sentence "John is mentally ill," we can divide the sentence into two parts: the subject ("John") and the predicate ("is mentally ill"). Note that nothing in the predicate portion of the sentence in any way qualifies or limits John's condition. So if we examine the concept more closely, we may draw the following conclusions about John—all at once and independent of each other.

1. John exhibits only mentally ill behavior.
2. John will exhibit this type of behavior in all situations at all times.
3. If John should stop displaying this type of behavior, it would contradict the truth of the original statement ("John is mentally ill") and all the other statements that follow it.

In other words, we connect John with mentally ill in such a way that we have difficulty breaking or separating the two concepts ("John" and "mentally ill"), and by neglecting to differentiate or qualify these two separate concepts, we allow ourselves to overgeneralize to the extent that we make the two associations almost synonymous.

If, on the other hand, we speak more carefully and concern ourselves with rendering an accurate evaluation of John's condition, we may say that "John often exhibits mentally ill behavior" or "John exhibits mentally ill behavior." Perhaps this distinction from the broad—and blurred—"John is mentally ill" appears slight and mere nitpicking, but nonetheless, we see that by qualifying the verb, we avoid leaving the impression that all we can expect from John is pathological behavior, while we still clearly state that we can expect this behavior from John from time to time.

How, then, does this fine distinction affect our thinking

and our actions? Language does much more than express how we feel or what we see. It not only comprises a tool for communication but also the mode by which most people think. Research and studies have shown us that the development of thought and language have a direct relationship with the ability to judge and respond to situations in a mature and rational manner. Thus, Rational-Emotive Therapy attempts to provide an understanding of our tendency to overgeneralize (and to abuse the verb "to be") and to show the tremendous influence that those tendencies can have on our actions and emotional lives.

I hope that the above discussion will seem much clearer as we examine various RET approaches to the many problems related to anger. Throughout *How to Live With—and Without—Anger* I will use and from time to time refer back to the principle of E-prime, and in each instance, I feel confident that the reader will more clearly understand the relationship among E-prime, thought, action, and the RET principles which teach you how to help yourself deal with and control many of the difficult situations that unfortunately occur all too often in our everyday lives.

Albert Ellis, Ph.D.
Institute for Advanced Study in Rational Psychotherapy
45 East 65th Street
New York, New York

Contents

"What disturbs people's minds is not events but their judgments on events."

Epictetus,
FIRST CENTURY A.D.

1

Must You
Feel Angry?

You'd better face the hard reality that situations that frustrate or prevent you from attaining your goals and from getting what you want from life really do exist. But *must* you feel angry? Have you no choice but to anger yourself at these everyday "horrors"?

Most psychologists agree that you absolutely must feel anger. They see the newborn infant as expressing emotions comparable to anger and rage in the first hours of life. And throughout all ages or periods of development many humans confront almost daily their own feelings of anger and those of other people with whom they come in contact. Most authorities in the field of psychology today say you need your anger to protect yourself from the onslaughts of a hostile and aggressive world. If you, say these authorities, do not always remain on your guard, you will stay especially vulnerable to others who will dominate and exploit you, jeopardize your freedom and property, and take advantage of your passivity or so-called good nature by abusing you for their own personal gain with no regard to your welfare. Psychologists with this point of view tell you that if you do not prepare to fight for what you want, you only have the alternative of remaining passive and silent when others take advantage of and prevent you from achieving your goals. Thus, most authorities today generally leave you with one of two alternatives for dealing with anger:

> Feel the anger but sit on it, squelch it, deny and repress it.
> Feel the anger and freely express it.

Squelching your anger doesn't get you much of anywhere and unexpressed rage will do you far more harm than candidly and freely expressed feelings. The *hydraulic theory* states that anger and other emotions have a tendency to increase in intensity, to expand under pressure like steam in a kettle, so that if you squelch your emotions, if you don't give free vent to them, you run the risk of doing some real harm to yourself. Real physical harm such as stomach ulcers, high blood pressure, or other sometimes more severe psychosomatic reactions. In addition, refraining from giving honest expression to your feelings—keeping these feelings pent up inside you—doesn't help you lose your anger. Quite the contrary. You will, in all probability, feel much worse. For your anger hasn't gone away, but stays right there in your "gut." And now you can easily turn overly critical of yourself for not standing up for your rights with those who have caused the injustice.

Conversely, if you let yourself feel authentically angry and let others know about your feelings, you may frequently encounter problems of quite another nature. For people will receive your free expression of anger in most instances as an outwardly aggressive or hostile action, and will probably close themselves off from you and defensively respond to you with *further* hostility.

Some therapists in the field have attempted to solve the

problem with still another alternative, what they call *creative aggression* (or *constructive anger*). This differs from the above *free expression* method in that you express yourself more controllably and hope (often against hope!) that others will willingly listen to your point of view.

In the following example I will attempt to illustrate the dynamics of the other theories and then, using the same example throughout the book, will investigate the alternatives and solutions that Rational-Emotive Therapy offers. I am confident that if you pay close attention to these principles, you will see that you can deal with problems relating to anger and other emotions effectively and efficiently by use of the RET guidelines.

Let us say that I have promised to share an apartment with you as a roommate and to share the rent, provided you fix up and furnish the place. This seems agreeable to you. You go to a good deal of trouble and personal expense to keep your part of the bargain. At the last minute I inform you that I have made other plans and cannot, will not keep my part of the agreement. You feel extremely angry with me; not only have you gone to considerable expense to keep your part of the agreement, but you experience great inconvenience in that you must at the last minute look for another roommate.

You may at first keep your feelings of anger to yourself. But because you have those feelings, unexpressed, your underlying resentment greatly interferes with our friendship. So you see that nothing gets resolved, that your seething anger interferes with many of your other activities as well, and that this solution won't work.

You decide to confront me with your feelings, to *free express* them. "Look here," you say, "I won't have you treating me like this! After all, you did say you'd share the apartment with me after I had fixed it up and furnished it. I never would have done that had you not agreed to share it with me in the first place. You've clearly done me wrong, and acted really rottenly. How could you have done a thing like that to a friend? I've never done anything so nasty to you, and I really don't see how you can expect anyone's friendship if you treat people so terribly."

Or given the convenience of my having the capacity and willingness to play it with you, you use *creative aggression* and thus you "prepare" me for what will come. Receiving my permission to open up about your feelings, you go ahead with the expression of your anger.

Although all of what you have on your mind may prove correct—from your point of view—your presentation of it (either through the free expression method or through creative aggression) *can* do more harm than good and, ultimately, can have quite a negative influence on your getting what you want out of this situation—or of life. Both approaches focus on my (or someone else's) wrong, even if creative aggression allows for a softening of the blow. Through that focus, they can almost not fail to set the stage for additional problems.

By openly criticizing me for my "outrageous" behavior, you can actually strongly encourage me to *defend* that same behavior, thereby exerting my "right" to it, my independence. Whereas I will not likely feel the need to hold onto my "outrageous" behavior if you allow me to reach critical conclusions about it on my own. Thus, steps I would then take away from it and toward more just treatment of you (and others) would constitute real steps symbolizing *true* growth, authentic change in my behavior.

Remember, also, that most people have strong self-downing tendencies. When you point out to them an error or an unappealing characteristic in their personality, they tend to carry the implications further than you even intended. Hence, from your critical remarks, no matter how well, how creatively put, they still experience pains of guilt or self-recrimination, and will frequently attempt to establish a similar set of feelings in you, their "attacker." We'd better acknowledge these very real problems as inherent in either of the two approaches that recommend expression of the anger. Nonetheless, acknowledging these problems still does not solve *your* problem: what *do* you do with your anger?

So far we have seen holding in anger, not expressing it, as a poor idea. Yet we have also seen that the free expression of it creates a whole complex of other counterproductive problems. Further, we have noted that creative aggression seems a more workable solution but that it still shares some of the same problems. Another alternative—that of *Christian forgiveness*—involves the turning of the other cheek. But in this aggressive, often hostile world in which we live, this seems somewhat impractical. People may feel far less intimidated by you and thus all the more tempted to take advantage of your passivity masked as "good nature." You may behave beautifully, but unfortunately, that does not mean that others will respect you and treat you as you treat them.

After examining the above alternatives in dealing with the problem of anger, we may state that although each approach may, from time to time, work in a given situation, you cannot effectively implement any one of them in all situations. Further, each one of these approaches has many serious and destructive drawbacks in its practical application. So let us look for a formula that will allow people to deal with difficult situations and get what they want without damaging their own integrity or exciting anger and hostile feelings in others.

The following chapters will introduce a method that can be used in virtually all situations and that encounters none of the drawbacks associated with the other approaches already discussed. If you read carefully and give your full attention to the formulas presented in this book, if you take the time and trouble to think seriously about, experiment with, and test out these new concepts in your own life, and if you energetically and conscientiously practice them over a period of time, I believe that you, too, will notice and enjoy the changes that RET can help bring about in your life, as so many of my clients and readers already have.

2

How You Create
Your Own Anger:
The ABCs of RET

The ABCs of RET (Rational-Emotive Therapy) can give you a far more satisfactory or what I call elegant approach to the problem of dealing with your anger. Not a magical formula, quite the contrary, since RET concerns itself with seeking solutions and dealing with all your problems in a realistic manner. Naturally I don't claim that no such thing as magic or mysticism can exist, for theoretically anything may prove possible. RET theory prefers to stick with hardheaded facts of reality—not with airy theories. And we keep looking for the facts until we find them.

How exactly did the theory of RET evolve? What does RET have that makes it different from and more effective than the other forms of psychotherapy?

The basic principles of RET have evolved from my own extensive clinical research and experience, further verified by my associates and numerous experiments done in this area. During my career as a psychotherapist I have had occasion to use many different techniques in treating my many clients. These years of intense clinical experience and research have shown me and my associates that most of the more classical analytic approaches wind up ineffective, inefficient, and fail to meet the problems of most people who seek therapy. I say this from my own personal experience. Although our vast field incorporates many techniques and approaches to helping people, I have found most of these methods too expensive and time-consuming for both clients and therapists. Naturally, emotional problems themselves wreak enormous costs and if these long drawn-out types of therapy show positive and lasting results, the investment seems well worth it. But, alas, this does not, in my opinion and from my own experience, appear true.

I have drawn many of the important principles of RET from the wisdom of philosophy as well as from the most modern psychological advances of our age. Since my youth I have made the in-depth study of philosophy a hobby of mine and by incorporating these principles into my therapeutic approach, I discovered that my clients could achieve more effective results in far less time than I had hoped for while using the other approaches. I found that by my presenting a philosophical as well as a psychological analysis, the client could enjoy the fruits of two sciences and achieve positive and lasting results from our therapeutic efforts.

Although I'd naturally advise your consulting a competent rational therapist when you have a serious problem, I have found that using RET, you can efficiently "therapize" yourself with little outside help. In this book I will explain how you create your own anger *philosophically*—by consciously or unconsciously subscribing to absolutistic, command-oriented thinking. If you can understand exactly how to control and operate this thought system yourself, you will enable yourself, with the guidance of this book, considerably to undercut and change many of your counterproductive and destructive responses to your anger. Other methods fail precisely here, in that they tend to generalize and depersonalize the problems of anger. RET has designed a scientific formula in which the steps toward a solution remain effectively workable no matter what the circumstances surrounding the situation.

Perhaps the most distressing fault that I realized while using the more classical techniques of psychotherapy: upon termination of many years of therapy, the clients still could not confront life's difficult situations on their own without the continued help of their therapist. I sincerely felt that after all that time and money my clients certainly deserved more helpful results. Rather than continue with these methods, which I saw as ineffecutal, I began to experiment with some ideas of my own. By combining this philosophical knowledge with various approaches used in therapy, I established the fundamental principles of RET. With rewarding results. For instead of depending on the therapist for giving them, with other therapeutic approaches, meaningless analytic interpretations, clients now had a realistic conceptual perspective with which to think and experiment. In a relatively short time they began to show a more rapid and lasting progress than I had seen with any of the other methods that I had previously used.

With most of my clients, I use realistic examples to help them work through their problems. Here, for the sake of clarity I shall stick to one consistent example throughout the book; so we shall continue with the illustration already introduced in Chapter 1. I have promised to share an apartment with you if you go ahead and fix it up and furnish it. We have agreed that from then on we will share the expenses. You have so far lived up to your half of the agreement, but at the last minute, without ample notice or explanation, I withdraw from my portion of the agreement. You become angry with me.

How, by using RET methods, can you overcome your hostility?

We begin by locating *C*—the *Emotional* (or *Behavioral*) *Consequence:* your anger.

Next we look for *A*—the *Activating Event* (or *Activating Experience*): I failed to uphold my portion of an important agreement between us.

As we look at *A* and *C*, it may appear that *A* causes *C*. RET theory assumes however and surprisingly enough, that although the Activating Event directly contributes to the Emotional Consequence, it does not really *cause* it. We do not always easily see the dynamics of cause and effect. Yet if we look closely at this relationship between *A* and *C*—as we will do throughout this book—we will find other factors involved and find that although my withdrawing from our agreement may have inconvenienced and disappointed you greatly—in that my actions have prevented you from getting what you wanted—my action alone does not necessarily lead to your feeling angry with me.

If we conclude that *C* directly results from *A*, then we would have to assume that whenever we encountered any one particular *A*, we would always expect a particular *C*. For instance, we know that water boils at one temperature and freezes at another and we find this true for all situations involving water and temperature. Yet when people and various situations interact together, such laws of causality do not hold true. Most of us know occurrences in which we have felt surprised by a person's reaction to a given situation. For instance, we have often heard of victims of brutal crimes who, instead of cooperating with the police and courts to bring their assailant to justice, have done just the opposite. They have gone so far as actually help their assailant avoid prosecution. If we examine one hundred people, all victims of the same crime, we would surely find a large variation of responses among these people. Some would act in the above manner, others would obsess themselves with the arrest and prosecution of the perpetrator, and yet others would respond at various points between these two extremes. An Emotional Consequence, although affected by an Activating Experience, does not directly and exclusively result from it.

Another important point to keep in mind: we do, in fact, have choices and control over our responses to every situation and our feelings and individual responses often remain much more within our control than we realize at the time. The more awareness we have of the existing alternatives, the more likely our ability to consider the situation in its proper perspective before we take action. The intermediate thought process which we carry on *between* A and C constitutes a process of evaluation in which we make a decision that will determine our response. The more aware we make ourselves of this intermediate phase, the better chance we have of making a choice which increases our likelihood of attaining our goals. Through such a choice we minimize the possibility of frustrating or complicating our progress by impulsive behavior.

In their own terminology, the sciences of linguistics, philosophy, and psychology have each attempted some explanation of the dynamics of thought and cognition insofar as they affect our Emotional Consequences. The difference in perspectives of these disciplines has tended to obscure, rather than to clarify, the questions regarding this relationship. This is not to say that little or no progress has occurred in this highly complex area, for each science has over the years developed increasingly more important facts about thinking and behavior. Perhaps the lay person has the most difficulty in grasping the fact that all of us carry out this process in an unconscious or automatic manner. We rarely give much thought to our thought processes, and therefore, we seldom make ourselves aware of the influence our thoughts have upon our actions and reactions in various situations.

You, like every other person, have structured during your development a *Belief System* which you rely upon to assist you in making judgments and evaluating situations, ideas, people, and events, again no matter how unconsciously. Athough you have your own personal belief or value system, you also have many beliefs relatively consistent with others in your given society or culture. Yet in some important ways the Belief Systems of different cultures significantly differ. Social scientists have repeatedly shown us that throughout both history and cultural development the norms and values of any society or societies vary greatly both from a historical and cultural point of view. We continually discover that customs and behavioral patterns that we judge barbaric and crude exist in civilized cultures today. We also know that an individual may hold a number of different Belief Systems at once, that cultural norms change during an individual's lifetime, and that individuals can either motivate themselves to change or get called upon by their society to change, sometimes radically, their feelings and opinions about many things in order to remain happy and productive in an ever-changing world.

As each society establishes sets of beliefs, values, and norms that bind its inhabitants together cooperatively, its teachers and religious and political leaders, as well as its parental figures, pass on guidelines which serve as foundations for the development of our own personal Belief Systems. From this we can easily see that our individual Belief Systems include ideas not entirely our own. Much of what we think good or bad, right or wrong, we have imbibed from our elders.

Even though you (and all of us) have your beliefs influenced by your environment, no necessary consistency or universal norm exists regarding Belief Systems. No action or person rates as either good or bad in and of itself, but we judge all actions by somewhat arbitrary and changeable standards. Hence, these judgments only indirectly relate to the person or action involved.

Having shown to some degree the ways in which your Belief Systems can influence emotional responses at point C, we turn our attention to B, which in our RET theory represents, quite appropriately, the Belief System. Before advancing a detailed explanation of B, let us clarify one main point. Although B exerts an extremely strong influence upon your reactions at C, we'd better not see B as the only factor in determining C but always remember that A still has a good degree of influence upon your reactions. Your reactions at C, then, invariably follow or equal a combination of A and B. As we shall see later, you often cannot realistically affect any major influence over A although you can determinedly try!

To take our discussion one step further, your conception of reality does not merely comprise your responses to external stimuli. This conception, which generally correlates with the rational world, instead stems from a vast storehouse of your previous experiences and your personal beliefs and associations related to these experiences. Every action you make follows a series of thoughts, no matter how spontaneous these actions or reactions appear. You tend to avoid or flee those situations that you consider repulsive, harmful, or distasteful, while you seek those that seem to you desirable.

Accepting the above and relating it to our previous statements concerning the differences between individual Belief Systems, we discover that no experience has any set value in and of itself. Your thoughts, your beliefs, remain extremely important factors in determining both your feelings and your responses to any given situation. Moreover if we accept that no (Activating) Experience rates as either good or bad in and of itself, we accept that an intermediate process determines our judgments beyond the Activating Experiences.

Using the RET model and once knowing the content of A and C, I have found it easy to locate quickly and accurately the important details about almost anyone's Belief System. From this point I can show people how to deal with life's difficult situations and teach them to use the RET model themselves. Of course, literally thousands of Activating Experiences and Emotional Consequences exist. Yet RET has discovered that in almost any situation you may place B in one of a few categories. Once aware of both A and C, you can find B with little difficulty—as I shall show you further on in this book.

By starting with C (Consequences), you learn that your feeling of anger (or any other self-defeating feeling) results from a "negative" experience at A. You can also see that the Belief System has strongly influenced these feelings at C. At this point RET seeks to help you discover exactly what beliefs contribute to these negative feelings and show you how you can alter any of the beliefs by examining their unreality and irrationality.

3

The Insanity
of Anger

In this chapter I will attempt to show how your rational and irrational Beliefs fall into only a few major categories and how you can learn to recognize and amend these beliefs where necessary. We have learned that in RET we start at C. Thus, to give as clear an explanation as possible of your Belief System, let us first consider an important point about C which we have so far neglected.

In RET we can divide all feelings into two major categories. At point C (Consequence), we have what we call:

Appropriate feelings
and
Inappropriate feelings

Although no strict or inflexible definition exists for either of these categories, we might simply say that an *appropriate* feeling consists of attitudes or approaches that will help you get what you want and help you achieve the major goals of your life—more precisely, feelings and behavior that will help you remain alive and live in a reasonably happy and productive manner without an overabundance of frustration or pain resulting from obstacles which life will inevitably place in your way. It follows, then, that an *inappropriate* feeling has a tendency to sabotage or inhibit you from achieving that which you desire from life.

We can also divide your Belief System into two basic categories:

> *Rational* beliefs (rB)
> and
> *Irrational* beliefs (iB)

Let us begin our discussion proper with your rational beliefs (rBs). We may safely assume that all human beings certainly have a set of rational beliefs. Our cooperative interaction with other people, along with our own personal conduct in relation to the objects we encounter in our everyday lives, strongly testifies to the fact that almost all of us have strong sets of rational beliefs that we use to control and direct our behavior. Otherwise, we could not expect that the amount of progress that the human race has made during its history would have reached the point that it has today. As noted in Chapter 2, we often learn our rational Beliefs from our elders, and they vary greatly in many respects throughout history and from culture to culture. Although great thinkers do bring about great changes in our laws and thoughts, the major guidelines for civilized norms and Belief Systems have undergone a process of evolution just as our bodies and cultures have changed throughout history. Human development and the development of our Belief Systems constitute processes in which many factors interact.

Generally every time something happens to you at *A* (Activating Experience), you respond to the situation in one of two modes: rationally or irrationally. Although your response, under normal circumstances, results from the combination of both modes, you can sometimes affect your actions more by one mode than the other. For instance, you may totally ignore the rational Beliefs and respond to a situation on a *purely* irrational level. Your irrational Beliefs about an event may have, thus, had an extremely strong, "winning" influence over your response.

Let us return now to our illustration and see if we can locate your rational Beliefs. We know that you feel angry with me at C due to my behavior at A, in that I unfairly withdrew from an agreement important to your happiness. Because of this situation, you may perhaps say to yourself something like: "What a bad thing he has done to me. How terrible of him to treat me in such a shoddy and inconsiderate manner!" This may seem a rational or reasonable statement. Nonetheless, we can see, on reflection, that although you appear to express only one idea here, you in fact have two ideas, each of which you'd better consider separately.

"What a bad thing he has done to me." (Meaning, "He has seriously frustrated my plans, and not only have his actions greatly inconvenienced me, but he has also placed me in a rather difficult situation.") The observation that I have done a "bad thing" to you seems both accurate and *appropriate*.

"How terrible of him to treat me in such a shoddy and inconsiderate manner." Here you see what I have done as "terrible," and you wind up with an irrational belief. As we shall see later, this idea of thinking of an action or event as "terrible" or "horrible" proves *inappropriate* and irrational because it may do a good deal of damage to your goals and happiness.

By allowing your *iB*s to take precedent over your *rB*s, you do not give sufficient attention to the full reality behind the Activating Experience. Your neglecting to contemplate, in advance, the possible outgrowths of your response at *C* (Consequence), puts you in a position of acting in a self-destructive manner and can lead to the same kind of problems that we saw with both the free expression method and the "sit-on-your-anger" approach. Rational-Emotive Therapy firmly believes that unless you have the awareness of and ability to change your irrational beliefs, you will continue to have difficult problems in dealing with your anger and other defeating emotions. RET also maintains the importance of changing your feelings at *C*, and we give strong consideration to helping you learn how to modify your behavior. *Yet RET consistently states that if you want to change your feelings and your actions in the quickest, most efficient and effective way, you'd better pay particular attention to changing your Belief System.*

At *A* we know that I have seemingly treated you unfairly by withdrawing from our agreement.

- At rB, your rational Belief System, we have discovered that you believe "I don't like that. I wish he hadn't treated me so shabbily."
- At aC, your appropriate (Consequence) feeling, you experience emotions of disappointment, displeasure, and discomfort.
- • *Rational: (don't like) and Appropriate: (disappointment)*

Yet we find that at iC, your inappropriate Consequence or feeling, you experience anger with me as well as your disappointment. You find the anger unmanageable and self-defeating, which therefore determines it *in*appropriate (it has a tendency to sabotage or inhibit you from achieving what you want in life). Using the RET method, we now seek the irrational Belief (iB) that led to your inappropriate Consequence (anger).

•• *Irrational: (?) and Inappropriate:* (anger)

In locating your iBs we use the method of logical, empirical checking, designed to discover any illogical, *nonempirical* ideas you might hold at *B*. By putting the case into the RET framework, an RET clinician can discover your rBs and iBs simply through a knowledge of your feelings and behavior at both points *A* and *C*. Logically, for example, your irrational Belief can hardly exist in the idea "How obnoxious of him to lead me on like that and then withdraw in that manner." This idea *does* make sense, as just about everyone would agree. Also your viewing such behavior as merely obnoxious will likely lead you to feel not anger but rather disappointment. So in continuing to look at your ideas about such behavior, we may discover that you have said or thought, "I view it as *awful* that you acted in such an irresponsible manner; this seems most unfair and *terrible!*" Although this may not at first glance appear very irrational or illogical, you have, in fact, arrived at one of the four irrational statements that angry people often make:

You have told yourself that you find it *awful, horrible,* or *terrible* that I have treated you in this manner. You have equated unfairness or injustice with *horror* and failed to distinguish between the two.

As I have just indicated, RET states that one can discover the nature of one's Belief Systems by knowing the facts at points *A* and *C*. People have a relatively limited number of emotions which they experience, and these feelings fall within a few major headings, and certain thoughts connect with certain emotions. People teach themselves to use these thoughts to evoke emotions. As we have stressed before, your Belief System makes it possible to apply value judgments such as good or bad, right or wrong, to any experience. Here again you can see a strong relationship or interaction between thinking and feeling.

In fact, one of the main RET hypotheses states that you seem to feel what you think or expect to feel—and not what you actually do experience. You prejudice your feelings about something with your views of what you believe you should feel. Moreover, although RET fully admits the transactional nature of human thoughts and feelings, it holds that in most cases—not all—your thoughts remain paramount over what we call feelings. Therefore, you can more quickly, easily, and importantly change your feelings as you change your thinking than you can change your thinking by modifying your feelings.

Just how much *do* your feelings about something cause you to change your thinking? You frequently know that you desire to act in a manner which you believe highly undesirable. It often happens that when such feelings become extremely strong or urgent, you may act in a manner contrary to your own personal beliefs. When you act this way, you often rationalize so as to alter, at least temporarily, certain beliefs. But once you gratify your feelings through actions, you frequently revert back to your former beliefs, and this will help you to feel guilty because you did not really change those beliefs but merely laid them aside temporarily to allow yourself to act in a certain way. Hence, we see that your thoughts may alter your feelings, yet we can also see that you often only temporarily make these alterations or use them in very specific situations.

The following four irrational statements represent fairly accurately the main ideas that angry people generally hold:

1. "How *awful* for you to have treated me so unfairly."
2. "I *can't stand* your treating me in such an irresponsible and unjust manner."
3. "You *should not, must not* behave that way toward me."
4. "Because you have acted in that manner toward
   me, I find you a *terrible person* who deserves
   nothing good in life, and who should get punished
   for treating me so."

A direct relationship exists between these four statements. Note that besides the negativity contained in each
of the statements, they include another unifying factor—
the tendency to merge the action with the person or to
equate the evaluation of the person's negative action with
the whole person. We saw this same type of overgeneralization in the E-prime theory whereby, in the sentence
"John *is* mentally ill," we assigned John, once and for all,
inseparably, to the concept "mentally ill" as though we
cannot reasonably expect any other forms of behavior
from him.

This failure to separate a person from his action implies
that only an (x) person can act (x) and that all (x) acts must
get performed by (x) people. Further, and more specifically, any person who does anything that any other person
deems bad or unjust must *be* a bad person. If a good
person performs good acts, then he can *never* do anything
bad, for he *is* a good person and capable of only good acts.
If a bad person performs bad acts, he can *never* do anything good, for he *is* a bad person and can perform only
bad acts.

The above argument holds true to the laws of logic
throughout, yet we'd better wisely remember that logical

truths and actual truth in reality can, and often do, as in this case, exist as two different sets of facts. We can see the logic of the above statements, yet we may just as easily see their irrationality. We know realistically that often people upheld as "good and respectable" often do gross injustices to others; conversely, we have seen people who have acted in an extremely just and fair manner in a number of situations labeled as "bad people" by almost all members of society. Thus, we know that logical thinking often proves false to life, although it may hold true to the rules of logic.

In the particular perspective through which we view this problem of your angering yourself at me and viewing *me* as rotten when I do a rotten act (unfairly break our apartment-sharing agreement) you had better attempt to locate the primary or underlying irrationality to your feeling of anger at point *C*. Using what you have learned about the relationships existing between person and action, you see your underlying irrationality consists of making a false association between me and my action, that you have not effected the separation of the two. So although RET holds that there seem no absolute laws or rules that will apply to all people in every situation, you may still use its simple *rule of thumb* for discerning the difference between *rB* and *iB* in your Belief System:

> *Beliefs remain rational so long as they do not extend an evaluation of the action into an evaluation of the person.* And further: *you remain rational so long as you view the action in a limited way: by the effect that it has upon you who experience it. The evaluation of a person can only legitimately arise from evaluating all his or her acts over an entire lifetime.*

We cannot judge an individual's Belief System as *totally* irrational unless we find this person to have either a most severe psychotic disorder or severe mental retardation, yet surely every person alive holds an irrational Belief about something from time to time. People's Belief Systems as a whole greatly determine their feelings and reactions; and remembering that that Belief System can maintain rBs and iBs simultaneously, we see that the Emotional Consequence—of an Activating Experience—whether inappropriate Consequence (iC) or appropriate Consequence (aC)—depends upon the ratio of influence between iB and rB.

If, at point A, you feel inconvenienced or disappointed by a situation, then you may have a rational or appropriate feeling. But your emotion of anger at the person causing the inconvenience shows (at C) irrationality because you had better separate the evaluation of the action and the evaluation of the person even though most people do not make this separation and by confusing a damnable act with a damnable person, make themselves needlessly angry. One might expect you to feel disappointed, inconvenienced, or discouraged at C by these unfair actions, but to feel angry and hostile, to assume that the perpetrator of these actions *is* terrible proves irrational.

For the sake of clarity, we'd better look at the causal relationship between your iBs and your anger. Although we have no incontrovertible proof that these iBs constitute the most direct or even the only cause of anger, by looking at the intrinsic relationship between thought and feeling we find a very close connection between the two. We have seen that using the RET model, we have been able to point out to people their own iBs and, further, to teach them how to eliminate them. In the process, we discovered that their anger diminished and disappeared.

While I would find it of great interest to investigate the transactional relationship between thinking and feeling, the huge amount of data that I would have to consider in order to render a clear and complete resolution to the discussion would go far beyond the scope of this book. Suffice it to say that although I only present RET as a theory, I know from clinical experience and from a mass of experimental data (summarized in the *Rational-Emotive Therapy Handbook* that I authored with Dr. Russell Grieger) that it works. While research continues and we await conclusive evidence concerning the exact nature of the relationship between thinking and feeling, we do best to content ourselves with the effective working theory that we now have.

Having established two aspects to your individual Belief System—rational and irrational—you confront another problem. Earlier we showed that humans have a basically rational nature; for if they had not, they could never have progressed to the point they have reached today. Why, then, should such rational animals have irrational beliefs (as our theory states) and act in accordance with them since they help destroy and contradict both their nature and their desire to get what they want? Many psychological theorists have debated this and similar questions, and unfortunately, few acceptable answers have come to light. We can perhaps best approach the question by dividing human actions into two categories that seem present in every action: the *primary* aspect and the *secondary* (or component) aspect. Using our illustration, I will attempt to explain the two of them.

When you made the decision to enter into the agreement with me, you perhaps felt that by making this arrangement, you would have what you considered a good living circumstance and would therefore feel happy. As your primary motive, you strove for happiness and contentment. This desire for happiness, as well as your arrangement with me seem rational—designed to help you get what you want. When I withdrew from the arrangement, you experienced frustration. You did not get what you wanted. Now, if we had never reached an agreement in the first place, you would have felt frustrated with the situation and perhaps disappointed, but you would not have felt angry with me. You would probably have simply judged my action as "bad" or undesirable. But now that I have withdrawn from our *agreement*, and although you remain in the same position as you would have been had we never entered into the agreement in the beginning, you feel incensed with me.

What makes you disappointed in one instance and angry in another even though your situation in regards to sharing an apartment with me stays the same in both— e.g., we *won't* share one? Because as we have discovered, your irrational beliefs identified my *person* with my bad *action*. Why? For as we have noted and will examine further, your anger sabotages your own goals.

If we look closely, we learn that you made the agreement to get out of a situation in which you felt unhappy, so you more or less used me to get what you wanted. Perhaps we might view your anger with me in the same manner, in that you utilize my bad action or shortcoming to blame me for your situation. In making an agreement with me, you felt able to take some kind of action to relieve yourself from an undesirable situation. My withdrawal from that agreement removes the possibility of my helping you get what you want.

So, just as you initially took a secondary action (making the agreement) to achieve a primary motive (happiness and contentment), you perhaps keep doing the same thing now—through your anger. Your anger can at least make you feel that you act in some way that will relieve you from the frustration of your situation. In other words, humans might use irrational Beliefs ("How *awful* for him to have treated me so unfairly" etc.) to achieve secondary gains. By feeling angry with me, you can blame me for your situation, and you can also give yourself a false assurance that you keep doing something to relieve yourself. By fighting me for treating you in a manner you consider unjust, you do not have to confront the original dissatisfaction; hence, you have an illusion that you actively do something about your situation.

You may derive an infinite variety of secondary gains through anger, such as the one above. An understanding of secondary gains provides some explanation of why rational humans hold irrational Beliefs, why all humans at times allow their *iB*s to influence them and hence act inappropriately.

While helping answer one question, we have raised another. For if you derive some secondary gain from your anger, why should you make any attempt to rid youself of anger? Through our understanding of secondary gains, we realize that every action has its *intention*. Each action you carry through or that it occurs to you to carry through, has at its base a specific aim or goal. For instance, we have put forth the theory that anger facilitates some secondary gain in that it relieves you from the feelings resulting from interaction against a difficult situation. While you generally have this aim consciously, you may hold it partly or wholly unconsciously. At the same time, the secondary gain or the intention of an action may prove either rational and productive or irrational and aim inhibiting. But even though anger (which stems interactionally from *iB*s and the Activating Experience) may have a positive intention, you'd better critically evaluate the possible destructive qualities of anger itself. We make the distinction here between the intention of an action or feeling as opposed to the actual consequence of holding that feeling. These two factors quite often seem very different. So, we'd better look closely at some of the realistic consequences of anger itself.

1. Anger stems from your irrational and illogical belief that a person's action equals *the same thing as* the person himself. Just as your evaluation of the person turns, thereby, one-sided and negative, so does your response to that person. Your irrational premise thus results in the alienation of a full person who will most probably in turn respond in a defensive manner in order to protect his or her own integrity and self image. So long as you maintain this alienating atmosphere, no good probability for openness of all points of view exists, and your anger will importantly inhibit a speedy and effective resolution to a problem.

2. Anger, a rather strong emotion, tends to overlap or extend into other areas of your life. Most people, when angry, express themselves in a hostile manner to associates with whom they do not feel angry. This often creates unnecessary tension and an overall uncomfortable and counterproductive atmosphere.

3. The depression and anxiety that result from increased tensions stemming from anger inhibit your effective performance in other aspects of your life.

4. Combined conditions of points 2 and 3 may create negative responses from other people that may in turn cause you to feel highly critical of yourself. In many people, this criticism takes the more elaborate form of self-downing and adds greatly to the existent anxiety.

5. The repetition of anger compounded with a combination of its above-mentioned side effects can create difficult tensions both within yourself and in your relationships with others. These relationships can involve such complications that you have difficulty realizing that you felt your anger toward some person wholly unconnected with the present situation. Hence, any resolution of the original problem will still fail to resolve the new difficulties that that anger created.

As we view the above points, we can easily see that the

side effects of anger far outweigh the secondary gains that you may achieve. For the secondary gains, *in the case of anger*, remain irrational and have no real effect upon the situation. They merely tend to camouflage the original situation. RET theory concludes that there are few *real* benefits to anger stemming from irrational beliefs exist.

In concluding this chapter, let us return to our RET model and the illustration we have presented and use the RET method to work through the problem from beginning to solution.

You entered into an agreement with me whereby we would share an apartment. Your portion consisted of your getting the place ready and furnishing it and mine with moving in with you. From that point we would share all expenses equally. At the last minute, and without sufficient notice or reason, I withdrew from my portion of the agreement—after you had fulfilled your part.

A (Activating Experience or Event): my withdrawal from our agreement in an inappropriate and obnoxious manner.

rB (rational Belief): "What a bad action!"

iB (irrational Belief): "How *awful*, I just *can't stand* his treating me in that manner. He *should not*, *must not* behave that way toward me, and I think that he is a *horrible person* for doing so and that he *should be punished*!"

aC (appropriate Consequence): disappointment, feelings of rejection, sense of loss of a good opportunity.

iC (inappropriate Consequence): anger, feelings of hostility, the desire for revenge or punishment.

Because you have judged my conduct in this situation as obnoxious and because my withdrawal from our agreement has greatly disappointed and inconvenienced you, you would act wisely if you decided not to enter into any further agreement with me in which you would at all depend on me to achieve your goals. If through this situation I had put you to an extreme financial expense, you might possibly seek legal counsel if you could not get proper satisfaction from me directly. By having minimal association with me, you avoid the danger of activating further unpleasant experiences which might cause you disappointment.

Yet by not feeling angry, you leave open the possibility of reestablishing good relations with me, for you still continue to acknowledge my good qualities. I discover that I can not take advantage of you, for you guard yourself well from letting me take you in by my undependable ways. And because you do not totally reject me for acting the way I did, you help me to acknowledge your good judgment and to respect you as a person.

Although you have other alternatives with the RET solution, you can see from this example that the RET method deals not only with the counterproductive aspects of anger but also with providing the groundwork for reestablishing relationships on the basis of mutual respect.

We have thus far explained the basic principles of the RET theory. The next chapter will examine various methods you can use to help you detect the irrational Beliefs that create anger.

4

Looking for
Self-angering Philosophies

I hope I have succeeded in explaining the general dynamic of the RET theory as it applies to anger and other related emotions. As I remarked in an earlier chapter, the mere understanding of a problem or a knowledge of its underlying causes do not provide you with sufficient material for actually solving that problem. You require much more.

RET addresses itself to important insights into your present situation rather than into those of your past. My earlier critical remarks regarding more classical techniques used in psychoanalytic theory attempted to make clear my premise that insights about one's childhood or distant past prove of little or no service in facilitating adequate "working through" of a client's problems. Still we had better make a distinction between RET insights and classical theory insights.

Granted the influences of your parents, teachers, religious leaders, and environment may greatly contribute to your growth and formation, yet you'd better realize that although these factors significantly influence development, they by no means remain fixed and unchangeable.

Take, for example, the condition of animal phobia, a common problem encountered among many mature adults today. Classical technique would attempt to trace your life back to early childhood in an attempt to discover what associations you have to the particular animal that you fear. It would then attempt to enlighten you with an interpretation of this fear.

My experience has shown me that such insights bring little help to clients with a problem today. In fact, they may often dwell on such interpretations to such a degree that rather than relinquish the phobia, they reinforce it by coming to believe—through reexperiencing the situation—that they do, in fact, actually have something to fear. Their fears thus increase!

The RET approach would attempt to locate any *iB*s that people may hold at present and show them exactly how they can rid themselves of these beliefs in order to overcome their problems. True, these insights about the past may have importance; but an insight which you can use to help solve a real present-day problem will prove more immediately useful. What happened ten or twenty years ago has little or no value now. It happened. The past remains fixed and unchangeable while you may affect the present and future by your own actions.

Those responsible for the upbringing of children have them more or less at their mercy. Youngsters have little or no choice in their somewhat helpless situation, and as their minds remain in the formative period, they have, to say the least, little ability to choose better alternatives. Children also lack the ability to make the necessary critical evaluations so important in making the best decisions. Their inability independently to meet their own needs, such as obtaining food, clothing, shelter, etc., places them in a state of complete dependency. Thus, their elders greatly affect and influence them. Yet as adults we do have the knowledge, exposure, and independence to choose more wisely and rationally.

We can seriously question the degree to which our childhood experiences influence us as adults. Our parents practice a certain religion and have taught us that we should practice it; yet many adults change radically in their religious philosophy. Certainly, the same applies to political convictions, social norms, cultural tastes, professional and career choices, and even the choice of a proper mate. In fact, I can hardly think of anything that parents do not attempt to drill into their children's heads. Yet I don't know of any adults who haven't substantially changed their views toward what their parents have told them, and the vast majority has managed to accomplish this without the aid of classical psychoanalysis.

RET stresses the important idea that as adult human beings we do have, consciously have, choices; we do make choices every day, and *we—not* our parents or others— make and direct these choices. As a mature adult you had better recognize that you control your ideas, attitudes, and actions, that you arrange your life according to your own dictates. The responsibility to change your life involves your willingness to separate yourself from the childish concept that your parents still have responsibility for your actions and attitudes today. And it also involves your attending to your present and future situations, not to your infantile ones. Many of my clients, when they become aware of their irrational ideas, tell me they got these ideas from their parents or elders as children. In fact, as we shall later discover, many of the important irrational ideas that people hold partly stem from ideas they acquired as children and never gave up in their adult lives. But they also originate in children and adults' *own* creative talent for inventing crooked ways of thinking!

Let us now return to our RET model and begin the task

of showing you how to use the insights we have thus far acquired so as to locate and rid yourself of destructive, goal-inhibiting *iB*s. In the last chapter we discussed what I have called in my previous writings *Insight No. 1*. This represents a clear understanding of the interactional nature of our Belief System in relation to our experience at point *A* and our feelings and reactions at point *C*. At this point we ask an insight-producing question: What does *B* consist of? We seek to know both what *rB*s and also, more important, what *iB*s you hold.

You can use two more or less overlapping approaches to locate and differentiate your *rB*s and your *iB*s. First you ask, "What do I actually appear to believe at *B* just before I experience my Consequences at *C*?" If you cannot grasp a clear answer to that, you can then look at the situation from this principle: you know both *A* and *C*. If *C* seems inappropriate—such as anger, anxiety, or some other related emotion like depression—you may well assume that some type of *iB* influenced your feeling. We have already listed the four irrational beliefs that most people hold with regard to anger. But once again:

1. "How *awful* or *terrible* that you treat me like this!"
2. "I *can't stand* your irresponsible behavior!"
3. "You *should not* act in that bad manner toward me!"
4. "Because you behave as you should not, must not, you deserve punishment because you are a *rotten person!*"

Although these statements hold for anger, they often seem not to apply when you experience anxiety, rather than anger, at *C*.

We find anxiety as more or less an internal danger signal activated when for some reason, either conscious or unconscious, you feel something will soon happen that will prevent you from getting what you want. Anxiety often stems from sets of irrational beliefs that you hold about yourself, while anger stems from irrational beliefs that you hold about others. Using our illustration, let us apply a variation and say that for some reason or other you suspected that you kept receiving an indirect signal or message from me that I would withdraw from our agreement before I directly expressed my plans to do so. Let us suppose that you heard me speaking to a friend of some future plan of mine that would not work out if our agreement still held. You do not yet know for certain what exact plans I have. You feel it inappropriate to confront me on the issue, for the means by which you acquired this information may have represented an intrusion on my privacy. You feel you have no choice but to keep this information to yourself. These circumstances may represent A while your feeling of anxiety may represent C. Because anxiety, like anger, constitutes an inappropriate Consequence (iC), let us begin to use the RET formula to question those beliefs which you might have held at point A. Using what you have learned about the ideas we consider irrational in relation to anger and understanding that anxiety differs from anger in that you direct it inward rather than toward a person or object, we might well discover a set of irrational ideas that overlap in many respects.

When you experience anxiety as in the above-mentioned situation where I reneged on our apartment sharing agreement, you may say or think to yourself the following:

1. "How *awful* if I can't manage things if you act irresponsibly toward me with regard to our agreement."
2. "I couldn't, under such conditions, *bear* the in-

convenience you would foist upon me. I *couldn't stand* my own poor methods of coping with either you or the situation."

3. "I *should have* the ability to deal with the situation."

4. "If I don't cope as well as I *must* cope, I am an *inferior person,* and I deserve what I get for not handling the situation."

As you can easily see, the above *iB*s that apply to anxiety remain almost identical with those that relate to anger. The only difference: you hold these ideas or beliefs in relation to yourself rather than to another person.

Another variation to our illustration demonstrates how people create inappropriate feelings and upset themselves unnecessarily. Let us say that instead of withdrawing from our agreement, I got transferred to another location and had to move out of town. You realize that I had relatively little choice in the matter because the transfer included a promotion I really wanted, and you understand and support my decision. Yet although not angry with me, you discover that you feel extremely depressed at point *C*. You may perhaps think something like:

1. "How *awful* that things have turned out so badly for me!"

2. "I *can't stand* things turning out this way!"

3. "Things *shouldn't* happen this way, and so terribly inconvenience me!"

4. "Nothing ever works out the way I want it to. Life is *always unfair* to me—as it *shouldn't* be!"

Obviously the above beliefs seem thoroughly irrational, yet I feel fairly certain that just about all of us have thought such ideas when we depressed ourselves. The general character of the *iB*s which relate to anger, anxiety, and depression prove, as we can see, almost identical. We can see the differences in where you direct *iB*s. Together these three constitute the three basic ways in which people upset themselves: putting others down, putting themselves down, and putting down the conditions of the world in which they live. Throughout the years my associates and I have encountered numerous irrational beliefs and ideas that people hold and use to make themselves angry, anxious, and depressed. Yet upon close examination we have found that we can place just about every *iB* which we have discovered under one of these four major headings. Because of this, I formulated the following simple, yet descriptive names that cover all these ideas:

Awfulizing
Can't-Stand-It-Itis
Shoulding and Musting
Undeservingness or Damnation

In later chapters we will examine each separately and in greater detail. For the present these descriptive headings serve sufficiently as a general idea of the overall *tone* of irrational ideas and beliefs.

Throughout my long and rewarding career as a clinician, I have had the opportunity to work with and assist numerous people whose problems have extended beyond the emotional difficulties that we have considered thus far. I particularly refer to persons who unfortunately have to cope with physiological as well as emotional problems. People, for instances, afflicted with certain physical or mental handicaps such as epilepsy, dyslexia, encephalitis, mental retardation, and low intelligence problems. Life presents them with extraordinary obstacles that make it almost impossible for many of them to live happy and productive lives.

Although many of them, unfortunately, spend many years in institutions or under otherwise strict supervision, they need not live with severe emotional problems as well. Naturally when they realize the difference between themselves and others around them—as many of them do—they often develop severe emotional problems owing to feelings of inferiority and lack of self-worth. Children, in particular, who suffer handicaps and who associate with children who have less severe handicaps often develop extreme emotional problems.

People tend to think that these emotional problems stem directly from the more obvious physical handicap. Thus, they very often make little or no attempt to assist the child or person in overcoming these difficulties. RET clinicians take the opposite point of view and contend that the emotional aspect of a physically or otherwise handicapped person's difficulty stems from his beliefs about himself. Even though neither Rational-Emotive Therapy nor medical science can effect any significant change in the handicap condition, RET practitioners have realized some wonderfully helpful aids that they have used to teach many how to live as happily and productively as their particular condition will permit. We refer here to a problem that stems from a problem, e.g., a problem of an emotional nature that can arise from disease as well as genetical, neurological, nutritional and other physiological origins. We sometimes cannot help the handicap itself but we can help the emotional problem caused by the handicap. As stated, RET contends that irrational Beliefs serve as perhaps the main contributors to these problems.

Children or adults who suffer from such handicaps live

in a world where life confronts them daily with the effects of their handicap, and they frequently use these disabilities to lower their self-image. They know what assets they *should* have, or what they think they *should* have, and they know they don't have them.

I find it almost impossible to overstress the disastrous results of what I call *Shoulding*. Should be? What *should* a person *be?* Who can judge and by what criteria? This irrational idea of *should* comprises perhaps the most destructive and counterproductive of all the irrational ideas I know. A *should* can make people devalue themselves in their own eyes to great despondency. Similarly, the idea of *should* can lead many to devalue other people to a state hardly imaginable.

Rational-Emotive Therapy firmly believes that you *should do* nothing. You have only to exist as you do and to live your life as best you can. If you can learn to accept yourself unconditionally, with your handicaps and other problems, and if you can learn how to live with these difficulties, you may consider yourself quite well adjusted in spite of these handicaps.

RET insights into emotional problems have helped many people and their families overcome difficulties in this area. We have accomplished this by teaching people to give up *Shoulding* and *Musting*.

We recognize three major forms of irrational thinking. All come under the general heading of *musturbation* and may arise individually or in combination.

Years ago I referred in my writings, talks, and in my work with clients to the *demandingness* or *commandingness* of humans who feel disturbed. In *Growth Through Reason*, I indicated that if you desire, wish, or prefer to do well in life or to have others approve of you, such desiring alone rarely gets you into any kind of emotional difficulty. You may feel distinctly sorry and frustrated when you do not get what you want, but you do not feel angry, anxious, or depressed. To create these latter disturbances, you almost always escalate your desires into assumed needs, your preferences into demands and insistences, your relative wishes into absolute dictates.

Whenever you feel truly disturbed emotionally, it seems almost inconceivable to me that you have not resorted to one, two, or all three of the forms of musturbation. Many human problems exist that have little or nothing to do with musturbation, but emotional problems virtually always stem from these forms of thinking and behaving. After talking with thousands of people with varying degrees of emotional upsets, I still haven't found any who do not themselves, with their own self-verbalizing hatchets, create their unnecessary emotional turbulence.

All men and women probably have literally hundreds of important irrational beliefs (iBs), any one of which can contribute to upsetting them. As I mentioned earlier, all these iBs seem to fit into only a score of major headings. We shall now outline the whole system of the irrational beliefs that contribute to or "cause" emotional disturbances.

IRRATIONAL IDEA NO. 1

"I must do well and win the approval of others for my performances or else I will rate as a rotten person."

Once you believe this idea, as almost all people in all parts of the world seem to, you may then somewhat "logically" conclude: "If I do rate as a rotten or inferior person, I view my life as awful and might as well begin to give serious consideration to the idea of my own self-destruction." This, of course, leads to strong feelings of depression, anxiety, and overall worthlessness.

Irrational Idea No. 1 primarily produces intense emotions of self-hatred and/or self-downing.

Some of the main corollaries of this irrational belief include the following:

1a. "I must have sincere love and approval almost all the time from virtually all the people whom I find significant or important in my life."

1b. "I must prove myself a thoroughly competent and adequate achiever or at least have a real skill or talent in something important to me."

1c. "I must succeed in avoiding noxious or unpleasant situations. My emotional misery comes almost completely from external pressures that I have little ability to change or control. Unless these pressures change, I cannot help making myself feel anything but anxious, depressed, self-downing, or hostile."

1d. "I must never encounter events that put me in real danger or that threaten my life, as I would have to make myself totally preoccupied with and upset about them."

1e. "I must continue to think, feel, and behave as I have in the past. My past life influenced me immensely and remains important today because if something once strongly affected me, it continues to determine and affect my present feelings and behavior. My early childhood gullibility and conditioning still remain, and I cannot surmount these tendencies truly to think for myself without being strongly swayed by these influences."

1f. "I must find a high degree of order, certainty, or predictability in the universe around me in order for me to feel comfortable and to perform adequately."

1g. "I must continue to rely and depend on other people. Because I remain weak in this respect, I shall also continue to need and rely on certain sets of superstitious and religious ideas in order to survive times of great stress."

1h. "I must understand the nature and secrets of the universe to live happily in it."

1i. "I can and should give myself a global rating as a human, and I can rate myself as good and worthy *only* if I perform well, do worthwhile things, and have people generally approve of me."

1j. "I must never make myself depressed, anxious, ashamed, or angry, or if I do give in to these feelings of disturbance, I amount to a thoroughly weak and rotten person since I then perform most incompetently and shamefully."

1k. "I must never question the beliefs, attitudes, or opinions held by respected authorities or by my society, family, or peer group because they certainly contain a real validity. If I do question them, people should rightly condemn and punish me."

IRRATIONAL IDEA NO. 2

"Others must treat me considerately and kindly and in precisely the way I want them to treat me. If they don't, society and the universe should severely blame, damn, and punish them for their inconsideration."

2a. "Other people must treat everyone, but especially me, in a fair and considerate manner. If they act unfairly and inconsiderately, we can view them as rotten people who deserve punishment and damnation, which society should see that they get."

2b. "Other people must not behave incompetently or stupidly. If they do, I justifiably can see and label them as thorough idiots who ought to feel ashamed of themselves and should expect none of the good things in life."

2c. "People who have the ability to perform well must not choose to shirk or avoid their responsibilities. They ought to accept and carry out their duties. They amount to rotten people and should feel utterly ashamed of themselves if they don't. People must achieve their potential for a happy and worthwhile life, or else they have little or no value as humans."

2d. "Other people must not unjustly criticize me. I can see them as rotten people who deserve practically nothing good in this life if they do so."

IRRATIONAL IDEA NO. 3

"The world (and the people in it) must arrange conditions under which I live so that I get everything that I want when I want it. And further, conditions must exist so that I don't get what I don't want. Moreover, I usually must get what I want quickly and easily."

3a. "Things must go the way I would like them to go because I *need* what I want and life *is* awful, horrible, and terrible when I do not get what I want."

3b. "I must continually preoccupy myself with dangers or fearsome people or things and upset myself about them. In that way I increase my power to control or change them. And I *must* control or change them."

3c. "I must avoid, rather than face and deal with, many of life's difficulties and responsibilities since I need or must have immediate comfort and can't discipline myself or go through present pain to achieve future gains."

3d. "People should act better than they do, and if they act badly or create needless hassles for me, I view them as awful and horrible, and I can't stand the difficulties which they create by their conduct."

3e. "I must continue to suffer endlessly if handicaps exist in my life, no matter how I acquired these handicaps. I can do practically nothing to change them, and I find that so horrible that life seems hardly worth living."

3f. "I must not find it difficult to change obnoxious or

handicapping elements in myself or in my life. Such difficulties ought not exist. I find it too hard to do anything about them, and I might as well make no effort or at most make very little effort to change them since the situation *is* more or less hopeless."

3g. "Things like justice, fairness, equality, and democracy must prevail, and when they don't, I can't stand it and life seems too unbearable to continue."

3h. "I must find the correct and perfect solutions to my problems and to those of other people whom I care for. If I don't, catastrophe and horror will surely result."

3i. "I must remain a helpless victim of anxiety, depression, feelings of inadequacy, and hostility unless the conditions that cause my unhappiness change and allow me to stop feeling disturbed."

3j. "Since I managed to come into this world and still remain alive, my life must continue forever or just as long as I want it to continue. I find it completely unfair and horrible to think about the possibility of dying and of no longer having any existence. I also find it horrible to think about the death of those whom I love. Death, except for my enemies, must not exist."

3k. "As long as I remain alive, my life must have some unusual or special meaning or purpose, and if I cannot create this meaning or purpose for myself, the universe or some supernatural or magical force in the universe must create it for me."

3l. "I can't stand the discomfort of feeling anxious, depressed, guilty, ashamed, or otherwise emotionally upset, and if I really went crazy and found myself in an institution, I could never stand that horror or make the adjustment back to normal life."

3m. "When things really have gone badly for me for a reasonably long period of time and there exist no guarantees that they will change or that anyone will take the responsibility to make things better for me, I simply can't bear the thought of living any longer and may seriously contemplate my own destruction."

These corollaries—outgrowths of the three major irrational beliefs—represent a sampling of the irrational ideas many people hold and which play a part in their everyday thoughts. Through the particular perspective of these ideas people condemn themselves, others, and the world around them. We can easily see that all these ideas contain elements of what *should* or *must be,* of how awful and terrible a situation or person *is.* Each of them also contains the elements of hopelessness and helplessness directed toward the world, the people in the world, or themselves. This idea of remaining powerless in life or at the mercy of one's life conditions constitutes perhaps the greatest irrationality.

Let us now review each irrational idea separately so that we may gain a clearer understanding of the content, origin, and effect of each idea.

IRRATIONAL IDEA NO. 1 deals mainly with your expectations of personal achievement. In addition, it involves the importance you place on other people's opinions of you. You set expectations for yourself and, if you do not live up to them, see yourself as inferior in your own eyes and in the eyes of others. Hence, you feel that the only measure of your self-worth equals the degree to which you can perform in a certain manner. You feel that other people will condemn and reject you if you do not do as you *should,* as you *must.*

Naturally, as humans we sometimes have a tendency either to overevaluate our own potential or to set goals for ourselves which people whom we respect or admire have either achieved themselves or would like to see us achieve. In many instances, these specific goals go beyond the realm of our capacity. It seems rational and understandable that you may feel disappointed if you do not reach certain achievements. Yet I can see no real reason for you to make yourself depressed, anxious, or angry at the realization that such goals remain, at least presently, beyond your reach.

Viewing **IRRATIONAL IDEA NO. 2,** we see the same negativeness and dogmatism as exist in Irrational Idea No. 1. Here, however, you direct these viewpoints toward other people instead of the self, and here you place unrealistic expectations on others.

Often humans like to feel or delude themselves into believing that they *are* the center of the universe and that all other people *should, must* cater to their needs and whims. Naturally, when two or more persons interact, a distinct possibility exists that this attitude will prevail in each of them. If so, conflicts can easily arise since each person has his or her own interest as the primary concern. Although I grant that you can appropriately extend considerations to other people as well as yourself, this ideal attitude unfortunately does not always arise. You may therefore wisely prepare to cope with a world of people who may often treat you harshly and unfairly and, in dealing with such circumstances, to seek alternatives to anger such as those offered by the Rational-Emotive Therapy formula.

While **IRRATIONAL IDEA NO. 3** has the same basic components of the two previous ideas, you may find it perhaps the most irrational idea of the three. We all recognize the irrationality of demanding that the conditions of our environment cooperate with our individual desires. Yet in my experience many people actually do upset themselves frequently and unnecessarily when these same forces refuse to "comply." I need only ask how many times you have encountered people who view it as "unbearable" when the weather does not suit their taste.

I think it a general human trait at one time or another to hold this and other irrational Beliefs. It hardly seems criminal to have irrational Beliefs. We all have them. But we'd better keep in mind that we would act wiser and feel a lot happier if we looked for these *iB*s and learned to recognize them when they badly influenced our reactions and behavior. This amounts to no magic cure, nor any formula for eternal happiness, but an effective step that just about any person can take to assist himself or herself in securing the things that he or she desires in life.

5

Understanding Your
Self-angering Philosophies

Having examined some of the irrational ideas that cause
anger and other related inappropriate Consequences, we
will now attempt to gain some insights into the nature of
these beliefs. For no matter how faithfully you may have
followed the RET formula as I have thus far presented it,
the whole system won't work unless you learn how to
Dispute and eliminate *iB*s once you locate them. We will
now turn our attention to three major insights or under-
standings that will help you Dispute irrational beliefs.

Naturally the kinds of insights we try to help RET
clients acquire hardly equate with those which other
therapies emphasize. Psychoanalysis, as we have already
noted, emphasizes insight into what happened to you in
the past and how this connects with your present difficulties. Transactional Analysis, somewhat similarly, stresses
insight into your childhood and your past, and like
psychoanalytic insights, Transactional Analysis demands
that you understand these past experiences and give them
extensive consideration before you can effectively change
them and let yourself live as a healthy adult.

Reichian, primal, and other abreactive or cathartic

types of therapies insist that you have to have insight into the enormous pain inflicted on you during your early childhood and, further, that you relive these early traumas and reexperience the pain of these unpleasant experiences before you can rid yourself of the adverse effects which these experiences continue to have upon your present life. Gestalt therapy demands that you must attain insight into every nuance of your present feelings and that this complete awareness of the here-and-now, practically unassisted, will change attitudes and actions.

Rational-Emotive Therapy believes that your present disturbance has relatively little to do with your past life. **INSIGHT NO. 1** stresses the extremely strong influence that our Belief System (B) has upon our reaction (C) to the Activating Experience (A). In other words, A does not really cause (though it, to some extent, contributes to) C; B constitutes the direct and basic cause of C. It would, therefore, follow that if the Belief System constitutes the major influence on the Emotional Consequence, any previous Activating Experience will have even less influence on C than a present Activating Experience. You will find this position, of course, distinctly contrary to that held by other methods of therapy.

We do not say that your past experiences have absolutely *no* effect on your present behavior. For instance, researchers have found that children who get severely punished by their parents will develop a tendency to feel more anger and act more violently toward others throughout their lives than will children who get less violently or severely treated. While this tends to indicate that there exists, to some degree, a relationship between a person's early training and his or her later conduct, we'd better not view such information as conclusive without further consideration.

We can give serious consideration to genetic factors and the part they play in creating environmental influences and shall discuss these in detail later in this book. The anger and violence characteristic of those raised in hostile and aggressive atmospheres may stem from an inherited rather than from an acquired disposition. For if either one or both of a child's parents has an inherited aggressive disposition, they may well pass on that tendency to the child. In tracing this causal chain of events, we see that the parent may then react to the child's inherited aggressive tendencies with violent and aggressive disciplinary measures. This will then reinforce the child's violent disposition, which may then get passed on to his or her own children. Here we see a somewhat vicious circle of violent environments whose basic underlying cause may well have a hereditary nature.

INSIGHT NO. 1 stresses the fundamental point of the importance of the beliefs you hold today. In RET we give little regard to how you arrived at those beliefs. The teachings you received from your parents and elders during your childhood and formative years may, in fact, have a great deal of influence upon those beliefs. Yet, as stated in previous chapters, you can acquire and can change these beliefs, no matter how you may have acquired them.

Here you have the difference between an RET insight and the insights as presented by various schools of psychoanalysis. Insight into the *origins* of your Belief System, assuming that you could ever truly acquire that insight, will help you very little. (As an ex-psychoanalyst I might add that you rarely ever acquire such insights; you generally fabricate or invent them.) These insights merely serve to sidetrack you from the much more important insight: "I clearly see that right now I make myself angry by my irrational beliefs at *B*. Now how can I zero in on these beliefs, understand their nature, and *change* them?"

If the type of insight offered in classical psychoanalytic theory seems either useless or counterproductive, we can legitimately ask how it has enjoyed such widespread popularity. Humans, in general, have a natural tendency to indulge themselves in certain activities which, although lacking any real value, yield certain gratification. Classical analysis offers its clients precisely these gratifications. As I do not wish to spend too much time going into detail about these other theories, let me say briefly that I think psychoanalysis gives people what they want but what will also do them little or no good in helping themselves.

1. They can enjoy listening to themselves talk endlessly about themselves.

2. They can avoid having to *do* anything about their problems because they have the excuse of looking more and more into their past, searching for "deeper" solutions.

3. They can paranoically put pieces of a puzzle together in perfect order by forcing them to fit into the procrustean bed of psychoanalytic theory.

4. They can seek frantically for a magical "key" that will automatically open up inner secrets and change their lives as soon as the "key" is found.

5. They can pleasurably play around with dreams and fantasies instead of sticking with much more hardheaded and usually more important reality problems.

6. They can indulge feelings of one-upmanship on others who have "less-depth-centered" and "more superficial" forms of therapy.

7. They can endlessly let themselves depend on the

analyst for help and support, instead of trying to solve some of life's relatively minor problems independently.

8. They can give in to, via transference relationship with the analyst, their dire needs to feel loved and to have one person in the world, at least, who seems completely devoted and on their side (forgetting, of course, they pay handsomely for this "loving" role).

Now let us examine RET **INSIGHT NO. 2:** *However you may have originally acquired your Belief System, particularly that part of it that consists of the irrational beliefs (iBs) with which you create your emotional disturbances, you now keep these beliefs alive by repeating them to yourself, reinforcing them in various ways, acting on them, and refusing to challenge their validity.* Others may have at first helped you acquire your irrational beliefs and even systematically drilled you with many of them, yet the primary reason you still subscribe to such beliefs lies in the fact that you continually reindoctrinate yourself with them today.

INSIGHT NO. 2 involves two closely related major points. Firstly, RET teaches that you carry on your early acquired anger-creating *iB*s by your own repetition of these ideas in your mind and your continued acting upon them. You seem to do this automatically or "passively" but if you look more closely you will see that you *actively* keep reindoctrinating yourself with irrational Beliefs. Secondly, inappropriate Emotional Consequences remain in existence *because* you continue to maintain irrational philosophies or beliefs from which they stem, and you continue to feel emotions such as anger, anxiety, and depression at *C because* you either consciously or unconsciously keep reiterating your irrational Beliefs to yourself. Again, although it "seems" or "feels" as if your anger "naturally" persists once you make yourself hate someone, you actually and actively *keep it alive* by constantly telling yourself that this person *should not* have acted badly and *is* rotten for acting that way.

As a child, I contend, you subscribed to the irrational teachings of your parents and teachers because you had a limited ability to recognize the irrational nature of such teachings. When your elders told you that a person *was terrible* if he broke a promise or agreement he had made with you, you naturally believed them. If, as you grew older, you had given some critical thought to these statements, you might have noticed that some or many people who went back on their agreements with you actually did *not* rate as completely terrible people. In fact, if you had given the idea ample consideration and thought, you might have discovered that your own parents, from time to time, went back on their word to you. Did that make *them* totally rotten and worthless? I hardly think so. If you had given thought to this, you probably would have realized that your anger—stemming, for instance, from your belief that people who do you certain injustices are worthless—only got you involved in further unpleasantness.

RET shows you how you can use the principles of reinforcement and penalization to work *for* you rather than against you. It shows you how you can *change* your ideas about practically all of your elders' teachings in relation to how people *should* act toward you. RET methods, used properly and conscientiously, help you rid yourself of these irrational beliefs. The fact that you may well make yourself angrier as an adult than you generally did as a child tends to show that early conditioning itself doesn't cause your adolescent and adult anger. Rather, your own constant repetition of the early acquired doctrines seems the main contributor to your latter-day anger.

In his social reinforcement theory Albert Bandura makes a similar point. Bandura, a devotee of learning and conditioning theories of human behavior, also acknowledges the highly cognitive element in human behavior and response. Although the social reinforcement theory has some similarities to our RET theory, there remain some important differences. Bandura implies that if I should act in an asocial manner toward you, you still have a number of alternatives—any one of which may fit into the framework of the sentiments of the social group. You would therefore have a choice of any one of a number of responses. You could hate me, dislike me, dislike my behavior, stay away from me, take me to court, etc. Normally, the social communication and rules of your community inform you that I had better not act toward you in certain respects and that I may risk a legal penalty if I do so.

As a human you tend to accept this communication and these rules. Thus, to some extent you learn to feel displeased about my act. You have a tendency to think about whether the rule I broke had little or no importance, whether I inconvenienced you mildly or greatly, whether you can or cannot get away with your anger and your possible aggression against me, and so on. In other words, you might use a social standard to measure the extent of aggression which society would sanction and choose to act according to those guidelines. All human emotions, Bandura implies, have a pronounced element of cognitive considerations and social learning. RET takes this same combined cognitive-conditioning outlook, but it especially stresses self-conditioning, as well as conditioning resulting from external social influences.

The second aspect of **INSIGHT NO. 2** deals with sustained emotions stemming from anything that happens to you at point A. This applies particularly to feelings of anger. RET hypothesizes that *the frustration you origi-nally experience has itself relatively little to do with your holding and retaining these hostile feelings for prolonged periods of time. Your ongoing, or sustained, view of that original frustration—rather than the frustrating condi-tions themselves—keeps you perennially angry with me.*

If I treated you in an inconsiderate manner, you could easily make yourself upset with me for a day or two—or for many weeks. Every time someone mentioned my name, for instance, or every time you otherwise recalled my existence, your original feelings of animosity would reas-sert themselves. Most of these difficulties you overcome or forget within a short period of time, and you never think of them again. Or at least, if you recall them to mind, you hardly feel disturbed by the remembrance of them.

What, though, of the times when you continue to har-bor feelings of anger and hostility, remaining angry for weeks, months, and even years? In these times you often forget the exact cause of the original anger. Here, every time you refer to either the name of the person or to the incident you repeat the irrational beliefs that originally created and provoked the feelings of anger. For unless you continually repeat to yourself these irrational beliefs and thus vigorously throw yourself into holding onto them and perhaps even acting aggressively while holding them, you almost certainly do not give the incident much thought after a reasonably short period of time has passed. *Your ongoing, or sustained, view of that original frustra-tion—rather than the frustrating conditions themselves—keeps you angry.*

INSIGHT NO. 3 states that *in order to change your disturbed feelings and behaviors and the irrational beliefs which you hold that lead you to have these feelings and behaviors, you almost always have to resort to a great deal of work and practice.* For no matter how aware you remain of the self-defeating nature of your irrational attitudes and actions, this awareness does not help you whatsoever unless you can effectively Dispute these ideas. And you can mainly do this with much practice and work.

All our beliefs, whether rational or irrational, vary in intensity and effect. For instance, many people hold certain superstitious beliefs, but their intensity may from time to time increase or lessen. Although most people agree that such omens as black cats and broken mirrors and such actions as walking under ladders have little meaning and have no connection with either luck or fate, these same people oftentimes avoid certain situations because their irrational superstition has gained an overpowering influence over their actions. The primary point to understand in relation to **INSIGHT NO. 3:** a considerable difference exists between *telling* yourself something and really *convincing* yourself about the rationality or irrationality of a belief or idea.

Because beliefs tend to change in intensity, you'd better strongly Dispute *iB*s at point *D* (Disputing). No matter what degree of awareness you have of the irrationality of a belief, that insight will help you little unless you develop skill in Disputing the iB. And unless you Dispute your *iBs* powerfully, you stand a good chance that they will gain a controlling influence in a situation. As we have stressed in this chapter, insight and knowledge alone have little value.

Remember, the more powerfully and consistently you dispute (at point *D*) your anxiety-creating or anger-producing *iBs*, the sooner you will dispel them. The next chapter will outline ways of Detecting your irrational Beliefs, Discriminating between them and more rational Beliefs, and then Debating your iBs.

6

Disputing Your
Self-angering Philosophies

In the RET theory D represents Disputing. It means that after you have found the Activating Experience (A), which preceded your disturbed Emotional or Behavioral Consequences (C), and after you have ferreted out your rational beliefs (rBs) and irrational beliefs (iBs) about A, and after you have clearly acknowledged that your irrational Beliefs directly help create your disturbed or inappropriate Consequences (iCs), you vigorously and persistently attempt to dispute these iBs.

Kishor Phadke, a brilliant associate of mine in Bombay, gave some special thought to point D, or Disputing, and decided to break it down into three main components:

Detection
Discriminating
Debating

I find his distinctions useful, since Disputing does largely consist of detecting your main irrational Beliefs, discriminating them clearly from your rational Beliefs and then debating these irrational Beliefs actively and vigorously. So far in this book I have outlined the ABCs of anger and have tried to show how you can detect your *iBs* with the help of three major RET insights. This chapter will show you in detail how you can persistently and strongly *debate* your *iBs*.

To begin this debating process, we shall consider again the four major kinds of irrational beliefs which you tend to hold whenever you make yourself angry at someone and show what you can do actively to debate or dispute them until you decide to give them up.

Using our apartment-sharing illustration, we may state Irrational Belief No. 1 as follows:

"How awful that you made me go to so much trouble and then withdrew from our agreement."

Assuming that you devoutly believe this *iB* and that you want to challenge it and give it up, you first ask yourself, "What evidence exists for the awfulness of his withdrawing from our agreement without any good reason?" or, in briefer form, "What makes it *awful?*"

Now, if we attempt to answer the question regarding the awfulness of the situation by describing the amount of inconvenience, the expense, and the obnoxious nature of my behavior, we will find ourselves in some difficulty. For as we have stated earlier, such feelings and attitudes lead to disappointment—not anger—as they remain quite rational. Anger stems from carrying things further and viewing the situation as awful, terrible, or horrible. You seem to have a tendency to equate unfair, inconvenient, or disadvantageous with awful. But they do not mean awful. As we shall see later in our argument, the separation of the terms "awful" and "unfair" does not merely amount to a form of semantic quibbling, for the implications of, and the manner in which we use a term make the difference between rational and irrational thinking.

The dictionary definition of "awful" begins as follows: "1. inspiring awe. 2. terrifying; appalling. 3. worthy of reverence and solemn respect." But then it goes on to the colloquial meaning of the term: "very bad, ugly, disagreeable, unpleasant, etc.: as, an *awful* joke." The problem with both the colloquial portion of the dictionary definition and the popular usage of the term lies primarily in the fact that one tends to attach an emotional idea to the word which extends beyond its practical meaning.

Perhaps it would be easier to clarify the difference between the practical and the emotional aspects of the word "awful" by applying a statement from our illustration: "How awful that he made me go to so much trouble and then withdrew from our agreement." You feel disappointment. You feel anger. Thus, you hold two distinctly different ideas about my behavior, one rational and the other irrational. Rationally you think that I have treated you rather unfairly and that you find that treatment, as the dictionary states, "very bad, ugly, disagreeable, unpleasant, etc." We may term these feelings rational or appropriate because they aid or abet your basic values: when we made our agreement, you had the idea that such a living situation would have advantages for you. My withdrawal has now frustrated that goal, so you rationally evaluate my actions as disagreeable and unpleasant.

Rational does not mean indifferent, calm, or passive. It merely means that it leads to appropriate feelings at point *C*. Considering the circumstances, you might feel exceptionally sorry, displeased, and disappointed because my unfairness has inconvenienced you enormously. You would thus have very strong rational feelings at *C*. The rational Belief would lead you to feeling sorry, displeased, annoyed, and irritated. It would *not* lead you to feeling angry. You create your anger by the emotional idea attached to the term "awful."

The tendency to "awfulize" constitutes the basis of the irrationality, for it implies something beyond the realistic or actual unpleasantness of the action and attaches an *additional idea of badness* to the existent rational idea. This awfulness which you add leads to the idea that the action has *more than* badness, that it *must not* exist.

By the attachment of an additional idea to the more rational ones, such words as "awful," "terrible," and "horrible" imply the following:

1. Dr. Ellis treats me totally or one hundred percent badly.
2. He seems to treat me more than one hundred percent badly.
3. He *should not, must not* treat me that badly.
4. He *must not* treat me badly at all but *should* only treat me well.

Assuming that we can agree that you irrationally relate awfulness to the treatment you have received, let us now go on to the next step in disputing the irrational Beliefs. We can wisely ask: What makes the action of breaking the agreement *awful?* If we recognize that awfulness implies that you have been treated one hundred percent (or more than one hundred percent) badly, we may surmise that I obviously could have treated you no worse. But if we look at the situation closely, we can easily see that I could have acted worse in many ways. For instance, I could have moved into the apartment with you as agreed on and then refused to pay my part of the rent. Or I could have made demands on you which would have further inconvenienced you after you had moved into the apartment. We need not enumerate all the possibilities; suffice it to say that I could not have treated you one hundred percent badly since there remain a number of obnoxious things that I did not do to you. So, although you can justifiably see the treatment you received as bad, inconvenient, and disappointing, you can not find it *more* than this, and yet you do irrationally think it so. You cannot rate it as *awful*, without implying by that term that I have treated you more than one hundred percent badly.

By evaluating my treatment of you as awful, you really take the position that I have *more than* inconvenienced you. We can see that you probably take this position by observing that if you only felt disappointed, inconvenienced, and frustrated at *C*, you would not feel angry. We can then ask: "How does my treating you unjustly and unfairly amount to my dealing with you in a *greater than* or *more than* bad or obnoxious manner?" In my experience almost every time you (or anyone) uses the terms "awful," "horrible" or "terrible" to describe a situation or someone's behavior, you imply that the circumstances have more than one hundred percent badness. RET tries to get rid of this type of attitude. At times, of course, when the circumstances seem exceptional or extreme, you may justifiably view those circumstances as exceptionally bad behavior. But do you see that if you believe that unfair treatment amounts to more than great inconvenience and unfairness to you, and that this *must* not exist you then have an irrational belief?

Dr. Donald Meichenbaum, an outstanding cognitive-behavior therapist who has done a good many important research studies of RET-related therapy, often refers to RET as a semantic therapy, and I agree with him. RET helps people discriminate between their generalizations and their overgeneralizations and between their reality-oriented thinking and their unrealistic or magical thinking. In the case of the term "awful," people often think that they mean *bad* or *very bad*, while their actual emotional meaning seems to include *totally bad* or *more than totally bad*. We help people see what they really mean when they use the term.

RET does not say that you only emote through the use

of words and meanings in certain "extended" ways. Obviously animals and very young children have emotions, and neither has the use of language. But we do believe that animals and children have limited emotional repertoires and, even more significantly, that they tend to emote in an unsustained, quickly dissipated manner. When children get old enough to use language effectively, they then acquire the ability to sustain their emotions and, unfortunately, also to make and keep themselves emotionally upset.

Moreover, as humans we invariably seem to talk to ourselves about our emotional reactions. When we feel highly emotional about something, we observe that state and evaluate how good or bad we find it. We do this partly because we have learned from others that some emotions rate as "good" and some as "bad," that some have advantages and some have disadvantages. But we also do it because all humans seem to observe their emotional reactions. We can view our emotional state objectively and think about the possibilities of living with or changing it, or we can "awfulize" and say many negative things about it to ourselves. We have this choice.

When you see me treating you in a certain manner and you think my behavior unfair, you tell yourself something about my unfairness. By doing this, you create a pronounced emotional feeling in your gut, either appropriate sorrow and/or irritation or inappropriate rage. You then observe your emotional reactions (which you may not realize you have chosen for yourself), and you evaluate them. You feel emotional about your emotions.

You use certain words to create emotional reactions. The words you use affect you only in accordance with the meanings you give them. They have no power in their own right. Words such as "awful" and "terrible" usually create disturbed emotions. Other words, such as "bad"

and "obnoxious," tend to create appropriate or undis-
turbed reactions. Not always, of course. You can say to
yourself, "How obnoxious! I find that unfair treatment!"
and mean that you find it more than obnoxious. Or you
can say to yourself, "How awful I find that treatment," and
mean that you merely find it obnoxious and that you
strongly wish I would treat you more fairly.

Do not think that every time you see something as *bad*
or *unfortunate* you stay within reality and that every time
you see something as *awful* or *horrible* you depart from
reality. Again, you control the meaning that you impose
on words and, thus, the power that you give to them. In
general, we have found that when you use words like
"awful," "terrible," and "horrible," you do give them
magical, beyond-reality meanings. If you see and can
change this tendency, you will significantly alter your
disturbed feelings.

Many people have a difficult time understanding that
when they say something like, "How *awful* that so-and-so
treated me unfairly," they keep going beyond reality by
implying that:

1. The unfair person has treated them totally unfairly.
2. They have been treated as unfairly as anyone
   could possibly treat anyone.
3. They can no longer enjoy life after this unfair
   treatment has taken place.
4. They have received more than one hundred percent unfair treatment.

Most people do not understand that the use of the term
"awful" implies all these things. By continuing to use the
term, they continue to upset themselves with it.

In my experience, *"How awful that I have been treated
in that way"* often also means *"when they should have,*

must have treated me fairly." For you to say that something should or must not exist demands that people at all times treat you in the way in which you wish they would. This means demanding something of other people which they can never fulfill. How obviously irrational!—for you can not expect them to treat you in accordance with your personal wishes at all times.

If you say to yourself that someone should not act unfairly toward you, you imply that you rate not merely the action as wrong but also the (entire) person who committed the action as such. You feel this person capable of acting justly, and you feel it is essential to you that s/he do so. S/he *must always* act fairly, and *must never* act otherwise. This very irrational expectation that you and others will always act fairly in every situation makes you feel anger. You can more rationally realize that many decent people—including yourself—occasionally do unfair or unjust things. You can more sanely feel disappointment and a sense of inconvenience when you encounter unfairness.

By looking closely at your own *awfuls, shoulds,* and *musts,* you can learn to examine and rid yourself of many of the irrational ideas which lead to counterproductive and inappropriate emotional feelings at *C*. Once you learn to master the RET technique for disputing and debating your irrational beliefs, you can carry it on for the rest of your life.

7

Thinking Your Way
Out of Your Anger

Anti-awfulizing and antimusturbation remain the core of rational thinking, the essences of uprooting your feelings of anger, rage, resentment, and fury. You awfulize and resort to musturbation in four major ways, and once you tell yourself that you find something *awful*, that it *must* not exist the way it does, you also frequently convince yourself of other related irrational beliefs. Let us now look at these common irrationalities and at what you can do to work on them.

RET refers to one of these beliefs as *I-Can't-Stand-It-Itis*. We frequently find this type of awfulizing or musturbation found in statements or ideas like: "I can't stand being treated so unfairly and being put to such great inconveniences."

What we call Debating, as part of Disputing, in RET, merely means asking yourself questions that will challenge your irrational Beliefs. The obvious challenges consist of "Why?" "How?" "In what manner?" "What evidence exists for this?" "Where can I find the proof?" Thus, you ask yourself, "Why or in what manner can't I stand such unfair treatment?"

If your answer to this turns out to be something like "I *can* stand it because it doesn't really seem that terrible," you would seem on the right track, but in fact, your answer doesn't quite suffice. First of all, by using the word "terrible," you will have, as we have noted earlier, a difficult time defining the term itself. Even if you yourself don't find the situation so terrible, a friend or some other outsider might judge it as terrible. Because of your subjective interests in the matter, others would then easily sway you into irrational modes of thinking, even if you had already successfully debated the idea of terribleness yourself. Agreeing with someone else's concept of terribleness most likely will encourage you into believing that you *can't* stand it and that he *shouldn't* act in that terrible way. For, as I have stressed before, the four basic kinds of *iB*s people tell themselves to create their emotional upsets tend to interrelate so that one leads to the other:

1. "I see it as terrible for him to treat me that way" *seems also to mean*
2. "I can't stand his behaving in that terrible manner."
3. "Therefore, he shouldn't act in that terrible manner."
4. "He *is* a terrible *person* to treat anyone that way."

In one way these seem like four different irrational statements. But terribleness, I-Can't-Stand-It-Itis, musturbation, and damning oneself or others all represent different forms of the same basic proposition. If we start with one of these forms, we often imply or overtly state the other forms as well.

RET states that if you can stop believing, really and thoroughly stop believing, in one of these forms, you will then *tend* to stop believing in the others. No certainty exists for this, but you definitely have this tendency.

We return now to debating I-Can't-Stand-It-Itis. If we forget, then, about terribleness, the unfair treatment amounts to an evaluation such as "Because he has treated me exceptionally unfairly and has caused me great amounts of unnecessary harm, I can't stand his doing that to me." You can now ask the question: "*Why* can't I stand it?" With the idea of terribleness left out, it appears that you see the situation as intolerable because you think you have experienced *too much* pain; *too much* suffering has resulted from the unfair action. You have somehow escalated much pain and trouble into *too much* pain and trouble. The term "too," as used here, seems to take on a more or less magical quality. Its use presumes that one may only allow exactly so much difficulty and inconvenience and *no more*. After a certain point—which varies from individual to individual—you consider the pain *too much*.

Thus, whenever you have the idea that you can't stand the degree of badness or unpleasantness that you experience with unfair treatment, you suffer not only frustration but a low frustration tolerance (LFT) as well. We can loosely describe LFT as the tendency to rant and rave at, rather than merely dislike, periods of frustration. The ranting and raving makes you feel much *more* frustrated than you would otherwise. If you Debate, and keep debating, your I-Can't-Stand-It-Itis, you will arrive at a more practical attitude for dealing with frustration and a new philosophy or cognitive Effect (cE), which we can call I'll-Never-Like-It-but-I-Can-Stand-It-Itis.

The question of whether you will make this basic change in attitude still remains. Anything you believe you can also definitely *refuse* to believe. You cannot control to any great degree what actually exists, but you do control—almost completely—what you *think about* what exists. So that while you have very little control over how I treat you (fairly or unfairly, well or badly), you do have a good number of choices over the manner in which you view my unfair or bad behavior. Thus, even if you judge my actions toward you as unfair and others agree that you have really been treated unfairly, you still do choose:

1. to believe that you can't stand this unfairness *or* that you can
2. to define the unfairness as awful *or* not to define it as such
3. to think I must not treat you in an unfair manner *or* to think it preferable that I do not
4. to judge me as a thoroughly horrible person *or* to judge me as a person who has acted inappropriately toward you in this particular respect.

If you will challenge and debate your hypothesis that you have little or no choice but to feel that you can't stand my treating you badly and that you can't stand it because you find it *too* bad and that it shouldn't exist, if you will challenge this, then and only then will you do something effective about surrendering these irrational ideas.

Let us now go on to debate the next irrational belief: He *should not, must not* treat me unfairly. "Granted that he has dealt with me unfairly and that virtually everyone in our society would agree that he has, what evidence exists, however, that he *ought not* abuse me in this unfair manner?" If we approach this question from the point of social morality, one might say that if the people in general ignored the *oughts* and *shoulds* of its social, moral, and ethical standards, their society could not survive as a civilized unit. Yet morality doesn't actually determine what *ought* or *should* exist; it merely establishes definitions or guidelines with regard to either right or wrong. In other words, civilized morality states that one *had better* act "properly" rather than "improperly" and goes on to dictate that otherwise bad results will accrue. If bad results occur by someone's actions, the members of a society may feel impelled—because of civilized morality—to lay some sanctions against the transgressor in order to persuade him or her to act otherwise in the future.

To avoid the accusation of indulging in semantic quibbling, let us clearly define the difference between "had better" act as opposed to "ought to" act in a certain manner. For the statement "You *had better* act in a certain manner in order to bring about good social results" has as its follow-up statement "If you do not act in such a manner, your community, members of the society, will decide that poor results have ensued and that you and their society will suffer." This statement seems empirically founded or realistic since we can observe right and wrong acts and discover whether they really do lead to good or bad results for you and your community. We can empirically check and validate by consulting any objective observer.

However, the second statement, "You *ought to* act rightly to get good results," implies the follow-up statements that "If you do not do what you ought to do:

1. ... poor results must occur for you and for everyone in your society."
2. ... some universal law commands that you deserve to get bad results and necessitates that dire things will happen."
3. ... you rate as a bad person."
4. ... you cannot possibly accept yourself and strive for real happiness in life."

The first of these propositions ("If you do not do what you ought to do, poor results must occur for you and for everyone in your society") seems false, for if you act wrongly, it would seem most unlikely that any great number of people in a society would suffer. The second and third propositions appear magical and unverifiable. And the fourth proposition again seems false, since some people manage to accept themselves and to strive for (and gain) a good deal of happiness in spite of the fact that they behave wrongly or immorally.

Thus, again we see that two somewhat similar, yet contradictory ideas exist here. For when you hold the idea that "People *ought* to treat me, *must* treat me better," you really imply:

1. "I would find it highly preferable if they did treat me better"

and

2. "Because I would find it preferable, they have to treat me better."

Although the first belief seems both rational and legitimate, the second one seems highly irrational. We hold, in RET, that if you were to stick completely with the rational belief (*rB*) ("I would find it highly preferable if they did treat me better"), you would merely feel sorry and displeased with the poor treatment you had received. Yet if you persisted, as many people have a tendency to do, in falling into the irrational belief ("Because I would find it preferable, they have to treat me better"), you would in all probability end up feeling very angry. Therefore, to get rid of the anger, you'd better ask: "Why *must* I (or anyone) get treated fairly at all times?" The rational answer: "Although it would seem desirable to get treated fairly at all times and although social rules declare it advisable for people to act fairly to me, no universal law exists, no reason commands I must get treated fairly."

If you can agree with the above, you will find that in

difficult and frustrating situations you will feel sorry and disappointed when others treat you unfairly, but you won't feel irrational anger and rage.

Let us once again review the whole RET formula that we have discussed up to this point:

Activating Experience (A): I have treated you unfairly by withdrawing from an agreement we have made.

Rational Belief (rB): "I find Dr. Ellis' action deplorable and unfortunate."

Irrational Belief (iB): "How awful! He should not, must not treat me in that manner."

Appropriate Consequence (aC): frustration and displeasure.

Inappropriate Consequence (iC); anger and rage.

Disputing and Debating (D): you detect your iBs and begin disputing and debating them by asking yourself questions that challenge your interpretations or beliefs regarding people's treatment of you.

Cognitive Effect or New Philosophy (cE): "I can see no reason why he *must* treat me fairly even though I would definitely prefer it."

Behavioral Effect (bE): loss of anger, relief, and return to the appropriate Consequence (aC): feelings of sorrow and disappointment.

Until you go through these ABCs and DEs many, many times, until you do them vigorously, strongly, and powerfully, and until you practice them over and over again, you will tend to sink back into your irrational beliefs and into your inappropriate Consequences. Only with continual practice will you probably uproot your iBs thoroughly and, even then, never for all time to come. You will often tend to regress into your former habits; all humans do. No one can ever expect to attain perfection at all times, yet by using the RET methods, you will always use you ability to recognize your iBs and iCs and you will have the process for debating and disputing them at hand so you may rid yourself of them as they recur.

In most all situations where you feel emotions of anger and rage, you have a human tendency to equate the particular anger-producing action with the person responsible for it ("He *is* a terrible *person* to treat anyone that way"). You give global ratings to individuals because of their actions. We have already discussed the implications of this type of reasoning in Chapter 3. Yet because of its importance and because it constitutes one of the most difficult of your irrational beliefs to debate, we will briefly review it again.

Your failure to distinguish between people and their actions leads you to imply that only an (x) person can act (x) and that all (x) acts must get done by (x) people. Further, and more specifically, any person who does anything any other person deems bad or unjust must *be* a bad person. If a good person performs good acts, then s/he can *never* do anything bad, for s/he *is* a good person and capable of only good acts. If a bad person performs bad acts, s/he can *never* do anything good, for s/he *is* a bad person and can perform only bad acts. As noted in Chapter 3, rational Beliefs start from chosen desires or preferences—e.g., "I want to remain alive and achieve happiness"—and they evaluate acts or traits as "good" or "bad" according to how they aid or block those chosen desires or goals. They evaluate behaviors as helpful or unhelpful to *people;* but they do not evaluate or judge people *themselves*, in their "essence" or their "totality." For such a global evaluation of a *human* would amount to a misleading overgeneralization and would tend to sabotage that human's survival and happiness.

Is there, then, no such thing as a bad person? RET states that no, there *are* no bad people and, similarly, there *are* no good people. Although some do more good and others do more bad, all people do some of both. A human represents a *process*, not a *thing* or an *activity*. Your expectation that people act in a certain manner at all times remains thoroughly irrational, for as humans we can never *be* all good or all bad at all times and in every situation. You can wisely keep in mind the multidimensionality of humans. They may make considerable contributions to all humanity or to the people with whom they come in contact. They may also have many deficiencies in other ways. For instance, people can make great contributions to art and science and thus benefit many others greatly. Yet in their personal lives the same people may consistently treat others with great unfairness and injustice. By avoiding rating people globally, you allow yourself to see their other aspects even though they may, in one or more instances, treat you unfairly.

In regard to our apartment-sharing illustration, my withdrawal from our agreement may have unfairly harmed you, but if you rate me globally for this, if you make yourself angry with me for this action, you can no longer allow yourself the enjoyment of the qualities of my personality that made you want to share the apartment with me in the first place. Thus, with your anger, you may be cutting yourself off from many rewarding personal experiences in the future.

Giving global ratings to other people closely relates to the human tendency to rate oneself globally, to place the same impossible expectations on oneself as we place on others. In this way you seek to gain self-esteem or self-confidence—frequently called ego strength—by living up to these expectations. But even though you may act fairly or justly in many situations, you may also fail to do so from time to time. When this occurs, you tend to feel depressed and self-downing because you have failed to live up to your expectations of yourself. Self-confidence includes and always leaves you on the brink of self-immolation. Self-esteem includes self-downing. Ego strength involves incipient loss of ego. You don't, it seems, have one without the other. Just as soon as you begin to like yourself because you do the right, good, or fine thing, you also begin to hate or deprecate yourself because you do the wrong, bad, or even ordinary thing. Self-esteem, if you feel it, requires continual booster shots, and the only real and effective booster seems to consist of more good deeds, more high ratings for various of your traits. If you give global ratings to the entirety of yourself or others, you will feel forced to change your estimations of yourself and others—as people—continually. However, if you stick to rating only the traits themselves, you will remain far less confused by and far more consistent in your estimations of yourself and others.

In RET we consider virtually all *anger at a person* inappropriate. If you feel angry about my trait of unfairness, you at worst consider it execrable and think that *I'd better* change it for the trait of fairness. That seems rational because as long as I act unfairly, I will needlessly hurt you and others, and you, they, and even I would find it preferable to avoid that. You could, of course, consider my unfairness *awful,* meaning totally—or a hundred and one percent—bad, but that would appear irrational since you would then go beyond reality. As long as you stick to thinking of my unfairness as highly undesirable and as long as you stick to hating *it,* we can call you appropriately or rationally angry. We can define rational anger as extreme annoyance, irritation, frustration, pique, or displeasure at my unfairness trait; your determination to stay away from me because of it; and even your attempt to get me to change, to act more fairly. All these reactions seem quite rational. But if you view my unfairness as awful or totally bad, and you also view *me* as bad for acting unfairly, you exaggerate reality or go beyond it into unrealistic thinking—feeling such things as anger, resentment, rage, fury, and wrath—about me and my behavior.

So, theoretically, you could acknowledge real anger and stay within rational experience, feeling appropriately or rationally angry with me for my unfairness. But the vast majority of the time that you feel angry, you have gone beyond reality: you have felt that because you don't like these things, they absolutely *must not* exist, that those people who created or maintain them *should not* have acted the way they did and do, that you find it awful that conditions exist in this manner, and that people causing such *horrible* conditions rate as bad people.

You can feel extremely annoyed and displeased and may call those feelings rational anger. The trouble with doing so arises from the tendency to refuse to face your feelings of "real" or irrational anger and to insist that you merely feel rationally annoyed when you truly feel insensately angry. So I personally prefer to think of practically all emotions of anger as inappropriate and self-defeating, even though I acknowledge that you may prefer to label some of them as "appropriate" and "rational." I fully acknowledge that whenever I honestly feel "angry" I not only *want* people to act well but also *demand* or *command* them to do so. If you can feel "angry" without such a demand or command, fine—you can then say that you feel "rational anger." But for the sake of clarity and finer discrimination, I would then prefer to label your "rational anger" as "strong annoyance" or "profound irritation."

I have said that if you rate my traits, such as my fairness to you and others, as good, this seems accurate and rational, but that if you rate *me* as good for having such desirable traits, this seems inaccurate and irrational. You tend to help me raise my self-esteem by rating me as "good." But then I also will tend to put myself down when you rate another one of my traits as "bad." This idea of global ratings rarely works too well since all humans possess a number of faults no matter how many good qualities they may have. For even if I always acted fairly to you and others, I wouldn't always do everything else well. No human does. So your esteeming me as a person because I continually achieve does not seem practical in this world of exceptionally fallible humans.

You and I had better avoid the idea of self-esteem and self-confidence. If I give myself self-esteem in order to see myself as a person who can almost invariably do well, to win the plaudits of others, and have a happy life, I also will strongly tend to castigate myself when I do poorly. As we agreed, I will do poorly on many occasions. Moreover, when I feel self-disrespect, lack of confidence, or low self-esteem, I almost automatically will assume not merely that I have certain disabilities and deficiencies, but that I *have* to continue to have them. For if I rate as no good or worthless for treating you and others unfairly, then how can a rotten me, an individual whose essence consists of rottenness, change and behave better in the future? If I see myself as an unfair person, won't I predict that I will keep acting unfairly and probably fulfill my own prophecy in this respect? Self-esteem and its concomitant, self-downing, practically never work very well. Therefore, using self-esteem to help myself feel better about my existence won't produce very good or lasting results. If this seems true, for what purpose should I rate myself?

When I say of myself, "I rank as a good person, and I really like my goodness. I would rate as a worthless person without it," I mean that I like myself *because* I act well and would dislike or down myself if I acted badly. Besides the disadvantages already mentioned, this type of good-bad self-rating has the great disadvantage of keeping me anxious if I do not always live up to the expectations I have imposed on myself. And I imply something still more in this idea of self-esteem: because I do such good things, act exceptionally well in many respects, I can legitimately see myself as a *better person* than anyone else. You may do well, too, and I view that as fine. But I tend to feel that I can do better, outstandingly better, and qualify as a *really* good person. I have to show everyone, including myself, that I rate as a *better* human. What we call self-esteem, then, often amounts to self-aggrandizement, for we often tend to feel ourselves as better or more worthy than other people.

I contend that one of our primary and really important purposes in self-rating involves proving ourselves not merely human (which we establish no matter what we do) but superhuman, or superior to virtually all other humans. When we say, "I have self-esteem," we really say that we strive for perfection, godlikeness, utter superiority, and nobility. We don't merely mean that our *traits* qualify as better than or superior to those of others; we actually mean that we, our essences, rate as better than others. And we may also mean that if we don't excel beyond other humans and become universally acknowledged for it, we will have little or no real value.

I have always found it interesting to note than when people do something poorly, they not only see themselves as pretty worthless individuals, but also tend to accept and forgive others, very often, for exactly the same deficiency. For example, if someone writes a poor essay, he may often, upon realizing the poor quality of the work, view himself as a total failure who can never write well. Yet if someone else were to write something equally poor, he would tend to have more understanding of the other person's similar deficiency. People tend to feel far more self-critical than critical of others because they demand almost perfect behavior of themselves. Thus, they often take themselves seriously to task. In such situations many people feel confident that another person would, in all probability, succeed where they had failed. For their own failures affect their self-image so drastically that they have difficulty in even making an honest attempt to master their inadequacy and, instead, often give into it, wallow in it.

Thus, if you encounter an excellent writer—far more skilled than yourself—you would most likely feel resentful and intimidated by the other's success to such an extent that you could neither appreciate nor learn from the skills of the other. For you this would involve admitting that other person's superiority insofar as writing. Having accepted your own inferiority, you would most likely automatically surrender your total self-worth. For these and many other reasons, you'd better wisely avoid attempting to rate either yourself or others by any one or a number of either good or bad traits. It can lead mainly to self-defeating confusion.

We do not question here the idea of evaluating and judging specific traits and characteristics in oneself and others. You may passionately like or dislike anything you choose. We stress the idea of carrying this individual judgment of a trait into other areas of a person's total character makeup. I would suggest that the wisest approach consists of evaluating each trait individually and comparing all these traits (both those which you find appealing and those which you find distasteful). With this overview, you can then decide whether you had better avoid or seek out a particular person.

If your decision favored the latter choice and you based it on an awareness of that person's bad as well as good traits, you had better prove willing to *accept* in him or her that which you find distasteful. In every individual you will find disagreeable things that will continue as an intricate part of that person. You may, of course, attempt to help someone alter these traits, but you'd better not make that possible alteration of personality a contingent factor in the relationship, for often you will find these deficiencies virtually unalterable. In all cases, people have a combination of good and bad characteristics; no one has ever had all of either. Until you readily accept this, you will find it difficult and frustrating to enter into any kind of honest close relationship with another person.

If we can accept this in ourselves and in others, we will no longer find a need to demand that a person *should* or *must* act in a specific manner at all times. We will no longer demand irrational perfections and will no longer find imperfections so intolerable that we feel helpless and angry in the face of disappointment and frustration. We will feel more tolerant and appreciative of our own qualities and those of others. This more realistic attitude will also enable us to live happy, productive, and satisfactory lives.

While we often find it difficult to tolerate negative aspects of our intimates, we also do not want to live without or disassociated from those same people and their traits which we enjoy. The illustration of the apartment-sharing agreement serves as a good example of this particular situation, for you discover that you have to live without something that you wanted very much but that you could not have. If you could face your loss rationally and with relative calm—and not demand that I, who broke the agreement with you, feel guilty or inferior—you could perhaps at some time in the future construct with me a relationship or agreement in the originally desired manner. Granted some time may have to pass before such a situation could occur, but if you act more or less rationally during the difficult period of our relationship, we would have an excellent chance of resolving a number of our difficulties.

In using the RET approach to the problem of anger and other inappropriate Consequences you uniquely concentrate, on you yourself, rather than on the other person or persons involved. This standpoint leaves you free from the disturbing goal-inhibiting frame of mind that comes along with anger, anxiety, and depression. Instead of expending time, thought, and energy on these emotions, you nurture all your available strength and fortitude so as to place yourself in a position to get what you want as quickly and as easily as possible. Anger and accompanying inappropriate Consequences will only cause you further unpleasantness, such as feuding or having to avoid a certain person or place because your anger will flare if you happen to encounter that person or one of that person's friends.

The RET method encourages your independence and helps you realize your own potential as a human while teaching you to accept your own shortcomings without feelings of worthlessness because of them. By overcoming these attitudes about yourself and others, you then can separate the real from the unreal, or magical. It may seem silly to say, but we do live in a very real world, and if we truly expect to get from this world the important things that we truly want, we had better prepare to deal with the situations and people in the world in a realistic manner. For it seems absurd and irrational to believe that in reality we can achieve our goals if we insist on viewing the world and ourselves in an unrealistic manner.

As I have stated before, we have little control over what happens or what actually exists, but we do have both choices and control over how we view that world and how we react to the difficulties, which exist as an important part of its reality. In this way we ourselves "create" reality. With RET tools, you will find yourself well equipped for your goals to live happily and sanely and rationally to confront the daily frustrations that plague your everyday existence. You will also cope with situations in which people or conditions make your goals frustrated or unattainable. To live with such an outlook certainly seems well worth the effort which the RET method requires.

8

Feeling Your Way
Out of Your Anger

In this chapter we shall discuss some of the emotive methods used in RET to overcome your anger. By "emotive" I mean a forceful, hardhitting, sometimes dramatic way of interrupting and changing your anger and a method that focuses on your "feelings" or "desires"—which invariably include "thoughts" and "actions" but which we can somewhat arbitrarily distinguish in their own right. "Behavioral" methods, which we consider in the next chapter, may overlap with "emotive" methods but tend to stress "actions" rather than "feelings." You also tend to do them with less forcefulness or drama.

The first, and perhaps the most important of the emotive methods of overcoming anger consists of unconditional self-acceptance or self-acknowledgment. This involves the strong resolve to accept yourself fully, no matter what you may do, including making yourself angry.

If you were to come to me, an RET therapist, and tell me that you keep making yourself angry, I would try to show you—by my attitudes and behavior toward you—a good example of what we call *full acceptance*. I would agree with you about the wrongness of your anger, but I would accept you as a human *with* this wrong behavior and would not in any way put you down for having it. As many psychologists have pointed out for a good many years, one's acknowledgment of others' right to live with poor behavior may well therapeutically enable them to accept themselves and thereby to have more time and energy available to change that behavior. But even if others don't always accept you, in fact even if everyone tends to severely criticize you for your feelings and behavior, you can still accept yourself fully while acting poorly. For if you do take the criticisms of others to heart, if you do agree with them that you rate as a worthless person for acting so poorly, you still have *decided* to agree with these ideas or notions about yourself. Because, on the other hand, you could have heard these people out, fully acknowledged their negative opinions about you, and then only seen your behavior as inappropriate, not that you amounted to a bad person for having such behavior. You would have *decided* to disagree with them. (If you can decide to agree with others' globally downing you for your anger, you can also decide to disagree with them.) If you already tend to down yourself, without much influence from others for your inappropriate feelings and actions, you can decide not to agree with your own self-downing attitudes. You can make the decision to accept yourself with your anger while acknowledging it as a fault, which you would like to amend. This strong decision amounts to an emotive method of self-choosing.

The more decisively, the more strongly, the more firmly you determine to accept yourself and to refuse to down yourself at all costs, no matter what you do in life, the more you will *feel* self-accepting. You can get this kind of powerful thought and feeling, as George Herbert Mead and Harry Stack Sullivan pointed out, by hearing other people's positive appraisals of you and adopting them as your own. You can also get it from figuring out for yourself that you can have any feeling, no matter what, and from firmly deciding, *choosing*, to accept yourself, even though you may hold some ideas and emotions (such as anger) you may wish to alter. The next step involves working continually at maintaining this feeling of self-acceptance. We believe an idea strongly not merely because it simply occurred to us or because certain people kept repeating it to us but because we, consciously or unconsciously, work at repeating it to ourselves and engage in some manner of "proving" it over and over again to ourselves.

Even if we have a physiologically biased idea—such as the notion that cake tastes good and meat tastes not so good—we keep repeating this idea to ourselves many times, showing ourselves, especially when we eat cake, how good we find it and how much better it remains than steak. Unawarely or semiconsciously, we put a good deal of effort into endorsing one idea ("Cake tastes great!") and "verifying" an opposing idea ("Steak doesn't taste good!"). Out of this kind of perpetual work and practice comes our strong—and highly emotive—conviction about the relative merits of cake and steak.

Similarly, you can really practice fully accepting yourself with your anger, if you have it, and the more often and more strongly you work toward this acceptance, the better you will feel about yourself. In RET we assume that anger does you more harm than good and that knowing this, you would prefer to minimize it. We view surrendering your *iB*s as an important part of this process to minimize anger and enjoy a happier life. At the same time we stress the importance of fully accepting yourself during the entire process and of repeating to yourself this acceptance or endorsement as often as possible.

Another emotive technique consists of Rational Emotive Imagery (REI), formulated a number of years ago by Dr. Maxie C. Maultsby, Jr., a rational-behavior psychiatrist. I have adapted it as follows: first, you imagine a negative event or series of events that normally lead to your feeling angry. Vividly and intensely imagine, for example, that I not only refuse to share the apartment with you and withdraw from our agreement in an inappropriate manner, but also go further by denying that I had ever made such an agreement with you. I strongly assert that you fabricated the whole story in an attempt to manipulate me into sharing an apartment with you.

Now imagine this negative experience, or any experience of your own, which will evoke intense feelings of anger and rage. Presumably you will feel very angry with me, both for going back on my word and for denying that we had ever made such an agreement (you know full well that we did and that I know that we did). Rather than avoid these feelings, let them erupt with their fullest intensity; let yourself fully experience them for a few minutes.

After you have really and truly experienced the anger and rage for a while, push yourself—really try to push yourself—to change these feelings. Use what you have learned from RET thus far, and work through the ABCs step by step. If you feel anger, don't think that you can't change this feeling by talking to yourself. You can. You can change this feeling at almost any time by working at doing so: by getting in touch with your gut-level feeling of anger and by pushing yourself to change so that you experience different and more appropriate feelings, such as those of disappointment and irritation at my behavior. You definitely have the ability to make these emotional changes. So give it a sincere try; concentrate and do it.

After you have pushed yourself to feel the appropriate Consequences of disappointment and irritation rather than the irrational feelings of anger, take a careful look at what you have done to make these changes and try to retrace or recapture the exact steps of your mental process. You will note that you have in some manner changed your Belief System at point B and have thereby changed your Emotional Consequences at C. You have probably accomplished this change in your feelings by telling yourself, "Oh, well, I'll never like his going back on and denying we ever had our agreement, but he definitely has a right, as a fallible human being, to act in that obnoxious manner." Or "He really has inconvenienced me greatly by his unfair behavior, but my world won't come to an end because of that inconvenience. How annoying! But I don't have to view it as really all that bad."

Let yourself clearly see what you have done by carefully and closely examining what important changes in your Belief System you have made, Make yourself fully aware of the new rational Beliefs (rBs) that create your new appropriate Consequences (aCs) regarding the unpleasant Activating Experience (A)—my acting unfairly to you and then denying my unfairness.

If your angry feelings do not change as you attempt to feel more appropriate feelings, don't give up. Keep fantasizing the same unpleasant experiences or events and keep working at your emotional feelings until you do change them from inappropiate to appropriate. You create and control your feelings, and you *can* change them.

Once you succeed in feeling disappointed or irritated rather than angry and once you see exactly what beliefs you have changed in your head to make yourself feel bad but not emotionally disturbed, keep repeating the process. Make yourself feel angry; then make yourself feel disappointed and annoyed but not angry; then look again at exactly what you did to bring about these changes.

Keep practicing by doing this over and over again until the process becomes familiar and increasingly less difficult to carry out.

If you keep practicing this kind of Rational Emotive Imagery (REI) for at least ten minutes every day for a few weeks, you will get to a point where whenever you think of an event about which you would normally make yourself angry or whenever this event actually occurs, you will tend automatically to feel disappointed or annoyed rather than enraged.

If you have trouble practicing REI every day, you can reinforce or motivate yourself to practice by rewarding yourself when you do with some personal indulgence that you particularly enjoy. On days when you fail to do your REI exercise, you can deny yourself something you like or penalize yourself by taking up some task you find distasteful.

I have rarely met an individual who could not keep practicing REI to reduce anger. Over the past years the hundreds of people whom I have encouraged in using this method and who actually and sincerely worked at it have in most cases been able significantly to reduce their tendencies to anger themselves at various kinds of unfortunate experiences.

You can also employ this REI method to create pleasurable or good feelings toward someone which will divert you from and aid you in overcoming your hostile feelings toward him. R. W. Ramsay, a cognitive-behavior therapist at the University of Amsterdam, has done some experiments in this connection and has worked with a technique he calls emotional training. As applied to anger, you might adapt his emotional training as follows:

Think of an intensely pleasant experience you have had with the person with whom you now feel angry. When you have fantasized such a pleasant experience and have actually given yourself unusually good, intensely warm feelings toward that person as a result of this remembrance, continue the process. Recall pleasant experiences and good feelings, and try to make these feelings paramount over your feelings of hostility.

Rational Emotive Imagery and pleasurable self-training work along the same principle as hostility indoctrination, which originally contributed to the formation of your *iB*s. Left to your own devices, you not only create anger and resentment toward others, but keep practicing and practicing these feelings until they "naturally" or easily rearise. You may not realize it consciously, but you do this kind of steady practicing with regard to your inappropriate negative emotions. By the same token, then, you can deliberately practice achieving appropriate negative emotions, as you do in REI, or you can deliberately practice positive or pleasurable emotions, as in Ramsay's emotional training technique. You do really have a choice of what you feel, and if you actively use these methods, they can provide you with the means to reach feelings other than anger.

RET employs some famous *shame-attacking and risk-taking exercises* to help you overcome your feelings of self-downing, but you can employ them as aids in reducing anger as well. When I invented these exercises, I realized that most people upset themselves by making themselves feel ashamed: ashamed of doing something wrong and ashamed of others' witnessing their wrongdoing and thinking lowly of them. I try to get my clients to do things that they consider "risky," "shameful," "embarrassing," or "humiliating," such as telling strangers that they had just been released from a mental institution, yelling out the time of day in public, or wearing outlandish clothing. They then can see that these "shameful" acts really didn't make them feel embarrassed or lead to self-downing unless they themselves decided to feel that way. They can also see that the shameful acts do not cause as much concern in the minds of others as the potentially "shamed" think they will, that others quickly forget about these acts, rarely, if ever, concerning themselves much with them. If you feel terribly ashamed or embarrassed by various harmless acts—like singing in public—you too can try a few of them until you see that not only can you bear to do them, but also you can learn much by performing them and you can even come to enjoy them.

At times we cover up feelings of shame or embarrassment with those of anger. You can use the same method described above to practice feeling neither shame nor anger. For example, suppose a waiter in a high-class restaurant gives you poor service and you feel ashamed to bring it to his attention or to complain about it—for fear he will treat you with disdain or, perhaps, make some disparaging remarks about you. Force yourself, under such conditions, to speak to the waiter about the poor service and even ask him to do something you normally wouldn't: that he replace your soup, which you find too cold, with warmer soup. By doing this, you will see that it really has no intrinsic "shamefulness." As you do it, also try to get yourself to feel that the waiter has his own human fallibility and that once you express your displeasure with his behavior, you do not have to condemn him for behaving that way.

Similarly, if you tend to feel hostile toward people who appear to act unfriendly to you, go out of your way "shamefully" to encounter some of them: horn in on a conversation they engage in with someone else, or insist that you have met them before when you really haven't, etc. By working against your shame in this connection, you will probably see that you invent some of their unfriendliness as a protection against your "shamefully" en-countering them and that while, in reality, they don't feel hostile or unfriendly toward you, neither have they had, initially, any great interest in you.

Risk-taking and shame-attacking exercises or this type of homework assignment consist of assertive endeavors. This brings us to regular assertion training, which RET has used since its inception and which constitutes an excellent way to prevent or tone down feelings of anger. For just as anger frequently covers up feelings of shame, it even more frequently stems from deep-seated feelings of unassertiveness. You would like, for example, to say no to a friend's request which you have no desire to fulfill, yet you don't feel comfortable about asserting yourself in this situation. Perhaps you fear being rejected if you don't participate, so you withhold your feelings and go along with your friend's wishes. Because you act this way, you can easily come to hate yourself for acting so weakly and to hate your friend for manipulating you into doing something you don't want to do.

If unassertiveness of this nature leads to hostility, you may often solve this emotional problem by training your-self to act more assertively. Thus, if you firmly keep refusing to "go along" with individuals who try to get you to do so, you will not act weakly, you will have no reason to condemn your behavior or yourself for it, and you will have no reason to condemn others for "forcing" you to do what you do not want to do.

Assertion training, though it falls under behavioral methods of combating anger (which we will consider in the next chapter), also constitutes an emotive technique of therapy when you have a strong desire to act assertively and fail to do so. If you sincerely want to say no to someone but hesitate to say it because you fear rejection, you might try forcing yourself to say it until you "naturally" feel good saying it and can easily and appropriately say it again and again. Your practicing such assertive training amounts to an evocative-emotive procedure.

Forcing yourself to behave differently from the way you usually do comprises the main emotive element here. As I keep noting, "emotional" thinking and "emotional" activity seem strong, forceful, biased behaviors. When emotional, you very much want (or "need") things to go or not go in a certain way, and you feel highly motivated to get what you want or avoid what you don't want. Emotionally, you move *powerfully* toward or away from various people and conditions. By the same token, forcing yourself to change your behavior (especially when you have trouble doing so) constitutes an emotive, dramatic way of self-modification. Assertion training frequently partakes of this kind of forcing.

In RET we have always employed some of the role-playing and behavior-rehearsal techniques, originally created by J. L. Moreno and then adapted by Fritz Perls and the Gestalt therapists. Whereas Moreno, Perls, and others tend to use these techniques largely for abreactive purposes—e.g., for the reliving of early emotional experiences and for cathartic release in regard to those experiences—we tend to use them in more behavioral ways, as espoused by modern behavior therapists.

Suppose, for example, that you want to tell someone off about something you dislike without being irrational and you have trouble doing so. As your therapist or as the leader of your therapy group I might get you to try to express the feelings you have about this situation. You might then role play yourself, and another member of your group might role play the part of the person whom you wish to confront. You would first tell exactly how you feel about the circumstances, perhaps trying to express yourself as honestly as possible. Then the members of the therapy group would give a critique of your presentation, commenting on whether you spoke (1) too hesitantly; (2) too honestly; (3) with distinct hostility instead of assertiveness; (4) quite appropriately. If you did well, we might ask you to repeat the performance several times, merely to rehearse it and get you used to it. If you did poorly, we might ask you to try doing it again in several different ways, until you seemed to express yourself not only the way you felt but also in a way that would most likely bring you the results you wanted with the person or persons to whom you expressed yourself.

When alone, you can do this kind of role playing or emotive acting out in your head, in front of a mirror, or with the use of a tape recorder. Or you can do it with the help of a friend or a group of friends. It does not require a therapist or a therapy group, though often you will find such a setting useful, just as you would find it useful to practice acting in a play in front of a teacher and a group of fellow actors.

You employ RET-type role playing, either with yourself or with others, not merely to express yourself and your feelings or to let off steam, but to show yourself that you really create your own feelings of anger and that you have much better choices. Many kinds of psychotherapies believe that if you feel angry at someone or something, you have to let out this anger before you can deal with the situation sensibly. You then might find yourself screaming or yelling loudly at someone, pounding pillows (which may represent the person you would wish to strike), or otherwise "letting out" your anger.

Considerable clinical evidence indicates, however, that the more you take out your anger in the above manner, the angrier you tend to become. RET offers a good explanation for this occurrence. If you, for example, deliberately insult someone who has done something "wrong" to you or if you pound on a pillow that represents that person, you in all probability tell yourself something like "He really did treat me unfairly and I hate him. He *should not* have acted that way toward me, and I really hope that he gets this type of treatment back twice as much as he gave it to me!"

As you express your feelings in this kind of self-verbalization, you will "confirm" your irrational ideas about the person you think has abused you. He has acted one hundred percent wrongly; he had no right what-soever to make such mistakes; he rates as a rotten person for acting in that way; he deserves to get punished. Perhaps after you release your hostility in this active manner, you will go back and review what actually hap-pened and somewhat forgive the other person for his or her "awful" acts. More than likely, however, your ex-pressed hostility will only serve to help you exacerbate the "terribleness" of these acts and make you feel, for the present and the future, even angrier.

Some individuals, after physically or verbally express-ing their hostility to others (or to the world), see how much they keep making a mountain out of a molehill, and then calm down and feel only disappointed and sorry about the way others treat them. But the vast majority of people seem to "confirm" their irrational view that others shouldn't act badly toward them and that bad acts mean the entire person rates as bad. Ironically, the more these people "release," "ventilate" or "abreact" (re-feel and re-enact some earlier experiences of) their anger, the an-grier they feel, and the more likely they will tend to make themselves angry again at other unfairnesses. So although occasionally in RET we help people express their pent-up feelings of anger (for example, by forcing themselves to tell someone off in one of our group or marathon therapy sessions) and although we help them show their feelings of annoyance or displeasure at the behavior of other people, as stated, we almost always try to help them see that they really create their own feelings of anger and that they have much better choices.

RET emphasizes that when you feel others treat you unfairly, you had better acknowledge your feelings of anger, if you have them, admit that you foolishly create these feelings, and surrender your shoulds and musts with which you create these irrational feelings. In this way, you can end up feeling very disappointed and sorry rather than angry, and you can perhaps choose to express these appropriate feelings instead of choosing to express your inappropriate hostile feelings.

RET by no means objects to your having intense feelings, including negative ones, but we encourage you fully to acknowledge, get in touch with, and stop denying such feelings. RET shows you how to differentiate or discriminate appropriate feelings of annoyance and displeasure from inappropriate feelings of anger and rage. RET teaches you how to keep the former, how to change the latter. It gives you a choice about whether—and how—you express your feelings to others. No matter how you feel, you'd better honestly recognize your feelings. But recognize doesn't necessarily mean endorse. Nor does it mean express. Some of your authentic feelings you can fully endorse and had better express. But not all of them!

9

Acting Your Way
Out of Your Anger

Like enjoyment or pleasure, human emotional disturbance—as noted long before modern psychotherapy
came into existence—has a strong habituating or repeti-
tive component. This habituating tendency or behavioral
pattern works more or less automatically and unconsciously and plays a large and important part in disturbed
thinking, emoting, and behaving. We can explain this
compulsion to repeat as follows: people probably first
began to treat you unfairly during your early childhood
when you almost completely depended on others for the
gratification of all your urges. You probably responded
only to yourself something like: "They must not treat me
that unfairly!" Having made this statement to yourself,
you might have haltingly and inefficiently made yourself
feel angry and lashed back at them. But over a period of
time, as you "practiced" and "practiced" this irrational
belief, you swiftly, easily, and automatically began to
take this idea—that you must receive one type of treatment and that others must not treat you in any other
manner—and you made it part of your basic philosophy.
So now, as this thought habitually and automatically

occurs, you "practice" feeling very angry and lash back at people who you (wrongly) think angered you.

Your thinking, your feeling, and your activity—the whole complex of your anger—therefore emerge as an instantaneous, reflexive, habituated response. Noting anger's individual elements—what you perceive and what you tell yourself about what you perceive—generally makes it easier to see that anger often stems from the irrational and childish belief that "I must not get treated this way." Originally, you probably did note these elements closely. But after a while you stopped noting them altogether and began merely to perceive that as soon as anyone treated you unfairly, you instantaneously felt anger and you then lashed back at that person. You therefore probably concluded—and mistakenly—that "The act of this individual's treating me unjustly automatically makes me angry." Although a false conclusion, the swiftness and habitual repetition of your emotional and behavioral reaction to unfair treatment led you to view the false conclusion as true.

Although we allow our unconscious and automatic habituation tendencies to take over many of our originally conscious activities, we never actually eliminate the cognitive elements directing our thinking and behavior. So when we do well at something, we do invariably have—and influence ourselves by—an underlying philosophy of "I want to do well at this activity and will try to do as well as I can." When we do poorly at something, such as quickly and instantly making ourselves enraged at another's unfair behavior, we also seem to have an underlying philosophy, this time of either lack of desire to do well at that particular task or an absolutistic *should* or *must* attitude that sabotages our desire to do well and creates our self-defeating behavior.

Perhaps uniquely among major psychotherapies and

self-help procedures, RET fully recognizes that we can and do have conscious directive motives behind "automatic" or habituated feelings and actions. RET shows you how to look for and identify and then dispute and significantly change those philosophies that do not seem to work best for you—notably, your irrational philosophies. But it also acknowledges, as many therapeutic systems do not, the enormous influence and power that rehabituated, "practiced" behavior has on thoughts and feelings. RET's behavioral homework assignments try to harness and use that power constructively.

For instance, if you keep having a difficult time learning to play tennis because you feel inferior and put yourself down for not making any progress at mastering the game, you can—in spite of your negative attitudes—force yourself to play daily no matter how poorly you perform. Although your self-defeating views and self-downing feelings will probably interfere with your learning to play well very quickly, they won't interfere with your learning to the point where you won't be able to play the game at all.

So despite your feelings and your inhibiting tendencies, you persist at practicing the task. As you do so, you ultimately play tennis better, and finally, you begin to play quite well. At that point in your progression you realize: "I thought I could never play tennis even adequately, but I now see that I can play fairly well. I still may not always play without making some fairly obvious mistakes, but I don't see that as anything so bad."

By forcing yourself—in spite of your self-downing attitudes and your inhibitory behavior—to keep practicing tennis, you can actually have an effect on those negative attitudes and thereby give up your disturbance about playing tennis. You can probably do this more swiftly, thoroughly, and efficiently if you also work on looking at and disputing your irrational beliefs. But just as your beliefs influence your behavior, your behavior also influences your beliefs. You therefore have a choice of working on changing both your beliefs and your behavior or of changing either one to help you change the other. RET encourages you to make both these choices. It not only uses highly cognitive, emotive methods (that largely involve changing attitudes and feelings), as shown in the previous chapters, but it also tries to get you to employ a number of active-directive, behavioral methods (that mainly involve changing overt actions). Within the latter context, an important form of treatment, one in which RET has pioneered extensively and acquired some degree of fame in promoting, consists of active, *in vivo* (in your own life) homework assignments. This means that we give almost all our regular clients—and we can teach people like you to give yourself—steady homework assignments to assist them in overcoming various emotional problems.

Using our illustration, let us assume that you feel angry with me for withdrawing from our agreement and that you seek help from an RET therapist. Your first homework assignment might consist of your maintaining contact with me while you keep working through your problems of anger. For if you immediately break off this contact because of the anger you feel toward me, such an action would present something of a cop-out.

Your goal does not merely include your efficiently stopping me from treating you unfairly in the future—which you could nicely do if you discontinued your relationship with me—but also includes getting yourself to feel only appropriately disappointed or annoyed with that type of behavior rather than inappropriately angry. If you discontinue relationships with people who make you angry, you will in all probability have minimal feelings about them and their behavior in the future but for the wrong reasons—because you have no contact with them and it. You will have done nothing to improve your own behavior and feelings. Thus, if you cease to feel angry at me because you completely forget about me and what I have done, what kind of change have you made? You will still, presumably, maintain the same philosophy as before. You merely won't activate that philosophy because you don't presently have any Activating Experience in which you might employ it. This amounts to something like your angering yourself immensely because a man steals from you and your then feeling no more anger toward him because he does not have the opportunity to steal from you again.

Avoidance of persons and situations does nothing to alter your anger-creating philosophy. You still have it, and you will continue to use it to enrage yourself whenever any negative experience occurs. If, however, you take the homework assignment of continuing to stay in some kind of relationship with a man who has treated you unjustly and even perhaps give him an opportunity to repeat his poor treatment, and if you maintain this ongoing contract and *still* don't anger yourself about what he has done to you, then it would appear that you've really worked on, and to a considerable degree, changed many of your irrational, anger-creating beliefs.

The homework assignment or behavior project consists of two distinct parts: first, the behavioral activity itself (*maintaining the contact*) and secondly, the cognitive activity (*working on your ideas about people and their treatment of you while you continue to participate with them*). We favor homework assignments with both behavioral and cognitive components because by using this dual approach, our clients can personally work through their emotional and behavioral problems simultaneously and learn by their own thoughts and actions to have a clearer understanding of how all the factors we have been discussing work together.

In many situations anxiety accompanies anger. You often make yourself angry because you feel anxious about confronting others with their poor and unfair behavior, and by angering yourself you cover up the feeling of helplessness which accompanies anxiety. Thus, you use anger to create the false sense that you work at doing something about the situation.

In vivo homework assignments can help you work out these compound difficulties of anger, anxiety, and depression in several ways. As mentioned, one of them involves staying in an unpleasant or obnoxious situation and working through your disturbed feelings about it. For example, if you felt anxious about confronting me with my unfair treatment, you could force yourself to confront me with a number of lesser faults I have, which you may have mentioned or discussed with me at various times during the course of our relationship. For instance, you might mention such things as my failure to meet or call you when I had said that I would, my speaking nastily to you, etc. Because we would already have started discussing unpleasant topics, you might find it easier to work up to the main issue presently at hand without feeling so anxious.

You can try another approach to dealing with feelings of anxiety or self-downing about having your anger. You can force yourself to realize that you have a right, as a human, to have feelings of anger. By acknowledging this shortcoming in yourself and by indulging yourself in the feelings, you would gain self-acceptance. In accepting yourself, you would also feel less intimidated about your own feelings and could gradually desensitize yourself to feeling anxious in anger-producing situations. In this frame of mind you would find it far easier to dispute your irrational beliefs, for you would allow yourself awareness of them.

These behavioral homework assignments can help you habituate yourself to facing "disturbing" experiences and to dealing with them rationally. You thereby see that you can survive happily in spite of your frustrations. In acquiring the discipline these assignments demand, you tend to increase your frustration tolerance. This greatly helps since emotional disturbances—anger, anxiety, depression—in large part result from low frustration tolerance (LFT). We often remain anxious about confronting someone because we refuse to bear the pain that would temporarily occur if we confronted the situation directly. We make ourselves angry because we refuse to accept the reality of painful or frustrating occurrences and we sometimes tend stoically—but passively—to accept them if we cannot easily and quickly remove them. By refusing to accept and tolerate the pain that accompanies difficult situations, we sustain our anger, for through our inability to stay with and work through disappointing situations we do not give ourselves the opportunity to change our irrational attitudes about their existence.

Good activity homework assignments therefore help you stay with unpleasant situations and tolerate them until you can effectively change them. They also help you take on various kinds of present pains for future gains, as when you force yourself to confront people quickly about their unfairness in order to get the hassle out of the way and perhaps induce them to treat you with more consideration in the future. The more you do the kind of homework that RET usually encourages, the more you tend to increase your tolerance for frustration and thereby minimize your tendencies to make yourself angry and depressed.

Joseph Wolpe, a famous behavior therapist, has

pioneered an effective technique of *reciprocal inhibition* or *systematic desensitization* exercise which you apply through thinking and relaxing rather than through live (*in vivo*) action. You can use Wolpe's method by letting yourself think of some situation in which you normally would feel very angry. As you picture the unpleasant situation, let yourself relax by using any one of a number of techniques, such as Yoga, or thinking of pleasant relaxing scenes. As you relax, your rage tends to dissipate. After you have practiced interrupting your anger with relaxing exercises over a period of time, you may well get to a point where you no longer feel anger in these situations.

Or you can use a hierarchy of "anger-creating" scenes, as Wolpe would again suggest. Write down a series of such scenes, ranging from mildly angering to greatly angering scenes. Begin by picturing the milder type of situation and immediately interrupt your feelings of anger by letting yourself relax. After you no longer feel angry at this mildly angering situation, go on to picture a more provoking situation and interrupt that one, again by relaxing. By continuing this process of training yourself to interrupt your anger, you establish a gradual sequence of desensitization to these situations. After you have gone through your own hierarchy of mildly angering, moderately angering, and intensely angering scenes and have succeeded in relaxing instead of feeling enraged by all of them, you will tend to feel desensitized to almost any kind of poor behavior or frustrating situation. This type of systematic desensitization (SD) enables you to feel less angry under any kind of angering situation; thus, you can reach a point at which you remain almost immune to anger-creating stimuli.

You will find systematic desensitization (SD) somewhat similar in theory to Rational Emotive Imagery (REI), although it also has an important difference. SD advocates that you begin with the least provoking situation and gradually work your way up to a more dramatic experience. You have to relax every time you go through the hierarchy of anxiety-creating or anger-inciting scenes that you imagine. REI, on the other hand, asks that you *begin with* the worst possible situation and let it flood your senses. Thus, you actively *force yourself* to change your feeling from an inappropriate one, such as anger, to an appropriate one, such as disappointment. You may find either of these methods effective, in accordance with personal taste or preference.

RET also makes use of B. F. Skinner's technique of *operant conditioning*. This self-management technique bases itself on the principles of reward and penalization. You carry out training or conditioning on the principle of rewarding yourself with a prize (such as food, approval, or a much sought-after privilege) when you perform the desired behavior; and with a penalty when you do not perform it.

Using penalties, as well as reinforcements or rewards, does not amount to the same thing as damning and putting yourself down for your poor behavior. I hope I can show you why by making a clear distinction between a *penalty* and a *punishment*. If you keep having temper tantrums and you wish to stop having them, for instance, you can legitimately penalize, deprive, or fine yourself some kind of penalty. For in this case the term "penalize" simply means to deprive yourself of something you consider beneficial or enjoyable in order to help you change your behavior for better results that you want to achieve—your basic goal consisting of helping yourself survive more enjoyably. To punish yourself, on the other hand, means (1) to penalize yourself in the sense just noted *and* (2) to denigrate yourself as a person for meriting the penalty.

Skinner's work has often led to considerable criticism

because an operant conditioner can subtly manipulate people by using reinforcing principles to get them to do many things they don't really want to do or don't find in their best interests. People can abuse the technique, especially in controlled environments such as schools, hospitals, and prisons. As used in RET and most other forms of behavior therapy, however, operant conditioning mainly takes the form of contingency management or self-control applications. Clients who wish to change their self-defeating behaviors and, particularly, to discipline themselves in various ways where they normally have great trouble doing so agree with (contract with) the therapist to engage in certain kinds of assignments and to accept pleasant reinforcements only if they complete their assignments satisfactorily. They also agree to accept certain penalties if they do not carry out their assignments.

Self-management principles also apply nicely to individuals who make contracts with themselves. Writers and artists have for many centuries helped themselves work at their crafts for a minimum period of time each day by allowing themselves to eat, read, or talk to their friends only after they have put in this allotted amount of time. Millions of people have induced themselves to diet, exercise, or do other unpleasant tasks by imposing some stiff penalty on themselves if they do not live up to the contracts they make with themselves.

To apply this principle to our RET theory, let us say that you have trouble spending time every day working on Disputing your irrational beliefs and working on your *in vivo* and other homework assignments. You know that you can use the RET theory effectively by giving ample time to this process. In this situation you can make a contract with yourself, and to make the commitment more formal, you can write your agreement down in very clear terms. As a reward (or reinforcer) for having carried out your exercises, you can select any activity or indulgence you particularly enjoy. Each day that you spend the required time Disputing and debating your *iB*s, etc., you can reward yourself. Failure to meet the requirements of your contract will result in a penalty (some activity or thing you find highly distasteful). You may sometimes find it preferable to seek the help of another person to assist you in enforcing this contract. A close friend or associate will often happily assist you in a project of this nature, for when people care for you, they enjoy seeing you improve. Also, an arrangement of this nature helps ensure that penalties and rewards get faithfully enforced—a crucial aspect of operant conditioning. If necessary, you can institute the penalty in the morning so that you will not avoid it altogether.

Because people have such a wide range of likes and dislikes, I will not take the time here to outline specific rewards and penalties. Instead, I will give a general description of what each may contain. Rewards, naturally, had better seem desirable, yet not too extreme for you do best to give yourself this reward every time you deserve it, and if the reward feels beyond your daily reach, you will have no reason to follow through with your agreement at times when you cannot earn it. At the same time don't make it part of your daily routine. Instead select something which you allow yourself less frequently. I would also suggest you select rewards that you can receive immediately upon completing your daily assignment since they will then tend to work more effectively. In the case of a ten-minute SD or REI exercise, I strongly suggest that you allot time to do the exercise in the morning. If you place it later in the day, a greater danger exists that you will put off your exercise and thus go to bed without having either rewarded or penalized yourself.

Like rewards, devise penalties within reason. Too severe or hard-to-enforce penalties do no good at all. In order to constitute effective motivations, penalties can have three main characteristics that relate to your life directly. They can consist of (1) not getting the reward and (2) depriving yourself of, or interrupting a part of, your daily routine that you enjoy. For instance, if you smoke, you can deprive yourself of smoking on days when you require a penalty. A penalty can also consist of a burden you impose on yourself in addition to the two mentioned above. Let us say that you generally take a cab or drive yourself to work because of your hatred of public transportation. As a good penalty you can force yourself to use this hated and inconvenient method. This works an effective penalty since you force yourself to put up with it twice: on your way to work and on your way home. A penalty, then, can (1) deprive you of your reward, (2) deprive you of part of your daily routine that you particularly enjoy, and (3) add a burden to your daily routine.

If you wish, you can institute a secondary reward and penalty system. If you practice your exercise every day of the week, for instance, you can give yourself a super reward on the weekend—such as going to dinner at a special place or to a movie. In a similar manner, if you haven't kept your agreement, you can impose a super penalty like having to get up early on a weekend morning to do some bothersome chore.

Let me reiterate the difference between penalty and punishment. As I tell my clients, you may decide to penalize laboratory animals for going down the wrong pathways in a maze in order to help them discover the right pathways. But you certainly wouldn't scream at or brutalize them if they hadn't responded correctly. You do this essentially, however, when you punish (rather than merely penalize) yourself for inefficient behavior—you put yourself down as a human.

So long as you stay with the idea "I *want* to give up my anger," you can logically follow it with: "and since I find it so hard to give it up and so difficult to train myself to work against it, I *want* to find a penalty that will help me work at giving up this anger." If you use this kind of formula, your desire to accept the penalty outweighs your desire to avoid the difficult taks of disciplining yourself against your anger. You willingly impose a penalty on yourself in order to overcome your unwillingness to accept the pain of the self-discipline.

When you punish yourself, rather than penalize yourself, however, you really tell yourself, "I *must* give up my anger and make myself more disciplined in this respect; if I don't do what I *must* do, I not only will penalize myself, but will also put myself down for not keeping my agreement with myself." The punishing equation includes a magical *must* and a foolish self-downing consequence of that *must*. Many people find it difficult to make the necessary distinction between these two ideas, for they feel that some force in the universe degrades them when they have promised themselves to do something sensible and then have failed to follow through with that promise. RET has a primary concern of helping people stop this type of self-flagellation.

RET also employs a good deal of assertion training (AT), strongly geared to help people act assertively rather than aggressively. When you assert yourself, you merely seek what you want and avoid what you don't want. However, when you act aggressively, you also add a hostile component to your feelings and behavior: your belief that others have no right to block you from getting what you want leads you to feeling contemptuously toward them for refusing to give you what you want. RET clearly teaches you how to distinguish assertion from aggression and how firmly and persistently to strive for the things you want without hating others, unnecessarily antagonizing them, refusing to compromise, and demanding or commanding that others must give you everything you want.

RET sets the stage philosophically for your trying to act assertively rather than aggressively and in this respect differs significantly from the less discriminating therapies of such people as Wilhelm Reich, Fritz Perls, and George Bach, to mention a few. Once you understand this RET principle and fully accept the fact that others do not make you angry but that you have the responsibility for creating your own aggressive or hostile feelings, you can much more effectively proceed to do many kinds of activity-oriented assertion training exercises that will help you overcome a good deal of your rage and fury.

Self-assertion involves a considerable amount of risk taking: doing what you really want to do; refraining from doing what you really don't want to do. Naturally, other people may feel annoyed by or think disparagingly of you for your assertiveness. Assertiveness therefore entails possible penalties, and you had better consider these before you assert yourself, particularly in some instances where you assert yourself with a supervisor or boss. You may deem the risks you take too high, and thus, you may decide not to assert yourself. Deliberately holding back on asserting yourself may at times constitute very rational behavior.

Many of the times when you behave passively, however, you view normal risk taking as being *too* risky because you feel perhaps overconcerned about gaining the approval of other people. Rational-Emotive Therapy shows you how to risk the disapproval of others in order to allow yourself the freedom of asking for what you want. RET helps you first break down your avoidance of risk and then make more overt and assertive moves.

Some common assertive homework assignments that we would encourage you to try in RET include the following:

1. *Take specific risks.* Think of a few things you would like to do but have usually felt extremely afraid to do and have therefore avoided. Like sending back a poorly cooked dish in a restaurant. Or wearing an article of clothing that looks rather garish. Or eating a sandwich when riding a bus or subway train. Or raising your hand in a large audience to ask what the speaker and other people may view as a foolish question. Or telling someone important to you that you dislike his or her behavior, while trying not to down that person for performing that behavior.

2. *Risk rejection by asking for something.* Think of something you really want—such as sex, a special food, a back rub, or going to a movie—something you think will result in cold or angry refusal if you ask for it. Risk this coldness or anger by specifically asking one of your associates, friends, or relatives for this thing. When refusal has occurred, try to talk the other person into rescinding this refusal. If you don't succeed, try on some other occasion to get what you want.

3. *Risk saying no or refusing something yourself.* Pick something that you don't usually want to do but that you often do in order to please others—such as going out to eat, having sex in a certain way, or carrying on a conversation for a long period of time—and deliberately take the risk of refusing to do this thing. You can at times nastily refuse, just to make the risk of saying no greater. Or you can usually nicely but firmly refuse, and persist at refusing, even though the other person keeps trying to get you to do what he or she wants.

4. *Do something ridiculous or "shameful."* As noted in the previous chapter, you can do some shame-attacking exercises: think of something you and most other people would think foolish for you to do in public and deliberately do this "shameful" or "embarrassing" thing. Like singing at the top of your lungs in the street. Or walking a banana, as if walking a dog or a cat on a ribboned leash. Or wearing a headband and a large yellow feather stuck in it. Or stopping a little old lady and asking if she would help you cross the street.

5. *Deliberately act as if you had failed at an important task.* Make yourself fail at a task that you normally would not want to let people see you fail at, and make sure they know about your failure. While playing in a baseball game, for example, deliberately drop a flyball that practically falls into your hands. During a public speech make yourself stutter for a while. Tell people that you have failed an examination when you have really passed it.

6. *Assert yourself coolly.* Many of the proponents of Assertion Training who swear by the fight-'em-and-assert-yourself school forget that playing it cool often constitutes a much better way of getting what you want. If you feel angry toward someone and if you acknowledge to yourself that you created this feeling and that you probably won't get what you want by overtly expressing it, you beautifully assert the fact that you live for your own enjoyment, and not for honest or authentic feeling in its own angelic right, and that you feel determined (a very authentic feeling) to have your way prevail. If you then deliberately squelch the expression of this feeling without, at the same time, denying that you have it, you often do much better by yourself than by honestly telling people off.

As Lois Bird correctly points out in regard to a mate who would get along better with his or her partner, "I don't care what you feel on a gut level; you don't have to spread it all over the verbal landscape. You can turn it off and talk to [your mate] with your cool intact." She doesn't quite note that this kind of behavior makes you much more assertive, in many instances, than overtly telling your partner off.

7. *Rehearse resistance to giving in.* George Bach and Herb Goldberg advocate a form of rehearsing resistance which consists of your getting together with a partner who makes a request of you and then giving him or her a reason why you don't want to fulfill this request. Your partner keeps coming up with reasons why you should fill the request, and you keep saying no—giving good reasons for your refusal. This rehearsal continues until you say, "You've convinced me," or your partner says, "I see that I won't succeed in convincing you, so I think we'd better stop."

8. *Courageous confrontation.* As noted above, hostility and violence often stem from lack of courage. You refuse to go after what you want or to confront others with their lapses; then, hating yourself for your own weakness and unassertiveness, you feel angry and combative toward those with whom you have acted weakly. Especially in males, as Sherwyn Woods notes, "violence is a restorative act, attempting to restore masculine self-esteem via aggressive demonstrations of power and strength," while at the same time denying feelings of passivity and dependency which in our society get linked with "femininity."

One antidote to this kind of unassertiveness and to compensatory anger consists of your courageously confronting those with whom you disagree. Certainly, overt conflict will thereby tend to occur, but at least you will put things out in the open, and resolution sooner or later will result. Even in severe and profound social conflict, confrontation seems the mechanism par excellence for dealing with many issues. If, therefore, you will courageously confront those with whom you seriously disagree and refrain from avoiding face-to-face conflict with them, this confrontation itself may well show them that you have relatively little fear, will try to have your own side prevail, and deserve consideration and perhaps compromise.

How do you do this kind of direct confrontation? By showing yourself that you can stand opposition and rudeness and that if others dislike you, you need not dislike yourself. While so doing, you often had better force yourself—yes, force yourself!—verbally to confront your opponents. No matter what the initial pain of so doing, remember that the pain of nonconfrontation generally turns out much worse—and more prolonged!

9. *Feedback.* Robert E. Alberti and Michael E. Emmons explain in detail how therapists can help their clients, especially their marital counseling clients, by rehearsing with and modeling for them assertive rather than aggressive behavior. You can do the same thing without a therapist by having one of your friends witness and "referee" a mock fight between you and, say, your mate or your boss. Set up a specific scene of conflict; decide with your onlooker exactly what the two of you, you and your antagonist, will do; have your witness critique your role playing (you, for instance, acting as the asserter and your partner as the resister); then replay the "drama"; then have more feedback and coaching by your onlooker; do the same thing several times.

Without an onlooker, you can use a tape recorder or video recorder to "observe" you and your partner during your role playing and can get feedback from the recorder to see how you have done and how you can improve your methods. Sometimes you can use the recorder, and sometimes you can use a live witness. At still other times you can have actual verbal differences with your partner, in real-life situations, and then ask one or more onlookers to report back to you what happened and how they felt about your own and your partner's assertiveness.

10. *Prior preparation.* Assertion, as Bach and Goldberg point out, often consists of preparing yourself in advance to deal with passive aggressors or procrastinators. Thus, one of your friends may not ask you to do things you don't want to do but may promise to meet you for appointments and never show up or consistently turn up late. If so, you then set very precise and active rules, such as "If you don't show up by ten-thirty and I haven't heard from you by phone, I shall go to the movies by myself." In making these rules, make sure that you don't make them idly and that you really stick to them.

11. *Clearly distinguish assertion from aggression.* Alberti and Emmons make a fine point of clearly distinguishing assertive from aggressive behavior, following some prior leads by Arnold Lazarus and my own writings. As Arnold Lazarus and Allen Fay note, "assertion involves taking a stand, resisting unreasonable demands, or asking for what you want. Aggression involves putting another person down. Assertion is positive, aggression negative." The main differences among unassertive, assertive, and aggressive behavior include the following:

Unassertive behavior: You want something and do not honestly express your want or make any real effort to obtain it. You resort to indirect, passive, somewhat dishonest actions. You frequently do not admit to yourself what you really want and don't want. You needlessly inhibit yourself and even deny some of your basic desires. You tend to feel anxious, hurt, and angry.

Assertive behavior: You want something, honestly acknowledge to yourself that you want it, and for the most part try to get it. You tend to act openly with others, though sometimes you do not fully reveal to them what you want but strongly and persistently try to get it for yourself. You feel self-interested and self-enhancing. You value other people's values and goals but usually prefer your own somewhat to theirs. You behave actively and expressively.

Aggressive behavior: You feel angry toward others for blocking your goals and often try to do them in rather than to get what you want. You strongly believe that they should not, must not thwart you. You act emotionally honestly but in an inappropriate way, often interfering with what you really want from others or with others. You behave actively and assertively but at the expense of others. You express yourself fully—and frequently overdo it. You often feel righteous and superior to others and tend to damn them. You may later feel guilty about your hostility.

If you will clearly differentiate these three kinds of behavior and not merely think you have a choice between unassertiveness and aggression, you can train yourself, along the lines outlined in this book, to act truly assertively, with responsibility toward yourself and others, as Arthur Lange and Patricia Jakubowski and other RET-oriented therapists advocate.

12. *Acting assertively.* Some of the elements of acting assertively, as outlined by Lange and Jakubowski and by Janet L. Wolfe, include these behaviors:

a. When expressing disapproval of, or your desire not to do, something, use a decided no. Don't hedge or leave the decision up to the other person. Don't make yourself defensive or apologetic.

b. Speak in an audible, firm tone of voice. Avoid whining or harsh and accusatory statements.

c. Give as prompt and brief a reply as possible, without using unduly long pauses or interruptions.

d. Try to have others treat you with fairness and justice and point out when they don't. But don't insist or command!

e. When asked to do something you consider unreasonable, ask for an explanation and listen to it carefully. Where appropriate, suggest an alternative act or solution you would rather use.

f. Where appropriate, honestly express your feelings without using evasion, attacking the other person, or trying to justify yourself in a defensive manner.

g. When expressing displeasure or annoyance, try to tell the other person the aspects of his or her behavior that you don't like. Don't attack the person, name-call, or imply that he or she deserves some kind of damnation!

h. Recognize the usefulness of I-messages instead of you-messages, but also note that the former provide no panacea. Joseph Wolpe, one of the pioneers in assertion training, tends to advocate I-messages and the use of anger in the learning of assertiveness. But therapists like Arnold Lazarus and David D. Hewes point out that I-messages, too, can include a great deal of self defeating rage while appropriate you-messages may not. Thus, if you object to the way a salesman deals with you, you can angrily say, with an I-message, "I get miffed in this kind of setup, when I try to buy a shirt from you and you behave the way you do with me." Or you can nonangrily, with a you-message, say, "You really seem to feel uptight as hell today. No wonder you act this way." Lazarus, thus, with his you-message, includes an understanding of the other person and even a positive reinforcement of him or her. So use but don't overvalue I-messages.

13. *Degrees of assertiveness.* Marlowe H. Smaby and Armas W. Tamminen point out that various degrees of assertiveness exist and that some of them seem appropriate for different kinds of situations or with different partners. Using minimal assertiveness, you merely hold your ground and refuse to let another control you, as when someone tries to horn in on a line ahead of you and you merely point to the back of the line and indicate that he or she had better go to it.

Using the next level of acting confidently assertive, you recognize another's side of the issue and feelings about it, but without vindictiveness, you solidly hold your ground. Thus, if a friend wants you to lie for him or her, you say, "I can see how you feel about this and why you want me to do this and how disappointed you will feel if I don't. But I also have strong feelings that I don't want to do this and will possibly get into some kind of trouble, so I wish you wouldn't ask me to do it. In fact, I feel somewhat uneasy about it now that you have asked."

Using a higher level, bargaining assertiveness, you still firmly hold your ground but also go out of your way to see the other's point of view and make some kind of compromise solution. Thus, you may say to the friend who wants you to lie, "I can see how you feel about this and why you want me to do what you want and how disappointed you will feel if I don't. But I also have strong feelings that I don't want to do this and will possibly get into some kind of trouble, so you can see how I feel about it and why I won't do it. But I think I can see another way to help you. I will stick pretty much to the truth but will really go out of my way to get that person to give you a job so that he can see how capable you are. I will recommend that he give it to you even though you may lack the experience he desires."

If you practice these different levels of assertion and use them discriminatingly, you can act the way you want to act and still remain on good terms—even very friendly terms—with others.

If you take these assertive risks within the context of Rational-Emotive Training, you won't feel terribly ashamed by them and you won't down yourself for acting in a way that seems at times foolish. Your goal in RET doesn't consist of taking social risks or of bucking conventions simply for the sake of doing so. RET stresses the gains you can make by the mere act of taking these risks.

In taking them without worrying too much what other people might think of you, you assert yourself while, at the same time, convincing yourself that nothing *horrible* will happen. Also, you keep learning that you can tolerate the disapproval of others although you may not particularly like that disapproval. This also allows you to feel that no person, including yourself, can legitimately put you down globally or evaluate you as a rotten person when you perform an unpopular act.

I don't claim that you will automatically surrender all your angry feelings and actions and turn into an individual who feels appropriately displeased but never enraged when certain unpleasant things occur. For even if you act appropriately assertive on practically all occasions, you may still remain an injustice collector who not only finds things wrong with others and with the world, but also whines and screams when such unfair things happen. But I do claim that one of the main instigators of anger lies in acting passively and unassertively. And I claim that if you practice acting more assertively—while realizing that you do not need the approval of other people who may deem you too assertive a person—you will tend to feel less anger with less frequency than you do presently.

RET stresses education and, consequently, employs all types of psychoeducational methods, including reading materials, audiovisual aids, charts and diagrams, slogans, and *modeling*. If you saw me as a therapist and present to me your problem of often angering yourself at people who treat you unfairly or inconsiderately, I would try to act as a model of RET's antianger philosophy for you. Thus, if you came late to therapy sessions, failed to listen—for whatever reasons—to what I or the therapy group leader kept saying to you, refused to do your homework assignments, or otherwise showed resistance to learning and changing, I would attempt to *show you that I definitely disliked your behavior but that I did not angrily condemn you for displaying that behavior.*

Not that I would necessarily show complete calm or indifference to such actions. I most probably wouldn't! I take my work as a therapist very seriously and if you failed to listen, for instance, I would still emphatically try to get you to see your self-defeating philosophies (your *iB*s) and would try to teach you how to uproot them. I would not angrily condemn you for your inattentiveness.

I would not want you to develop an emotional dependence on me and to change yourself because *I* wanted you to do so. This brings to mind something I discussed earlier in the book. I pointed out that when you openly criticize others for their "outrageous" behavior you court the disadvantage of actually setting up their urge to *defend* that same behavior, thereby exerting their "right" to it. I went on to point out that they would probably not feel the need to hold onto their "outrageous" behavior if you allowed them to reach critical conclusions about it on their own. Thus, steps they would then take away from it and toward more just treatment of others would comprise real steps symbolizing *true* growth, authentic change in their behavior. So with my playing a part in getting you to change authentically. I would attempt to get you to do so for your own benefit and only incidentally for mine.

To help me in doing this, I would behave as a good model for you to follow: I would act as someone who could provide you contrast, someone who could show you more about your irrational behavior (anger) through that contrast. Assuming, then, that it would be helpful to you for someone to serve as a rational model, the question remains: how could you get this kind of benefit for yourself without actually seeing an RET therapist?

The answer: by finding good models in your own life. Unfortunately, most people whom we encounter hardly fall into this category. In fact, they tend to anger themselves just as often about trivial unfairnesses or injustices as they do important ones. Exceptions, however, do exist—an unusual friend or teacher, an occasional relative, an associate—people who feel determined to overcome life's unniceties and who actively keep working at doing so.

Talk to these people.

Try to learn from them how they manage to keep reasonably cool in the face of life's annoyances.

Observe them in action. See if you can model some of your own feelings and behaviors after theirs.

Find them in books and other biographical materials, for literature seems full of figures who often suffered great frustrations and even persecutions without making themselves unduly angry or upset.

Seek out these rational models and, as far as you find it appropriate, learn about their lives.

Other behavioral methods of working against anger that RET finds effective follow:

1. *Exposure to hostility.* If you have the help of a therapist or therapy group or if you have knowledge of RET and attempt to use it with yourself, exposure to hostility, in the course of group therapy or in the course of your regular life, may help you. This does not mean that the hostility *itself* changes you, for it frequently serves as a bad model. But your practicing *coping* with this hostility, especially under therapeutic supervision, may well help you handle yourself more effectively as you begin to look closer at and understand the nature of your hostility. As mentioned earlier, taking oneself out of a situation merely leaves the problem in a latent state, unsolved.

2. *Constructive activities.* As Andrew S. Wachtel and Martha Penn Davis and many other researchers have

indicated, angry and violent individuals tend to feel alienated, anonymous, and impersonal. If such individuals feeling this intense or prolonged anger can experience devotion to some highly constructive group or cause, they may divert themselves from first their sense of alienation and anonymity and then some of their anger.

3. *Early conditioning.* Victor H. Denenberg and M. J. Zarrow did a series of fascinating experiments involving newborn mice, raised in one group by rats, in another— control—group by mice. They found "the mice reared by rats were heavier than the mouse-raised control mice; they also were less active in the open field and preferred to spend time near a rat instead of near a mouse. Our most dramatic finding was that the rat-reared mice would *not* fight when placed in a standard fighting-box situation. . . ." This was in contrast to the occurrence of a great many fights among control mice reared by mouse mothers, thus showing that the "natural" tendency of mice to fight can get significantly altered by having them "unnaturally" reared.

Other experimenters have found that mice raised in close proximity to dogs or cats will not later get attacked by these natural "enemies," while mice raised regularly will suffer attack. Denenberg and Zarrow note that "we must therefore reject any hypothesis that states that aggression is a genetically determined, instinctive response that cannot be modified by experience. . . . This is not to suggest that genetic factors are not important. It is obvious that they are. What we are saying is that *both the genetic background and the environment in which those genes grow and develop must be considered jointly if we are to advance our understanding of behavior patterns.*"

If we take this information and parallel it with the human condition, it seems obvious that those subjected to early conditioning designed to lessen their anger would surrender much of their natural biological tendencies to act angrily and violently. Naturally, you can now do little about your own childhood, but you could give some thought, if you have children, to helping condition them to act less hostile.

4. *Diversionary measures.* As noted above, constructive action may serve as a good diversion to hostility, and so may less constructive behaviors. Norman Zinberg, following the ideas of William James and Freud, wonders whether some kinds of competitive and semidestructive activities, such as organized sports and politics, will more successfully serve as forms of sublimation for anger and violence than other kinds of activities, such as movies or private enterprise. No one as yet truly knows, but the *RET position would tend to assume that highly aggressive pursuits, such as dog-eat-dog industrial competition and prizefighting, would help make humans more rather than less hostile in their feelings and behaviors.*

Robert Barton and Paul Bell found that mild degrees of sexual arousal served to inhibit physical aggression in experimental subjects, while exposing the same subjects to less diverting pictures of scenery, furniture, and abstract art. They found that mild levels of sexual arousal would serve to inhibit subsequent physical aggression.

As noted previously in chapter 9, the use of reciprocal inhibition as a diversionary measure also tends to reduce feelings of anger. From the evidence available, *it would appear that all kinds of enjoyable, constructive, and even neutral diversions can serve to interfere with and at least temporarily to ease hostility.* Consequently, if you want to control your own angry feelings, you can consider using such distractions, either to help you get rid of your anger on a transient basis or to help train yourself so that ultimately you will permanently tend to feel less enraged when confronted with certain obnoxious stimuli. As diversions, you can use thoughts, fantasies, games, activities, emotional involvements, pleasures, or any number of other embroiling behaviors. Mainly discover what particularly works for you in this regard.

5. *Coping procedures.* One of the main factors that seems to help almost all kinds of disturbed emotional reactions consists of your engaging, and knowing full well that you engage, in effective coping procedures. Richard Pisano and Stuart P. Taylor, for example, found that forty individuals who had records as high aggressors against others reduced their aggressiveness not when they received punishment for aggressing or when given money for not aggressing, but when allowed to give equal punishment to those who attacked them.

I conclude from this experiment that when the aggressors realized they could cope effectively and capably with their opponents, they felt much more secure and less hostile and punitive. And a good many other experiments similarly show that *when people feel that they definitely can cope effectively with some situation, they handle it much better and upset themselves considerably less about it.* I would therefore recommend that you try to develop a good set of coping measures that you can employ when faced with obnoxious events and badly behaving people. If you know fairly well that you can deal adequately with someone who treats you unfairly, you will have less of a likelihood of angering yourself at him or her. This does not constitute an ideal solution—since you often may not cope effectively with an aggressor and may recognize your own ineffectuality—but it will help in many instances.

6. *Cognitive awareness and desensitization.* R. Novaco conducted an experiment which involved showing people how to manage their anger through relaxation methods alone, through cognitive awareness and RET alone, and through relaxation combined with RET. He found that

RET worked better than relaxation and that both methods combined worked still better. We find the same thing in regular sessions of Rational-Emotive Therapy: if we first show clients how they philosophically create their feelings of anger—by whining about injustices and frustrations and demanding that these absolutely must not exist—we then can show them how to relax, how to instruct themselves in anger-coping methods, and how otherwise to live with and finally to remove their rage.

By using RET formulations, you can do the same thing for yourself. Acknowledge fully that you create your own feelings of ire and see how you do so—by insisting and commanding that something exists when it doesn't or that something must not exist when it indubitably does. As you understand this and work to remove or modify your own commands on others and on the universe, you will find yourself much more able to employ the various behavioral methods that I have outlined in this chapter.

Let me emphasize once again that although RET has a distinct theory of human nature, of emotional trauma, and of effective psychotherapy and although it does make eclectic use of many therapeutic techniques, we cannot justifiably call it an eclectic theory. It covers, in some respects, perhaps thirty or forty different methods, many of which vary greatly from one another, but it uses them because they appropriately fall under its general theory; it uses them in the framework of the general RET theory.

Its behavioral methods, for example, do not merely consist of symptom removal. If an RET therapist persuades you to employ several behavioral techniques—such as activity homework assignments, operant conditioning, and assertion training—to help you overcome your feelings of anger, he will not do so merely to get you to stop feeling angry right now, while you remain in therapy. He will try to see that you leave therapy with a good understanding of how you incite yourself to anger and how you can stop this in the future as well as in the present. And stop it under any set of difficult conditions that might later arise in life.

By giving you theoretical understanding and practical techniques that you can employ yourself, RET attempts to provide you with a treatment methodology that will enable you not only to *feel* better, but to *get* better—and to see the effects of that for the rest of your life.

10

More Rethinking
About Your Anger

RET, though fundamentally a cognitive approach to personality theory and psychotherapy, has very strong and integral emotive behavioral components. Actually, however, we have only thus far presented one basic cognitive procedure for examining and uprooting angry thoughts and feelings. That is *D*, or Disputing, in the ABCDE method of understanding and minimizing anger. Although Disputing has many complexities and includes such things as debating and discriminating, it nevertheless represents only one philosophic or cognitive approach to the problem.

If you really work at Disputing strongly, intensively, and persistently, you probably won't need any other cognitive method of accurately defining and dislodging your irrational Beliefs (*iB*s). Yet RET therapists over the years have discovered several different methods of helping clients examine and reject their irrational thinking. Let me outline some important and helpful variations.

First of all, you can use the technique we call DIBS—Disputing Irrational Beliefs—which gives you a more systematic way of taking one of your absolutistic ideas and systematically "ripping it up" many times until you no longer tend to subscribe to it. Like several other RET methods, you do DIBS for a minimum of, say, ten minutes a day for about twenty or thirty days in a row. I have outlined the general DIBS technique in the last chapter of the revised edition of *How to Live with a "Neurotic,"* in the final chapter of *A New Guide to Rational Living,* and in a separate pamphlet published by the Institute for Rational Living, Inc. Let me present it here as you can specifically apply it to a problem of anger.

Let us suppose, once more, that I have promised to share an apartment with you, have persuaded you to go to considerable expense to fix it up, and then have unfairly and irresponsibly backed out on our deal and refused either to move in with you or to reimburse you for the trouble and expense you have taken. You feel extremely angry at me especially when we meet or when someone mentions my name, and you soon see—in the ABC model of RET—that your primary irrational Belief (*iB*) that makes you feel angry consists of the thought "He *should not* have treated me that unfair way!"

You now use DIBS—Disputing Irrational Beliefs—to question and challenge that thought. In using DIBS, you ask yourself the following questions, and preferably, you write down each question on a sheet of paper and also write down your answers, so that you can review, add to, change, and consolidate them each day.

Question 1: *What irrational Belief do I want to Dispute and surrender?*

Illustrative answer: "He should not have treated me that unfair way!"

Question 2: *Can I rationally support this belief?*

Illustrative answer: "No, I don't think that I can."

Question 3: *What evidence exists of the falseness of this belief?*

Illustrative answers:

1. "Perhaps he didn't even act that unfairly to me. True, I see his action as completely wrong and irresponsible. But he may have, and others may have, a different view of this matter. And their view may have some validity. So I don't even know that I have 100 percent certainty of his wrongness and irresponsibility."

2. "Assuming that I can indubitably prove that he did behave wrongly and unfairly to me, what law of the universe says that he *should* or *must not* behave that way— that he *has to* act fairly? None! Although I and other people would find it right and proper for him to act fairly to me, he definitely doesn't *have to* do so."

3. "If he *should have* or *must have* treated me fairly instead of unfairly, he would have done so, for how could he avoid doing what he *must* do? The fact that he *didn't* treat me fairly seems to prove conclusively that no reason exists why he *must have* done so."

4. "When I tell myself, 'He should not have treated me that way!' I really seem to mean that (a) the conditions that existed at the time he treated me that way should not have existed and (b) he should not have followed them if they did exist. But of course, the conditions of his life, his history, his personality, his biological makeup, etc., did exist at the time he treated me unfairly. And if these conditions did exist, how could he *not* have gone along with them, as I seem to demand? Suppose, let us say, his mother strongly objected to the very thing that I wanted him to do and suppose that he, because of his undue attachment to her, went along with her objections and decided to cop out of our arrangement. By my statement 'He should not have treated me that unfair way!' I actually insist that his mother must not have her objections and/or that he should not go along with them. But how can I legitimately *make* her give up her objections or *make* him ignore them? Naturally, I can't!"

5. "By demanding that he not treat me unfairly, I actually seem to believe the statement, 'Because he theoretically could have *not* acted in that unfair manner, he therefore *should* have not acted that way!' But this statement clearly represents a non sequitur: its conclusion doesn't logically follow from its premise. No matter how true it may seem that he theoretically could have chosen not to have treated me unfairly, that never means that he therefore *must* choose to act fairly."

6. "In demanding that he treat me fairly, I really devoutly believe the proposition 'Because I strongly want him to act that way, he has to give me what I want!' But how valid does that proposition appear? Clearly invalid!"

7. "I also seem to believe the idea that 'Because I have treated him quite fairly throughout our dealings, he *should* and *must* treat me with equal fairness!' Another nutty idea!"

8. "I see him as a complete louse for treating me lousily. But even if I can prove to virtually everyone's satisfaction that he did treat me unfairly and shabbily, I invalidly overgeneralize when I label *him*, his entire *person*, as a louse for treating me in this vile manner. He almost certainly has some good traits and performances, too. How, therefore, can I legitimately define *him* as a worm?"

9. "When I say, 'He should not have treated me that unfair way!' I hypothesize, by using this *should*, an absolutistic *must*. I don't say, 'He *preferably* should treat me fairly,' or 'He *most probably* would get better results for himself and society if he treated me and others fairly.' I dogmatize and absolutize that 'He *must* treat me fairly!' But as far as I know, I can prove no absolutes, and positing them and feeling completely convinced of their truth appear futile."

10. "While I cannot prove the truth of my belief 'He should not have treated me unfairly,' I *can* prove that if I continue to subscribe to this belief, I will in all probability

feel very angry at him and could continue to feel angry for perhaps months or years to come, thus interfering with my chances of dealing with him effectively. Although my anger-creating statements seem unprovable, the evil results of my devoutly believing them appear eminently provable! Therefore, I had better give them up!"

11. "By demanding that he must treat me fairly, I imply that I can't stand his unfair treatment of me and that I can only survive and lead a happy existence if some force in the universe makes him rectify his erroneous ways and begin to treat me fairly. Obviously, my ideas in this respect amount to hokum. For although I'll never *like* the unfair treatment, I *can* certainly stand it and, if I stop foolishly making myself enraged at him, can also arrange to have a long and reasonably happy life in spite of his past, present, and future unfairness."

Question 4: *Does any evidence exist of the truth of my belief about him—of my assumption that he should not have treated me unfairly and that he rates as a louse for doing what he should not have done?*

Illustrative answer: "No, no good evidence that I can think of. I can easily obtain empirical data showing he treated me unfairly, and I can most probably get a consensus from many other people that he treated me unfairly. I could therefore validly contend that his *behavior* seems lousy. But I don't seem to have any evidence whatever that *he* rates as a louse for having that behavior. So, at most, my belief about him has only partial truth—and significant aspects of it appear highly exaggerated and essentially untruthful."

Question 5: *What worse things could actually happen to me if he continued to treat me unfairly?*

Illustrative answers:

1. "I would not get reimbursed for the time, trouble, and money I have spent in fixing up the apartment he agreed to share with me and would therefore continue to

suffer real inconvenience as a result of his withdrawing from the agreement."

2. "He might possibly give people a false impression of our differences, thus convincing them that he acted correctly and that I acted wrongly. This would blacken my name and reputation."

3. "As a result of his disliking me and perhaps inducing others to dislike me, too, I would suffer more inconveniences."

4. "Living in my new apartment by myself or having to share it with someone else, as a result of his reneging on his agreement to share it with me, might well prove highly annoying."

5. "I might continue to have hassles with him, particularly if we remain in contact for a long time to come. Even if we somehow resolve our differences, we both will tend to have a bad taste in our mouths and will lose out on our previous degree of trust and friendship."

Question 6: *What good things could happen or could I make happen if he continues to treat me unfairly or to change his ways?*

Illustrative answers:

1. "I could gain in assertiveness by confronting him with his unfairness and by trying to get him, even though unsuccessfully, to change his attitude and behavior toward me."

2. "I might well enjoy living by myself or finding another person to share my new apartment."

3. "The time and energy that I now expend in maintaining a friendship with him I might well put toward doing friendly things with others or to enjoying myself in other ways."

4. "I could practice my discussing and arguing skills through my attempt to get him to see things differently and to redress his unfair actions toward me."

5. "I could use this unfair situation with him as a chal-

lenge to work on my own attitudes, to acknowledge fully that I create my own feelings of anger when others mistreat me, to change my own anger-creating philosophy of life, and to prepare myself for more constructive action and less destructive rage and temper tantrums in the future when other people treat me unfairly."

The DIBS technique simply formalizes some of the more important aspects of disputing irrational Beliefs when obnoxious and unwanted conditions occur. It consists of a systematic approach to D, Disputing through a particular set of questions that you keep using with yourself whenever you feel emotionally upset at C. You can apply DIBS, of course, to feelings of anxiety, depression, despair, self-pity, and low frustration tolerance. As you may have already noted, this technique encourages a concerted, methodical approach, aims at your using it regularly (on a day-to-day basis), and asks that you do it in writing or with the use of a tape recorder, so that you can keep reviewing your previous Disputing so as to solidify it.

Another cognitive method of uprooting irrational Beliefs (iBs) consists of a technique invented by Joseph Danysh (and outlined in his book *Stop Without Quitting*). It uses the principles of general semantics—the science of language discrimination—originated by Alfred Korzybski. Korzybski notes that virtually all humans naturally and easily overgeneralize and make continual use of partially meaningless higher-order abstractions in their words and meanings. He points out that people consequently tend to defeat themselves and behave rather inappropriately as a result of their inaccurate conclusions resulting from their inaccurate semantic usage. Several of Korzybski's followers have tried to apply his teachings to the field of emotional disturbance, and much of their thinking has been incorporated into Rational-Emotive Therapy—which many authorities describe as one of the leading semantic therapies.

As stated, Joseph Danysh's theory embodies these principles of semantic overgeneralization, and in his referenting technique, he provides us with a practical, cognitive tool for bringing to our attention some of our most foolish ideas and gives us a hardheaded method of eliminating them.

As applied to the problem of anger, you can use the *Referenting* technique as follows: suppose you felt exceptionally angry whenever you saw or heard reference made to someone who has "made you" angry in the past and suppose you now want to eliminate your irate feelings toward that person. Telling yourself, "Don't feel angry. Don't feel angry," won't really work. If anything, you only could expect from it that you might succeed in suppressing your anger. You would not undo it.

Your emotional problem here probably consists of your *referenting* (confusing or coalescing) your ideas about the person's *behavior* with your ideas about the *person himself*—in a sloppy, bigoted, and overgeneralized manner. Thus, if someone else asked you to give the meanings or associations that immediately popped into your head when you thought of the person's behavior, or of the person specifically, you would probably say something like, "His behavior is no good, rotten, unfair, horrible, and evil. He is a no-good individual, a rotten person who is always unfair. He is someone whom I particularly cannot tolerate."

This type of exclusive, one-sided, and overgeneralized coalescing of the terms surrounding a person's behavior with the person himself naturally will cause you to feel exceptionally hostile toward him. As long as you insist on making this connection, you will find it almost impossible to forgo your feelings of anger and view behavior and people in a truer, more objective light.

Danysh's technique of referenting forces you to go beyond your prejudiced one-sidedness with regard to people's behavior and to bring to your mind a good many equally valid terms to describe both people and their actions. Referenting consists of taking a relatively vague word, such as *behavior*, and forcing yourself to list the much more specific referents, or concrete descriptions, that comprise it. Danysh's method particularly encourages you to bring to your own attention *many* of the diverse meanings of a term, instead of a few limited (and prejudiced) meanings. For example, while thinking specifically of someone's—say, a woman's—behavior, compose on a sheet of paper a list of negative and pejorative terms to describe that behavior—such as "rotten, no good, unfair, horrible, awful, evil, and lousy." Then, on the same sheet of paper, go out of your way to think of and write down any terms which you might think of to describe the positive or good aspects of her behavior—such as "fair most of the time if not this time, probably fair from her own point of view if not mine, acts in her own self-interest as do I, forthright, determined, assertive, sometimes very nice and considerate of other people, concerned with other people in general," etc. Finally, you might write down some of the aspects of her behavior that are neutral—many of the things she does or says that might not get construed as "good" or "bad" but just as objective parts of her performances—such as "interested in many aspects of life, highly absorbed in music, not devoted to sports, makes many public presentations," etc.

By referenting, as accurately and completely as you can, *all* these different aspects of your concept of this woman's behavior, for instance, you force yourself to keep in mind a more holistic, more accurate, and less one-sided view of her in general. Thus, your highly prejudiced views about her behavior—"rotten, no good, unfair, horrible," etc.—will tend to diminish. You will begin to see her behavior as it really exists and not as you might tend to fictionalize and distort it in your mind because of a *particular* instance.

Similarly, you could take her name—which you at first only referented negatively—and force yourself to referent it on a piece of paper or tape recording in more favorable terms, such as "a person who acts both rottenly and well; an individual who has bad points and good points; a woman who sometimes acts unfairly but much of the time behaves quite fairly," etc. And, too, you could force yourself to referent that person in a more objective, neutral, merely descriptive way, such as "a woman who stands five feet five inches tall, who does a wide variety of things, who associates with a good many people, who has diabetes, who has written a good many books," etc.

If you force yourself to use this referenting technique, especially when you feel very angry toward someone, you will almost invariably find that you can "deemphasize" his or her bad traits and thus start to acquire a much more enlightened, accurate, and realistic view of that person. Referenting won't make you automatically forgiving and unangry with all people whom you encounter and all the nasty actions they perform against you. But it frequently will help. When you get into the habit of doing it, you will tend to find after a while that you stop making yourself as often or as intensely angry at people.

Another good method which you can use both cognitively and behaviorally consists of what Viktor Frankl calls paradoxical intention. Various other therapists use it in different ways and often call it different names. In RET we sometimes refer to it as reducing irrational beliefs to absurdity. Using paradoxical intention, you can take any idea and reduce or enlarge it to absurdity—by exaggerating in your mind the wildest implications of the original idea. For instance, if you want a man to do something for you and you make yourself angry because he refuses to cooperate with you, exaggerate your wish for power and control over him:

"Of course he has to do what I want him to do! I have absolute control over his behavior. If he tells me that he will jump through hoops to please me and then refuses to go through with this jumping, I can easily put him in chains and whip him until he jumps and jumps and jumps! In fact, if I want him to give me a million dollars or to grovel in the dust before me ten times a day, he has no choice but to do my bidding! Because I desire him to do anything whatever, he completely has to do it! And if he refuses, I can immediately send down thunderbolts and annihilate him."

If you take the idea of having control over a person to a ridiculous extreme such as this, you will soon see that you really have virtually no control over him and that he has a right to do whatever he wishes even when he unfairly inconveniences you by exercising that right. You will see that human nature does not exist in the manner that you command it to exist; thus, you will start interrupting your own foolish commandingness.

Just as you can use paradoxical intention cognitively (in your mind) as described above, you can also practice it behaviorally through oppositional behavior. If people treat you unfairly and you feel exceptionally angry because of this treatment, instead of starting to plan to punish them in various ways for their iniquity, you can deliberately force yourself to take the opposite track and to act very nicely and *un*hostilely to them. You can, for example, keep befriending them in various ways: invite them to interesting functions that you know they will enjoy; do them special favors; show unusual consideration and kindness toward them. By such paradoxical behavior, you will first of all practice feeling unangry instead of angry at them—and you may actually make yourself feel nice or at least neutral about their "abominable" behavior. Secondly, you will, by turning the other cheek, in this manner, set them a good example and show them that one group of people's unfair treatment doesn't necessarily have to produce rage in another person. Thirdly, you may well encourage them to look again at their behavior and to see how badly they treated you. Finally, you may help them act very nicely toward you in the present and future and even make reparations for the wrongs they have already done you.

I do not contend, in this respect, that this kind of turning-the-other-cheek philosophy will always work or that you invariably act wisely in effectuating it. But I do say that if you use it judiciously and realize that you do it for paradoxical reasons (and not necessarily routinely, in every instance where someone treats you unfairly), you may gain considerably by it and help reduce your feelings of rage.

Paradoxical intention also works against human stubbornness. If people treat you unfairly and you even recognize that they have a problem since they do so, you may still *perversely* continue to feel and act angrily toward them in order to maintain your false integrity—to make yourself feel "stronger" when, in actuality, you keep acting weakly. This phenomenon occurs commonly between you and your parents, for instance, during your childhood. They advise you, mainly for your own good, to get up promptly when the alarm clock rings in the morning and to get yourself off in time for school. You don't like to get up that early, and you lazily (with your low frustration tolerance!) resist. But you also see that by resisting, you keep getting into trouble with the school authorities and sabotaging some of your own goals—for example, to get good marks in high school and therefore to get into a good college of your own choice.

Perversely, you tell yourself something like: "I won't get up early to please my parents! Damned if I will! That would prove me a ninny who only goes along for their ride. I'll show them! I'll deliberately stay in bed late and prove my strength and follow my own integrity!" If you act that way as a child—or, for that matter, as an adult—you merely fool yourself. Because your parents advise you to get up early, you foolishly—and perversely—convince yourself that if you do so, you will follow their rules and do it for *them*. You consider that kind of rule following a weakness, when actually it would mean a strength. You "strongly" resist them and actually act foolishly— weakly—when you do.

Similarly, often, with anger. Often you feel furious and see your fury as more self-defeating than anything else and perhaps as encouraging others to treat you even more unfairly. Yet instead of trying to change your commanding philosophy about people's behavior, you cling to that philosophy and convince yourself that you strongly and rationally feel enraged and that you'd *better* show offenders their faults. By convincing yourself that to do otherwise would prove you weak and make you give up your own integrity, you choose to persist with your rage even though you fully realize that you act irrationally. Actually, to give up your anger while keeping a strong dislike about unfair acts would make you much stronger and get you better results. But if you see it differently, and perhaps deliberately make yourself even more enraged and vindictively go after the person who has wronged you, you will continue to feel angry.

When you interrupt "strong" perversity with paradoxical intention and deliberately get yourself to think nicely about and act kindly toward others in spite of their unfairness, you paradoxically fight your own irrationality and tend to give it up. In terms of what you really want for yourself and what you will want from your future relationships with people who treat you with some degree of unfairness, you can get better results by acting in this more rational manner.

Rachel T. Hare outlines another form of paradoxical intention which I have used to help my clients cut down their angry feelings and actions. It consists of giving yourself (or some other person) limiting conditions under which you can allow yourself to have temper tantrums. One of my clients felt exceptionally irate and combative every time he thought that someone on the street spit in his direction and actually got some spit on his pants or shoes. I persuaded him to contract with himself that he would only let himself feel and act angrily when he could prove, with clear-cut observational evidence, preferably with the confirmation of other observers, that some spit had actually landed on him. Since he could rarely prove this, his fits of anger subsided greatly.

To use the same paradoxical or limiting technique on yourself, pick a set of conditions where you feel you have been treated unfairly and where you frequently feel and act with rage. Deliberately limit or hem in this set of conditions. Contract to allow yourself to feel and act angrily, for example, only when (1) everyone agrees that people have truly treated you unfairly, (2) everyone also agrees that the unfairness has caused you a considerable amount of harm, and (3) you can prove to yourself, in monetary terms, that you have lost a considerable sum of money by the unfair treatment.

If you allow yourself, in this paradoxical manner, "freely" to feel and express your rage while deliberately restricting yourself, you may soon see that you can live with your own restrictions, that you do create your anger yourself, and that you have the power to limit and control it. Such paradoxical techniques work because they get you away from thinking, desperately, "I must feel angry" or "I must not feel angry." They give you a wider range of possible reactions and help you convince yourself that you can function in this wider range.

Other kinds of humor also dramatically interrupt your overly serious manner of looking at certain unpleasant events, thereby needlessly making yourself angry, and consequently, RET therapists frequently use various types of jocularity to help their clients poke fun at their own solemnity and, both cognitively and emotively, learn to accept themselves better. I gave a now somewhat famous paper, "Fun as Psychotherapy," at an annual convention of the American Psychological Association in Washington, D.C., and made a great hit in the course of giving it, since I sang—yes, sang—two of my rational humorous songs in the course of my presentation.

I pointed out in this paper that "if human disturbance largely consists of overseriousness and if, as in Rational-Emotive Therapy, therapists had better make a hard-headed attack on some of their clients' fatuous thinking, what better vehicle for doing this ideological uprooting than humor and fun? . . . Let me briefly mention here that my therapeutic brand of humor consists of practically every kind of drollery ever invented—such as taking things to extreme, reducing ideas to absurdity, paradoxi-cal intention, puns, witticisms, irony, whimsy, evocative language, slang, deliberate use of sprightly obscenity, and various other kinds of jocularity."

Following this RET lead, you can frequently laugh at yourself when you see yourself getting angry, look for the gross exaggeration in your ideas about what others *must* do to satisfy you and how things *should* go right to make your life easier, and thereby cognitively and emotively attack such silly notions. When you demand good behavior in others, you can remind yourself, "Oh, yes, I always act perfectly well myself. I *never* treat others unfairly or go back on my promises to them. Well, hardly ever!" When you think that you absolutely need others' approval and that they amount to complete rats for not giving it to you, remind yourself what a love slob, a Mr. or Ms. Jehovah, or an RP (rotten person) you have made yourself into. When you inwardly or outwardly whine and scream because poor economic, artistic, or social conditions exist for you, tell yourself something like: "Oh, yes, I run the universe, and whatever I want has to, in fact *immediately* has to, come about. Everyone else has to live with frustration and annoyance, but not *me!*" Call to your mind, also, what I often tell my RET clients: "Life, whether I like it or not, generally gets spelled H A S S L E. Tough taffy!" When you command that you must have certainty and that you can't stand it when you don't have guarantees of success, love, fairness, and ease, show yourself: "I think I'll engrave a beautiful certificate which absolutely, with no shadow of a doubt, guarantees that I will always get exactly what I want at the very second that I want it. Then I'll get along wonderfully well and won't have to feel angry about anything!"

Keep using humor, directed against your nutty ideas but not, of course, against yourself as a person, in many different kinds of ways. And if you want to sing to yourself (or others) some of my humorous songs, you can use these from the songbook *A Garland of Rational Songs:*

Rational Songs:

WHINE, WHINE, WHINE!
(To the Tune of the Yale "Whiffenpoof Song")

I cannot have all of my wishes filled—
    Whine, whine, whine!
I cannot have every frustration stilled—
    Whine, whine, whine!
Life really owes me the things that I miss,
Fate has to grant me eternal bliss!
And if I must settle for less than this—
    Whine, whine, whine!

PERFECT RATIONALITY
(To the Tune of Luigi Denza's "Funiculi, Funicula")

Some think the world must have a right direction—
    And so do I, and so do I!
Some think that, with the slightest imperfection,
    They can't get by—and so do I!
For I, I have to prove I'm superhuman,
    And better far than people are!—
To show I have miraculous acumen—
    And always rate among the Great!—

Perfect, perfect rationality
    Is, of course, the only thing for me!
How can I even think of being
    If I must live fallibly?
Rationality must be a perfect thing for me!

I WISH I WERE NOT CRAZY
(To the Tune of Dan Emmet's "Dixie Land")

Oh, I wish I were really put together—
Smooth and fine as patent leather!
    Oh, how great to be mated
    To this lovely state!

But I'm afraid that I was fated
To be rather aberrated—
  Oh, how sad to be mad
  As my mom and my dad!

Oh, I wish I were not crazy! Hooray, hooray!
I wish my mind were less inclined
To be the kind that's hazy!
I could, of course, decide to be less crazy;
But I, alas, am just too blasted lazy!

LOVE ME, LOVE ME, ONLY ME!
(To the Tune of "Yankee Doodle")

Love me, love me, only me,
  Or I'll die without you!
Make your love a guarantee,
  So I can never doubt you!
Love me, love me totally,
  And I shall get by, dear;
But if I must rely on me,
  I'll hate you till I die, dear!

Love me, love me all the time,
  Thoroughly and wholly;
Life turns into slush and slime,
  Lest you love me solely.
Love me with great tenderness,
  With no ifs and buts, dear;
For if you love me somewhat less
  I'll hate your rotten guts dear!

Since I have done marriage and family counseling for more than thirty years, people frequently ask me how they can check or control their anger at their spouses or at others with whom they have a close relationship. Well they might! As another well-known marriage counselor, Dr. David Mace, points out in a valuable article in the *Journal of Marriage and Family Counseling,* overt or covert feelings of anger probably interfere with love and disrupt more intimate ties than do any other causes. Dr. Mace rightly takes to task the "marital fighting" concepts of George Bach and his followers and points out that if you tend to argue and fight with your mate, you can use the RET approach of dissolving or dissipating your anger, rather than of palliatively expressing it or diverting it.

More concretely, he outlines three main methods of doing this:

1. Acknowledge your anger. Tell your partner, "I feel angry at you," just as you would say, "I feel tired," or "I feel frightened."

2. Renounce your anger as inappropriate. Even though your mate has treated you badly or unfairly, face the fact that you create your own anger, that you need not do so, and that you usually harm your relationship by feeling it and by expressing it against your partner.

3. Ask your partner for help. Show him or her that you have a problem in dealing with your anger, and see if she or he can suggest some plans to help rid you of it and to make your relationship better.

David Mace has some wise suggestions along the above lines, and I highly endorse them. In a follow-up article to his, also published in the *Journal of Marriage and Family Counseling,* I add these additional RET methods to help you deal with your anger at anyone with whom you have a marital or other close relationship:

4. Acknowledge your anger to yourself. Don't merely inform your mate about your angry feelings, but frankly tell yourself, "Look: let me face it. I really feel angry at my partner. Not merely displeased; not merely annoyed at his/her *behavior.* I feel angry at my mate as a person. I feel condemning, demanding about *him* or *her.*" Unless you do something like this, you will not tend to feel in touch with your anger and will "acknowledge" it in a lip-

service-giving kind of way. Once you acknowledge your ire to *yourself* and work at defusing it, you may then choose (or not choose) to express it to your mate— depending on his or her vulnerability, on his or her own tendencies to take your anger too seriously, and on various other factors.

5. Assume full responsibility for your anger. Do not hesitate to admit that you created it, that you angered yourself. Say to yourself something like: "Yes, my mate may have acted badly and treated me unfairly, but he/she only frustrated me, gave me what I didn't want. I made myself feel annoyed and irritated about his/her poor behavior, and quite appropriately, because I do honestly want him/her to act differently and feel sorry when he/she doesn't. But I also, quite inappropriately, *made myself* angry by commanding and whining that he/she *must not* act that way; *has to do* what I want; renders my whole life terrible and awful when he or she doesn't; and consequently turns into a thoroughly rotten person. *I* chose to think this way and thereby anger myself against my partner. And I can, if I want to do so, always choose to think differently and change my feelings of anger into more appropriate feelings of disappointment, sorrow, and annoyance." If you fully, in this manner, acknowledge your own responsibility for making yourself angry, you will by that very admission tend to rid yourself of a good part of your angry feelings.

6. Accept yourself with your anger. As soon as you condemn or damn yourself for having neurotic symptoms—anger, anxiety, depression, feelings of worthlessness, or anything else—you tend to stop all progress in ridding yourself of such symptoms. For if you see yourself as a worm for feeling, let us say, enraged at your mate, how can you picture a total worm like you acting unwormily in the future? And while you keep berating yourself

for stupidly making yourself angry, how can you garner the time and energy to understand exactly what you told yourself to create your anger and to work at ridding yourself of it?

Accept yourself, then, *with* your anger. This does not mean, as some psychological writings imply, that you had better view angry feelings as "good," "appropriate," or "constructive." You can see them as "normal" in the sense of constituting part of the human condition—as an aspect of your human fallibility. But they still, almost always, defeat you—and, as David Mace points out, tend to harm your intimate relationships.

7. Stop making yourself anxious, depressed, and self-downing. As you learn to accept yourself, no matter how angry you feel or how foolishly you can act when angry, you can also learn to accept yourself with any of your other "wrong" or "bad" behavior, and if you do this, you will give up most of your vulnerability—the feelings of hurt and self-pity which often help you feel very angry.

8. Look for the philosophic source of your anger. After fully acknowledging your feelings of anger, seeing that you do not down yourself for having these feelings, and eliminating some of the self-deprecating elements in your creating these feelings, you can look for the philosophic sources of your anger. Assume (as shown throughout this book) that just about every time you feel enraged in your gut, you have a profound philosophic assumption behind this feeling and that this assumption includes some should, ought, or must. Consequently, *cherchez le* should, *cherchez le* must! Look for the *should*, look for the *must*! In anger at your mate, you frequently hold the *must* of resentment—"You *must* treat me kindly, considerately, lovingly, and approvingly!"—and the *must* of low frustration tolerance—"The conditions under which I live *must* turn out nicely and nonfrustratingly so

that I easily get practically everything I want without too much effort."

More specifically, when angry at your mate, you usually tell yourself: (a) "My partner *must* treat me considerately and lovingly. He/she actually behaves unfairly and disapprovingly. I *can't stand* this behavior! I find it *awful*! What a total rotter that makes him/her!" And (b) "I got together with this mate in order to get great joy and happiness. Economic, social, sexual, or child-rearing conditions in our relationship obnoxiously exist. They *must* not continue to exist this horrible way! How *terrible* that they do! I *can't bear* it! Mating therefore seems an absolutely frightful state, and I hate the very thought of going on with it!"

So look—and keep looking until you find—your own *shoulds*, *oughts*, and *musts* about (a) your mate; (b) your children; (c) the conditions under which you live; (d) your in-laws; (e) your sex relations with your mate; etc. As soon as you really zero in on and clearly understand these *musts*, you locate the real or most important sources of your hatred and rage—as I and Dr. Robert A. Harper point out in *A Guide to Successful Marriage*.

9. Discriminate your wishes from your demands and commands. Try clearly to discriminate your wishes about your mate and your relationship from your *must*urbatory commands. You can very legitimately tell yourself, "I would much rather have my mate have sex with me twice a week than have it once very two weeks." But you can then illegitimately add, "And therefore, he/she *must* do so!" Just about every one of your absolutistic commands on your partner has a somewhat realistic and reasonable wish or preference behind it. Search in your head and your heart for *both* the wish *and* the escalating command that insists you *have* to fulfill or satisfy this wish. Separate the two very, very clearly!

10. Dispute and debate your absolutistic *musts*. Your merely *understanding* your demands on your mate (and on the universe) will not solve your problem. For you can easily say to yourself, "Oh, yes, I see now that I feel terribly angry toward my partner because I keep commanding that she/he do exactly what I prefer. Well, maybe I'd better give up those commands and translate them back into wishes." Fine—but not enough!

Unless you very actively, persistently, and strongly dispute, question, and challenge those demands, you probably will never give them up. Only by arranging a thoroughgoing change in your philosophic assumptions, your absolutistic *shoulds*, will you probably dissolve your angry feelings. And by dissolve, I do not mean suppress, repress, avoid, or sweep them under the rug. I mean actually *eradicate* them! Also, make it much less likely that you will re-create them in the future.

11. Employ behavioral and emotive means of undermining your feelings of anger. As noted throughout this book, and especially in chapters 8 and 9, you not only create or manufacture your own angry feelings but then reinforce them by various emotive and behavioral acts. You therefore had better use evocative-emotive-dramatic and active-directive-behavioral methods to give up your anger. Thus, emotively, you can deliberately act lovingly rather than angrily to your mate. You can train yourself to empathize more effectively with your partner's point of view and feelings. You can practice what Carl Rogers calls unconditional positive regard or what in RET we call full acceptance of him or her. You can use nonblaming I-statements instead of condemning you-statements about your mate's behavior. You can express your hostile feelings about your partner to other people (e.g., friends) rather than directly to him/her. You can role-play some of your angry reactions to your mate. You can use Rational

Emotive Imagery to let yourself imagine your mate's acting very badly, letting yourself feel very angry at him/her and then practicing changing your feelings to disappointment rather than anger.

As for behavioral methods, you can use several to help you reinforce your anti-musturbational attack on feelings of anger. You can deliberately stay in anger-inciting situations or court them if they do not exist, to give yourself practice in coping with such conditions and in changing your hostility-creating philosophies as you deal with them. You can practice assertiveness instead of passivity, to ward off your building up unnecessary feelings of rage when you do not legitimately assert yourself with your mate. You can use operant conditioning or self-management methods and reward yourself when you react unangrily to your partner while penalizing (but not damning) yourself when you react angrily. You can employ behavior rehearsal methods and train yourself (by working with a model or role-playing partner) to react more appropriately when your mate does some presumably "upsetting" act. You can make written or oral contracts with your mate to do some things that he or she wishes you to do, provided that this mate will do other things that you would prefer. You can use relaxation, meditation, thought stopping, or other desensitizing and diverting methods to take yourself, at least temporarily, out of anger-arousing situations and to give yourself extra time to work against your commanding philosophies.

In many different ways, then, you can apply virtually all the anger-reducing methods outlined in this book to the problem of acknowledging your making yourself incensed at your love partner or other person with whom you have an intimate relationship and to giving up your angry feelings and enjoying more of the good feelings that this relationship may engender.

RET writings, such as my book *Humanistic Psychotherapy: The Rational Emotive Approach* and the one I coauthored with Dr. Robert Harper, *A New Guide to Rational Living,* contain much antianger material, and tens of thousands of people have helped themselves make themselves less irate by reading this material. In addition, the Institute for Rational Living, Inc., in New York City distributes a good deal of other materials, such as posters, buttons, tape recordings, wallet cards, videotapes, and films, which may help you work against angering yourself. I have frequently heard from people who have had little or no actual rational therapy but who have used these kinds of materials to good effect and have modified their irate behavior tremendously by persistently working with them.

At the institute in New York we also present a great many talks, seminars, workshops, marathons, and other public presentations which help large numbers of people with their anger. At the Friday night workshops, "Problems of Daily Living," which I have conducted almost every week for more than a dozen years now, people either bring up their personal problems and receive direct help on them from me and members of the workshop audience or else they participate less actively and more vicariously and learn how to handle their problems mainly by observing how the audience and I work with other people.

RET employs all types of psychoeducational methods to help people work against their self-defeating emotions like anger. And you can explore various methods yourself and use any or all of them to help you see what you tell yourself to make yourself angry, to understand how to dispute and challenge your own anger-creating irrationalities, and persistently to act and emote in antihostile directions.

11

Ripping Up Your
Rationalizations
for Remaining Angry

Since there exist such rational reasons for giving up our feelings of anger and such sensible ways of dealing with these feelings, why do we find it so easy, then, to ignore these rational reasons and sensible ways? Why do we favor—even, at times, revel in—staying angry?

Probably, first of all, because anger has definite biological roots. In order to see the situation in its proper perspective, let us look closely at these biological bases for anger.

As many ethologists, physiologists, sociologists, and other scientists have shown, we have a great deal of evidence that indicates—although it hardly proves conclusively—that you make yourself angry partly for biological reasons. Donald T. Lunde and David A. Hamburg, for example, have shown that in animals—as well as human children and adults—fighting behavior (as well as other forms of hostility, such as rough play, threats, etc.) tends to prevail in males much more than in females because of the influence of androgen, the male hormone on such behaviors. Additionally, Yoram Jaffe and his associates have discovered that sexually aroused males and females show more overt aggression than nonaroused subjects; and Edward Donnerstein and his research group have found that highly erotic stimuli tend to facilitate and maintain aggression in male subjects.

R. C. Boelkins and J. F. Heiser, after examining research data from animal and human biological studies, conclude that we can view aggression "as an adaptive behavior having its origins in genetically coded neural mechanisms . . . acted upon by both hormonal and psychosocial factors." The famous psychologist Harry F. Harlow holds that "aggression most likely remains in man as a solid component of his biological heritage as a primate." Sigmund Freud, considering a great amount of clinical and anthropological evidence, gives us this summary statement:

> The bit of truth behind all this—one so eagerly denied—is that men are not gentle, friendly creatures wishing for love, who simply defend themselves if they are attacked, but that a powerful measure of desire for aggression has to be reckoned on the part of their instinctual endowment. . . . Civilized society is perpetually menaced with disintegration through this primary hostility of men towards one another. . . . The tendency to aggression is an innate, independent, instinctual disposition in man . . . it constitutes the most powerful obstacle to culture.

Dr. David Rosenthal, chief of the National Institute of Mental Health's psychology laboratory, presented a paper on "Heredity in Criminality" at the meetings of the American Association for the Advancement of Science in which he studied considerable psychological and physiological data in regard to criminals and concluded strongly that a significant hereditary, as well as environmental, factor exists in the causation of some forms of criminality.

Philip Solomon and Susan T. Kleeman, in an article on

"Medical Aspects of Violence," point out that violence—when unprovoked or bizarre or when associated with impaired consciousness, confusion, or irrationality—may stem from limbic disease or cortical disease of the brain. Several researchers, including British psychiatrist John Gunn find that individuals with abnormal brain waves prove more likely to commit motiveless violent crimes than those with normal brain waves.

In another study of criminals' brain waves, B. D. Murdoch concludes that aggressive psychopaths seem to have a significantly higher level of cerebral instability than do nonpsychopathic prisoners. Denis Williams also found that aggressive criminals produced significantly more abnormal brain waves than otherwise "normal" criminals.

Specific biochemical and hormonal concomitants of aggression and violence have turned up in the studies of many different investigators. E. J. Kermani, for example, found that testosterone in males and to a lesser extent in females helps foment aggression. L. A. Gottschalk and his associates, studying the biological rhythms of the menstrual cycle in women, discovered a tendency of both anxiety and hostility levels to decrease transiently around the time of ovulation and saw as the presumed cause of this decrease some hormonal change. C. L. Ekkers confirmed the hypothesis that a positive correlation exists between aggressive behavior and methylnoradrenaline secretion in young males. J. R. Lion, G. Bach-y-Rita, and F. R. Ervin, in their studies of violent individuals, conclude that "at least ten and probably twenty million Americans have impaired brain function which limits their potential to understand, channel, and redirect aggressive energies."

Many outstanding social and physiological scientists

have held that biological, hereditary, and chemical factors play a pronounced part in human aggression—along with psychological and sociological learning. Jerome D. Frank emphasizes the high level of male hormone output among young males and attempts to relate this to a pattern of recurrence of war. Dr. Jose M. R. Delgado has done many experiments with monkeys with tiny electrodes implanted in key areas of the brain. By pushing a button and sending a radio signal, he can induce a peaceful monkey to go into a rage and attack other monkeys. As Albert Rosenfeld points out, "when he releases the button, the monkey is peaceful again." Abraham Maslow held that deprivation needs of humans, including their urges to aggression, have an instinctoid basis and include "some genetic basis . . . however weak this may be."

Paul Meehl, Leon Festinger, David Premack, and a group of other very well-known psychologists agreed that humans "are not a very lamb-like species and do have innate tendencies toward anger and aggression. Dr. Benjamin Spock summed up his views on child development by noting that humans have "inborn temperament," "ever-ready hostility," and a power drive that virtually cannot be eradicated from their nature. Frederick W. Ilfeld, Jr., held that "violence as one form of aggression, may be considered as an inherent part of human nature."

Other social thinkers, such as Ashley Montagu, hotly dispute this view. Montagu states that human "aggressiveness is a learned form of behavior. There is absolutely no evidence whatever; indeed, the evidence is entirely in the opposite direction, that man is in any way 'programmed' to behave aggressively."

Montagu seems partly right, for no *conclusive* evidence exists for the programming of aggression, anger, and violence in humans. But most authorities agree that they have innate tendencies to get easily self-programmed in such ways. For many reasons, their biological tendencies predispose them to react angrily.

K. E. Moyer points out that a variety of physical inventions, including hormone injections, electrical stimulation, and surgical brain lesions, can control irritable aggression in humans. And in his *The Psychology of Aggression*, he notes that certain allergens affect the nervous system directly, probably causing a noninflammatory swelling of the brain, and that such allergens can, in some people, lead to many types of irritability, including acute and chronic physical violence. Anthropologist Ralph Bolton, studying exceptionally hostile tribes like the Qolla of Peru, found that a higher protein intake of food went along with lower homicide rates and more peaceful behavior, while a lower protein intake tended to create opposite behavior. Sociologist Pierre L. van den Berghe summarizes his views on human aggression and available resource competition by saying, "Drawing comparative evidence from primates, I suggest that Homo sapiens rates high on territoriality, hierarchy and aggression, and that these forms of behavior are biologically predisposed. With the food growing revolution, the cultural elaboration on these biological predispositions became increasingly important; but an understanding of human behavior must necessarily be both biological and socio-cultural."

Professor Steven G. Vandenberg, a behavior geneticist, presents evidence from studies of identical and fraternal twins that the former behave far more like each other in aggressive tendencies than the latter and that therefore, heredity seems a significant factor in hostility.

Many other scientists—especially ethologists such as Konrad Lorenz, Robert Ardrey, Desmond Morris, N. Tinbergen and Lionel Tiger—have likewise beaten the drum in recent years to apprise us of the fact that hostility has fairly evident biological roots. And even those who have criticized their "findings," such as Edward C. Ryterband, have admitted that at least part of their argument appears valid. Ryterband, for instance, has noted:

> No intelligent arguments can or should deny that environment has significant effects on all of man's behavior. Increasingly, evidence has accumulated not that there are instincts which control us, but that much of our behavior springs from both genetic and environmental sources. The data regarding the dual effects of both genes and experience on intelligence and some behavior disorders are substantial and old already. It is only being argued here that similar data may speak for some of man's aggression as well as for other more attractive features in his behavior, that some part of his aggression is a product of his genetic past as well as his environmental present.

Erich Fromm, in his *Anatomy of Human Destructiveness*, largely concerns himself with showing that we don't have specific or unsurmountable instincts to destroy ourselves or to wage ceaseless feuds and wars. He stoutly opposes the instinctivist-hydraulic model of aggression that writers like Freud and Lorenz espouse—the model that says that we as humans have innate destructive or aggressive energies and that if we do not express and utilize them directly, they will force us into extreme forms of violence, like war, genocide, and suicide. At the same time, Fromm admits that the data of the neurosciences which he reviews "have helped to establish the concept of one kind of aggression—life preserving, biologically adaptive, defensive aggression. They have been useful for the purpose of showing that man is endowed with a potential aggression which is mobilized by threats to his vital interests."

So even Erich Fromm, obviously, does not completely oppose a biological basis to anger and aggression. He merely shows that this basis does not doom us to the worst forms of aggression, particularly mass murder, which some other theorists, including Freud, seem to think it does. Also, as Morton Deutsch points out in reviewing Fromm's book, his basic thesis holds that destructiveness (and, presumably, all other character traits) result from the interaction of various social conditions with human existential drives—such as our awareness of our power-lessness, our ignorance, and our death. But these existential drives themselves have a clear-cut biological basis, as I think Fromm will gladly admit. So his seeming antagonism to biological forces in our nature remains very partial—and in many ways, no antagonism at all.

Granted that almost all contemporary theorists acknowledge anger's strong biological as well as sociological roots, you would mistakenly "use" the biological basis as a reason for not changing your own irate behavior. Granted that you have innate tendencies to anger yourself at the real and imagined injustices of the world. Admitted that you have strong predispositions to condemn others as a whole for some of their highly partial behaviors and to wish them dead for doing "wrong" and "immoral" acts, I still ask: why must you *go along* with those physiologically based tendencies? And what justifies your using its "historical" basis as an *excuse* for your rage?

Don't forget, in this connection, that you have numerous other biologically based urges that you nearly always control—and with good reason. You naturally and biologically spit, chew, and pass flatus. But do you do so unrestrainedly, without any controls on yourself?

Therefore, no matter how strong are your inherited predispositions to scream at others, tell them how completely stupidly they act, and pummel them into the ground when they seriously thwart you or treat you unfairly, the fact still remains that you don't *have* to do any of these things, and you can usually (if not always) appreciably cut down on these kinds of behaviors if you willingly work hard to do so. No evidence exists that you will necessarily end up with an ulcer or high blood pressure for often blocking or controlling such behaviors any more than it exists for your winding up equally diseased and dis-eased if you control a host of your other biological functions.

As a member of society I personally squelch many of my biological, pleasure-oriented urges and I do so every day in the week, perhaps even every hour of the day. I eat less than I want, copulate on only limited occasions, frequently keep silent when I would thoroughly enjoy continuing to talk, go fully clothed in even the hottest of weather, and restrict my biological urges in countless other ways. And not only do I manage to get by with minimum or moderate discomfort as I limit myself in these scores of ways, but I actually often feel pleased to do so. As a diabetic, for example, I *enjoy* curbing my diet and forcing myself away from sugary foods which my palate would relish but which the rest of my constitution would find almost fatal. Curbing my anger (and my biologically based desire to knock the stuffing out of those who block me in various ways) does not unbearably frustrate me. In fact, in some ways, I manage to enjoy *that* kind of self-curbing, too!

People also hold onto their anger because they do not realize their alternatives. Even downtrodden individuals, such as minority groups or women, whom our culture has sorely tried and abused, need not give vent to their anger, nor must they cravenly submit to exploitation and subjugation. They have more than the grim choice of: (1) passively submitting to their controllers, letting themselves get "walked over," and (2) angrily ranting and raving, symbolically or actually resorting to violence—presumably giving healthful vent to their feelings and thereby feeling much better and more confident about themselves. Of these two choices, the first seems definitely the worse and basically consists of unassertive subservience. So I definitely do not recommend that. But in RET we seek a third path, one that exists *between* cravenly giving up what you want and nastily telling others off—fighting them to the death. We advocate, instead, *determined opposition.* If I, for example, lived as a woman in our still antifeminist society, I would realize how many injustices and handicaps I had to bear because of my femaleness, and I would fervently dislike, oppose, and even hate these barriers to my greater fulfillment. But I would not (in much the same way that my male oppressors bigotedly scream and whine against female rights and privileges) idiotically convince myself that "Because social rules treat me unfairly, they *must* not exist! How *awful* that they do! I *can't stand* society's discriminations! The people who promulgate and sustain these rules emerge as totally rotten *tyrants*, whom we have to annihilate entirely if we want these horrible customs changed!"

In other words, no matter how disappointed, frustrated, and determined I felt about antifeminist traditions, I would not waste my time and energy screaming and wailing about such traditions. Instead, I would determinedly organize myself and my female cohorts to fight and change them. Claudeen Cline-Naffziger partly sees this third, nonangry, determined path toward social change when she notes: "Florynce Kennedy's analysis of action-oriented anger is educative for both women and their therapists. She suggests that instead of women putting down other women, husbands, family, or custodians as is wont to occur, women must be encouraged to put their anger energy on the sources of power. Anger energy is more potent when focused on those above rather than those around or below."

Previously in this same article, Ms. Cline-Naffziger noted that "most women have such a reservoir of anger and so much energy stored up in tending it that they need screaming, kicking, yelling sessions to release the excess and get the burden down to a manageable size." She fails to see that this kind of screaming and kicking behavior carries with it a distinct *philosophy* of anger—namely, that things *must* not remain indubitably unpleasant even when they almost certainly *will*, at least for a while, remain that way. And she doesn't see that such tactics will mainly siphon off energies that women could put to constructively fighting to change the social system.

Moreover, as thousands of years of human history have proved, once a downtrodden group angrily and violently pits itself against a group of ruling oppressors, its childish demandingness and commandingness frequently spark equal irrationality and lack of rational judgment in its opponent. So either the original rulers get back into power and savagely annihilate the rebels or (as in the somewhat typical cases of the French and Russian revolutions) an even more extreme group of rebels takes over from the original group—and a frightful and almost completely senseless bloodbath and prolonged suppression of human liberty ensues.

As a longtime revolutionary myself, particularly in the fields of sexual permissiveness and psychotherapy reform, I have frequently made angry outbursts against my "reactionary" opponents, and sometimes I still do. But I have almost always found that my anger does more harm than good for my own cause and that I work much more effectively for what I want and against the stupidities I don't want when I vigorously, forcefully, determinedly —and *non*angrily—keep fighting for what I consider just, good, and efficient.

Scores of psychologists such as George Bach and Herbert Goldberg and other authorities in the field point out the great harm that we do to ourselves by refusing to acknowledge and express our feelings of ire. In agreement with Freud, they insist that "when open aggressive expression or interpersonal encounters are suppressed, either for conscious reasons, such as the desire to be polite or 'nice,' or for deeper motivations, such as the fear of angry interchanges, these feelings are not lost. Rather they are driven underground, so to speak, and re-emerge transformed behind socially acceptable masks."

Such remarks require careful consideration. Bach and Goldberg seem to mean that you may sometimes have *disturbed* reasons for suppressing or repressing feelings of anger. Thus, if I treat you unfairly, you may first feel you have to act politely to me in order to show everyone, including me, how you rate as a "nice person." We can call this "disturbed" because you then tend to run your life mainly for others and not enough for yourself. You make yourself so concerned about my and others' opinions that you refuse to ask yourself what *you* really want in life—and you feel frustrated and unhappy for surrendering too easily to any opposition.

Your second disturbed reason for suppressing anger: your fear of possible rejection and anger if you risk telling me your feelings of displeasure. You would really like to show me my unfairness and try to get me to act better toward you, but you feel terribly afraid of such a confrontation because it might turn into an angry interchange. You again start worrying too much about what *I* might think of you and too little about what *you* really want. Once again, this means that you feel you have to make yourself into a totally "nice person" who never quarrels with anyone, never risks disapproval. Unassertion, or the giving up of what you really want to do in life in order to desperately win another's acceptance means that you fail to live, that you give up much of your healthy desiring, and that you fail to ever let your own individuality emerge.

So, if wanting to rate as a "nice person" and fear of rejection constitute your motives for squelching your feelings of anger, you will drive underground some of your *other* feelings—especially your feeling that you have a right to exist in this world and to have others treat you fairly. Bach and Goldberg quite rightly point this out. But they also seem to forget that you could have quite different, *healthy* reasons for not feeling or expressing anger—namely, your wish to have more loving, cooperative, and friendly relations with me and others and your desire to have more of the things you want and less of the things that you do not want in life.

In other words, Bach and Goldberg fail to see that while you can (1) illegitimately need and insist on others liking you, you can also (2) *legitimately* desire and want to get along better with them. If you have the first need, you then, peculiarly enough, tend to suppress the second set of feelings, and, perhaps more important, you also suppress your desires to get along with yourself and to try to achieve what *you* want to do in life. Since, however, you *do* want others to like you and you *also* want to get what you desire out of life, the overpolite demeanor that Bach and Goldberg deplore denies this—and especially denies your own wants and preferences. But Bach and Goldberg, unfortunately, forget that when you healthfully surrender your dire *need* for others' approval, you can still legitimately retain your *desire* for their affection. You can therefore consciously suppress (instead of consciously repress) some of your angry feelings—and thereby get along better with them and with yourself. Overpoliteness may well stick in your mind emotionally but normal politeness may distinctly aid both your interpersonal and intrapersonal relations.

The various arguments in favor of anger often have a fairly sensible core, but this core easily gets escalated out of proportion to the underlying half-truths it contains. Of course, anger has its good points! So do murder, tyranny, revolution, baby seal hunting, and cannibalism. All these expressions of the human spirit can exist in a legitimate, self-fulfilling way and sometimes—though not too often!—do decidedly more good than harm. Moreover, if we completely extirpated them from the human condition, our race would suffer a distinct loss.

So with anger. Many authorities have rightly pointed out its humanitarian elements. Israel Charny holds that "aggression is an omnipresent, instinctive force in all of life which we might best define as the purposeful, pulsating energy or strength for being that is one's life force." Albert Solnit indicates that "in children the aggressive behavior serves to make contact with the love object and gain libidinal satisfaction." Martin Roth points out that political, religious, and revolutionary wars have a pronounced altruistic element because they would not have occurred without the peculiarly human characteristic of self-sacrifice.

Edward Sagarin shows how suppressed people can acquire respect for themselves through hatred for others. W. W. Meissner contends that "human aggression has a positive and constructive role to play in the development of man's religious spirit." Edward D. Joseph sees aggression as including behavior and activities, mental and otherwise, that emerge as forceful and that involve a direct approach to the object. Nevitt Sanford indicates that we want children "to be angry about the right things (human exploitation for example) and to express their anger in ways that help to counter destructiveness." Chris Meadows designates anger as "the emotion which primes aggressive behavior in defense of life and integrity." Rolland S. Parker points out that expression of anger and aggression may help people confront and master difficult situations.

All these points have a good deal of truth. But they also have considerable falsehood. For they mainly confuse "anger" or "aggression" with assertiveness, the strong motivation to change obnoxious stimuli, and the determined effort to effect that kind of change. True, hostility contains such constructive elements. But even more true: you can keep these elements and still eliminate what we normally call hatred and rage.

The apologists for anger and aggression apparently do not see this. They do not define their terms clearly enough, or they hopelessly think that you can only assert yourself—especially in the face of difficult or obnoxious conditions—through a great deal of childish demandingness or whining that things should not, must not exist the way they do, and through consequent feelings of anger. Wrong! You can keep your determination and your assertiveness without grandiose enragement if you think clearly and act forcefully along the lines outlined in this book!

Anthony Storr whitewashes anger in this way: "Only when intense aggressiveness exists between two individuals . . . love can arise." True—if you train yourself to feel and act entirely unemotionally, with no passion whatsoever in your life (which, as a human, I doubt you will find yourself able to do!), you will knock out "bad" emotions like hostility—and "good" ones like love. But rational, as I keep emphasizing to my clients and to audiences all over the world does *not* mean unemotional. It means *appropriately* emotional. Storr, for example, seems to believe that you need aggressiveness in order to love, and I believe that you don't. But although one of us probably holds a wrong view, neither of us may hold it irrationally—unless we also believe that our view *has to,* absolutely *must* prevail. Our passion doesn't make us irrational—but our dogma does!

"Constructive" aggression advocates believe that if people "do you in" and you let yourself have a brief or mild period of anger against them, you handle yourself very well, while if they treat you just as badly and you let yourself intensely and prolongedly hate them, you handle yourself badly. This idea has some truth to it since long and extreme hatred usually makes for worse results than short and moderate hatred. But very few, if any, of the abreaction-encouraging writers or therapists seem to realize that *all* anger, even one percent anger, has a *should, ought,* or *must* in it and that even your one percent anger differs significantly from the ninety-nine percent irritation that you would feel if you applied your irritation only to my *actions* rather than to me as a whole person.

If you limited your reaction in that appropriate manner when I treated you unfairly, you could, for instance, very strongly say to yourself, "I loathe his behavior! I thoroughly wish that he would not act that way! I feel very determined to get him to treat me better." In that way, you would tend to feel exceptionally irritated at my actions and you would be unusually determined to get me to stop them rather than weakly and briefly (one percent anger) telling yourself—or me—"I really hate him for treating me that way! He should not have done that!"

Remember, in this connection, the old joke about the woman who tells her highly conservative parents that she "is a little bit pregnant." Either her pregnancy exists—or it doesn't. Her statement that she has a "little bit" of pregnancy doesn't face the real issue: that she *really* has gotten pregnant. If you make yourself act only a "little bit" angry for "a little while," you obscure the fact that you still take a philosophically wrong position about someone and his or her unpleasant behavior and still *command* that he or she not act that way. In my view, cruelly murdering a hundred people definitely proves more wrong than cruelly murdering one. But that hardly makes the single murder right or proper!

Dr. Robert I. Daugherty has stated that "sometimes,

anger can be fun. Once in a while, an argument—if it lasts only a short time and has some resolution—gets your adrenalin going. It can be the highlight of your day."

Yet we had better not forget, in this connection, that Hitler *enjoyed* sending millions of Jews and Gypsies to the gas chambers. And Stalin and other tyrants *felt great* about imprisoning, torturing, and finally managing to kill many of their political opponents. Lots of harmful human acts can seem fun, such as overeating, overdrinking, drug taking, and staying home from work or from school when you have some difficult task to do there. Most of these "fun" conditions, however, consist of short-range hedonistic gains, and in the long run they lead you—and especially the people you feel angry at—into all sorts of difficulties. Although your *basic* goals in life had better consist of pleasure, happiness, and enjoyment, your going for certain *immediate* gains, such as those bestowed by rage and violence, hardly helps you achieve your basic purposes.

Patti Hague expresses this idea: "Maybe by nurturing myself and having more faith in my lovableness and my relationships I'll not be so fearful of angry responses from others and I'll let my new found freedom to express anger become powerful instead of dwarfing it with tears." As people frequently do, Ms. Hague seems to assume that displeasure results in anger or tears with no other alternative available. And she also implies that if she has lovableness and can act well in relationships, she has the leeway to express her anger without disadvantage and thereby to gain honesty and self-respect.

Another half-truth! For if she looked at the situation more rationally, she could fully accept herself *with* her failings—including her unlovableness and her poor relationships. Making self-acceptance contingent on good traits amounts to a very risky procedure! Assuming that

Ms. Hague could manage *un*conditionally to accept herself, she could then much better afford to express her
displeasure to others, to say to them, for example, "I
really don't like the way you keep treating me and wish
you would stop it!" *Anger*, however, would go far beyond
this kind of displeasure and would stem from the idea
"Because I don't like the way you keep treating me, you
must not continue to do so, and if you do, I have to view
you as a rotten person!" No matter how much Ms. Hague
might fully and unconditionally accept herself, making
herself angry in this grandiose way still amounts to damning others, and she would mainly replace self-condemna-
tion with excoriation of other people. Still a mistake!

Various types of therapy, such as Reichian, primal, and
bioenergetic therapy, claim that by letting people react
violently and angrily in a therapy session or group, they
actually lose their hostility and act less angrily in their
real-life situations. However, as far as I can see, the vast
majority of people who go through these kinds of
therapies end up by feeling much more angry as the
therapy "progresses." I have talked with hundreds of individuals who think they have "successfully" undergone
Gestalt, psychoanalytic, and various kinds of "rage" and
"fight" therapies, and the vast majority of them have felt
and acted more hostilely than they did before their
"cure." This substantiates the experimental work of Dr.
Leonard Berkowitz and a host of other psychologists who
consistently find in research studies that individuals who
punish, curse at, and otherwise aggress against
wrongdoers almost always begin to feel more angry instead of simply blowing off steam and feeling less irate.

People who act out their anger and physically or verbally retaliate against those who do them seeming injustices may, of course, *sometimes* wind up by feeling less
angry. For a variety of reasons. (1) They temporarily run

out of energy and get too exhausted to continue their rage. (2) They acknowledge and face their feelings of anger and thereby help desensitize themselves to such feelings. (3) By expressing their fury, they note their own asinine reactions and show themselves how foolishly they behave—and need not behave in the future. (4) They magically believe that now that they have told someone off for acting badly, that person "deserves" forgiveness. (5) They like the fact that they have asserted themselves, instead of fearfully bottling up their displeasure at the "wrongdoers." And liking themselves for this assertiveness, they feel more able to accept others with this "wrongdoing." (6) They once in a while, by expressing their anger (instead of more intelligently merely expressing their displeasure), induce "wrongdoers" to change their ways; they feel very good about this change and therefore surrender their anger. (7) They often get a lot of approval from anger-inciting therapists or therapy groups; they feel good about this approval and temporarily forget their anger.

For many reasons such as these, anger-inciting therapy may sometimes work. But even when it does, it tends to augment the *philosophy* of anger—in that while you keep screaming and cursing at people for acting badly, you keep reinforcing your notion that they *must* not do what they have done and that they amount to lousy *individuals* for acting this *horrible* way. Consequently, even when your *current* anger at these "lousy individuals" subsides, you increase your chances of making yourself furious at them and other wrongdoers again in the future. So while anger-inciting therapies "work," at least to some extent, they usually end up by creating more harm than good.

Bach and Goldberg insist that "constructive aggression increases as hurtful hostility is reduced and informative impact is increased." They therefore advocate some "aggressive rituals," such as bataca fights, in the course of which angry people fight each other in limited ways and make sure that the other does not get too badly mauled. The participants in these ritualistic fights know that they set definite limits, give themselves only a short time span in which to fight, set up various restrictive rules, use a good deal of playacting, and sometimes as in the "Virginia Woolf" technique, fight in a deliberately outlandish and extreme way. Thus, they add an element of absurdity and humor to what they do. Under such conditions, they not only allow themselves to let off steam, but also acknowledge and show themselves that a real fight, with no holds barred, has very bad results and that they'd better not engage in *that* kind of a struggle.

On the other hand, fighting in a limited or playacting form also has its distinct limitations. Because while the participants actually scream at each other or hit each other with harmless bataca bats, they usually tend to reinstill themselves with the idea that the other individual *does* act in a one hundred percent wrong manner and that he or she *must* stop doing that or will turn into a louse. Such controlled fighting may temporarily help the participants—but largely because each still thinks that he or she indubitably behaves correctly and that the hated person behaves very badly. They ask, as end result, that the other will unquestionably act better in the future. No real forgiveness or acceptance of human fallibility seems involved in such ritualistic fighting; thus, the final outcome may easily bring much more harm than good. So even when such techniques temporarily work, they have their serious limitations.

Yet another limited and dubious view of why we hold onto anger was expressed through William James: that since as humans we have innate tendencies toward violence, we'd better let ourselves have other emotional outlets of an intense nature and thereby provide ourselves with a moral equivalent of war. Erich Fromm quotes the hypothesis that if Hitler's concentration camp guards had released their repressed urges toward sexual sadism in their sexual relations, they would have shown much more kindness to the prisoners. Fromm takes a very skeptical attitude toward this theory.

I quite agree. Several studies have shown that people who get sexually aroused can act more sadistically and violently toward their victims than those who lack such arousal. True, some individuals, if they participate actively in situation A—such as picketing for a political cause or engaging in a sex orgy—will therefore feel diverted from participating as actively in situation B—such as violently assaulting some of their peers or those over whom they have control. But true also: other individuals will do exactly the opposite. They will perversely learn, from the first set of experiences, how to act more assertively and aggressively in the second set of experiences and will therefore behave more instead of less angrily.

People take different messages from the same experiences. One woman grows up with an alcoholic, badly behaving mother and therefore decides never to take a drink for the rest of her life. Her sister grows up with the same mother, decides that drinking seems a good way to get through life, and makes herself into a severe alcoholic. As we keep emphasizing in RET, Activating Experiences, at point *A*, do *not* make you feel Emotional Consequences, at *C*. Your beliefs or interpretations *about* these experiences do. Consequently, out of one hundred people who have "cathartic" emotional experiences, either of an angry or a nonangry nature, at A, twenty may make themselves less hostile at the people who "anger" them—and eighty may make themselves more hostile.

The body therapies, such as Reichian and bioenergetic therapy, do abreactively let people give vent to their anger or to release the bodily armorings that block the expression of pent-up feelings of rage, and they do on occasion thereby lead to a catharsis of anger. By using these therapies for assertion rather than for anger, some actually wind up much less angry, but such therapies lead most people to do just the opposite. For the *most* part, these therapies tend to encourage and augment anger. The vast majority of clients—and I would personally tend to use the term "victims"—of the usual body therapies seem to make themselves considerably more hostile as their therapy progresses.

Body therapists, of course, vary enormously, just as other therapists do. Alexander Lowen and his followers frequently incorporate *sotto voce*, a good deal of rational, anger-interrupting philosophy. Many years ago, before he became well known as a neo-Reichian therapist, Lowen told me that as he manipulated people's bodies, he also employed many modes of cognitive therapy— including Freudian, Jungian, and Adlerian techniques— and if you read his works carefully, you will see that he still does, even though he primarily stresses psychomotor methods. Other relatively competent body-oriented therapists seem to do likewise.

One of Lowen's followers, Dr. Alice Kahn Ladas, writes in this respect:

> Bioenergetic analysis is not primarily a ventilative therapy. The basic concept is not the ventilation of anger . . . but the capacity to stand on one's own two feet literally and psychologically. For many people, this involves becoming aware of anger, rage, or even hatred that has been repressed in the past or in the present. Anger that has been repressed in the past inevitably produces certain types of chronic muscular tension. One may pull one's punches until one has a widow's hump, or lead with one's chin until one has a stiff jaw. It is the job of a bioenergetic therapist to loosen such chronic postures

and, when this is done, feelings of anger or rage may be experienced. At such a time, the person in therapy is encouraged to discharge them *in the therapy session*. A competent bioenergetic therapist definitely discourages the acting out of character problems outside of the therapeutic encounter. The analytic aspect of therapy involves the use of intellect to understand and integrate feelings that come up during the session. This is done through discussion.

As you can easily see, Dr. Ladas uses body material largely to *reveal* anger—and then uses rational discussion to discharge it. In RET we similarly encourage people very often to *acknowledge* their feelings of hostility, to *understand* how they create them, and to *work* at giving them up. We do this, we naturally would contend, much more efficiently and with much less danger of illegitimate conclusions on the client's part, than occurs in various body therapies. But it seems clear that *some* body-oriented therapists do much of what we do—often without quite acknowledging, as honestly as Dr. Ladas does, the "use of the intellect" which they also employ.

A large amount of clinical data and self-observation shows that expressing one's anger overtly or even letting it out by symbolically telling others off or by reading gory stories or witnessing violent films really helps one to reduce one's rage and to feel vastly relieved. Some of this "evidence" seems partly correct, and some of it seems specious. Naturally, you can temporarily feel better, and even less irate, if you directly or indirectly express your anger toward others. But you almost always release yourself only transiently, and in the long run you reconfirm your hostility-creating philosophies—that the people who bother you *should not, must not* act the way they indubitably do—and you build up future angry reactions. Occasionally, you let off steam—and then realize that you don't have to condemn your opponents the way that you do. But usually, you see them as more contemptible than ever, and you tend to hate them more.

As noted above, scores of experiments have shown that when subjects let out their anger on others, they usually turn more rather than less irate. Leonard Berkowitz, James A. Green, and Jacqueline R. Macaulay allowed one group of frustrated subjects to strike the frustrator and another group not to do so. Those who did the striking proved just as apt to anger themselves about the same individual in the future. Berkowitz, Arnold Buss, and Seymour Feshbach did separate experiments in which they inhibited their subjects' aggression, and all of them found that direct or indirect inhibition tended to reduce rather than to augment aggressive behavior. Summarizing many such studies, Feshbach notes that "our own observations indicate that *acknowledging and labeling the affect [anger] provides a sufficient degree of expression in most instances of anger arousal*" and that *overt expression of it therefore does not seem necessary.* [Italics mine.]

Feshbach also significantly observes: "Most psychotherapists agree that the reduction in anger that occurs in patients for whom anger has been a major problem is primarily a result of insight and more refined discrimination rather than the cathartic expression of the affect. Cognitive reorganization may be a far more effective means of reducing violence than promoting its sublimated or free expression." Helene Papanek, a noted Adlerian therapist, also notes that for the expression of hostility to bring about therapeutic change, such expression had better result in a learning experience and help strengthen the individual's social feeling—e.g., give him a better focus on learning to express and to experience himself or herself in new positive ways.

The view that if people, especially children, see angry and violent actions in books, on the movie screen, or on

TV, they will get a vicarious cathartic effect and will tend to release their own inner anger harmlessly, instead of violently taking it out on others, apparently has a little truth to it—but very little! Some children and adults, under some conditions, may view or read about violence and may thereby release their own anger, instead of giving vent to it. But as Dr. Robert M. Liebert and his associates have shown, the reverse seems to hold in many more instances. In one of their reports, for instance, they conclude: "At least under some circumstances, repeated exposure to televised aggression can lead children to accept what they have seen as a partial guide for their own actions. As a result, the present entertainment offerings of the television medium may be contributing, in some measure, to the aggressive behavior of many normal children. Such an effect has now been shown in a wide variety of situations."

The same thing happens in this respect as probably happens with other kinds of disturbance. Most children or adults, when shown models of other people who behave in a disturbed manner sexually, socially, morally, or otherwise, decide that such behavior doesn't seem right for them and may strongly determine *not* to engage in it. But a certain minority of individuals, when witnessing self-defeating or antisocial acts, use them as "good" models, or think that they *have to* perform similarly, or berate themselves for even having wishes similar to those of the badly acting individuals. Such vulnerable individuals may take on some of the worst aspects of the models and may thereby harm themselves considerably. The notion, therefore, that humans normally release their aggression harmlessly when they witness various kinds of anger or violence does not fit the facts, and much evidence exists against it.

Studies of people's indirectly expressing themselves

angrily by viewing films, reading violent stories, having hostile fantasies, or otherwise using indirect means of anger catharsis have produced even greater lack of confirmation of the value of abreaction than have studies of overt hostility. Leonard Berkowitz, in a pioneering article on "The Effects of Observing Violence," found that watching violence generates more violent reactions in people.

The National Commission on the Causes and Prevention of Violence submitted a report indicating, according to *U.S. News and World Report*, that "television has been loaded with violence. It is teaching American children moral and social values 'inconsistent with a civilized society.'" The Surgeon General's Scientific Advisory Committee on Television and Social Behavior also did a special study of children's viewing television violence and concluded that there exists "fairly substantial experimental evidence for short-run causation of aggression among some children by viewing violence on the screen," and other evidence from field studies "that extensive violence viewing precedes some long-run manifestations of aggressive behavior."

Many authors, including Victor B. Cline, Arnold Arnold, and Jacques-Philippe Leyens and his co-workers have shown that the witnessing of violent films by children and adults will help increase feelings and acts of aggression. Albert Bandura and Clarissa Wittenberg have summed up some of the data as follows:

> This body of research points up the fallacies in several popular ideas. One is that violence only affects those who are already violent or deviant and involved in aggression. This has not been borne out. All viewers tend to be affected. Normal children also learn and are encouraged to perform aggressive acts by viewing them under certain circumstances. Another idea is that if parents instill in their children adequate standards of what is right or

wrong, the violence they see will "wash over them." It was clearly demonstrated that even where children can label behavior as bad or wrong, they may imitate it if it was successful, and the conflicts would be resolved more often by a reevaluation downward of the worth or the role of the victim. Whether or not the observed aggressive acts are successful becomes more important than the moral value of these aggressive acts. Perhaps the most prominent idea which has been questioned is that of catharsis. There is no evidence that viewing violence, at least in most forms, dissipates aggressive drives and makes a person more healthy. In fact, it has been demonstrated that a frustrated viewer watching violence would become less inhibited and more likely to act on violence impulses.

Many other studies, such as that by Mary B. Harris and George Samerott also present evidence against the hydraulic view of anger: the view that you have to vent your anger in some overt or fantasized form or else it flows out of you in violent or self-harming ways. Jack E. Hokanson summarizes many of the studies in this field by noting that "the results show clearly that overt aggression does not inevitably lead to either physiological tension reduction or a reduction in subsequent aggression." If anything, these studies indicate that in our culture "aggression will have at least a temporary arousal-reducing effect, and that the likelihood of future violence will be enhanced."

In another trenchant view of anger-inciting studies, Richard Walters concludes that "the series of studies reported above lend considerable support to the belief that the observation of violence in real life or on film or television can have harmful social consequences."

Which means? That the view that you'd better let out your anger and abreactively and cathartically let others know how you feel, or at the very least let it out symbolically by viewing violent films or other representations, represents a nice theory—but one hardly borne out by the facts!

Rollo May theorizes that violence stems largely from naïveté or innocence and that if we have greater knowledge, accept the evils of the world, and work at achieving our own individuality while at the same time acknowledging our social responsibility, we will feel less hostile.

He has some good points here. Knowledge itself probably won't make us unangry at others. But if we accept ourselves and others *with* our and their evils, we will stop commanding that these evils not exist and will stop making ourselves hostile. Acknowledging social responsibility in itself also does not eliminate hostility—and may actually increase it. If I acknowledge that I'd better treat you fairly and let you live and do your own thing, as long as it does not interfere too seriously with mine, I will tend to accept the reality of my living as a social person and will not hate you when you want me to treat you nicely or justly. So responsibility, in that sense, lets me have a higher frustration tolerance and therefore feel less angry at you and at the world.

At the same time, however, I can easily say, "Because *I* act responsibly, you should do so too! And because you don't do what you *should*, you emerge as a rotten person who hardly deserves a good existence!" With this kind of "responsible" thinking, I can easily make myself angry at you. Similarly, by striving for more individuality, I can either believe "I want what I want, but if I don't get it, and you don't give it to me, tough!" Or: "I need what I want, and if I don't get it, and you block me from achieving it, how awful!" In the latter case, I will make myself quite hostile.

Innocence, in other words, does not merely include my seeing the world as a nonevil, marvelous place. More important than that, it includes my demandingness—my believing that the world *must* not have evil in it and that it *has to* work the way I want it to work. With this kind of absolutistic innocence, I will almost certainly make myself quite angry.

Psychoanalytic and primal therapies both believe that people have to get in touch with their past hostility toward their parents and the intense rage they felt when young and frustrated in order to work through their hostility today. This constitutes an exceptionally mistaken view: that virtually all children feel intensely frustrated and enraged during their early childhood and that unless they get in touch with this rage and act it out today, they will have repressed, inner pain that will stop them from developing and getting rid of their anger. No good evidence exists for these hypotheses, and considerable facts contradict them.

First, many children don't rage that badly when they feel frustrated. They certainly don't like it, but they fairly gracefully persevere and do not act like little gods who *must* not get frustrated.

Secondly, when they do whine and scream, inwardly or outwardly, about their parents' poor behavior, their own tendency toward and choice of screaming seem the real issue, not merely the acts of their parents. To say that these acts caused their screaming amounts to a false conclusion. *They* caused their own screaming and had better assume responsibility for it. Similarly, if they have an allergy to, say, grapefruit and their parents keep feeding them grapefruit, we cannot very accurately conclude that their parents made them (except genetically) allergic or caused them to break out in a rash. Their parents *contributed* to their allergic reactions but didn't truly *cause* them.

Thirdly, even most highly vulnerable children, once they get frustrated early in life and inwardly or outwardly scream about this, manage to come to terms with, stop screaming about, and ultimately accept and forget about these early experiences and their reactions to them. Only a few *unusual* children grow into adults who seem to remember the original frustration and, screaming forever, plague themselves about it twenty or more years after it first occurred.

Finally, even when these few self-plaguing adults yell and scream today about what happened twenty years ago, they frequently make themselves more rather than less angry at their parents for frustrating them—and more angry about the "insults" and "horrors" that the world foists on them. Their "unrepressing" their anger usually helps them to escalate it rather than to give it up. Only if they stop believing, today, that their parents *should have* treated them better, and rate as total *worms* for not doing so, will they likely surrender their feelings of anger. Such a change in their Belief System proves highly unlikely in various kinds of primal therapies.

Almost all people who feel very angry know quite well how they feel and only occasionally do not know it. Most of them seem *too much* in touch with their feelings—and consequently keep making themselves angry all the time.

Almost any therapist can, of course, bring out "hidden" anger by inducing clients to scream, to go through painful physical exercises, to beat pillows, to remember "horrible" childhood incidents, etc. How much of this anger represents unconscious or repressed hostility, however, and how much did the therapist *presently* incite? Answer: almost all of it usually falls in the latter rather than the former category.

Remember, in this connection, that according to RET theory, we naturally and easily *make ourselves* angry, have an underlying biosocial *tendency* to do so. Consequently, if I as your therapist get you to playact anger toward me or a member of your group, forcibly restrain you so you cannot move, poke you in the gut and interfere with your breathing, or imply that your mother really had a thoroughly lousy character for unduly restricting you, I will have no trouble whatever in helping you make yourself angry *right now*. Having a talent for foolishly inciting yourself, you will usually follow my instigative lead and will make yourself just about as angry as I want you to feel. But this hardly proves that, all along, you really *did* violently hate me, another group member, or your mother and that I now have merely made you conscious of this feeling. Probably, for the most part, you really like me, this other group member, and your mother, but you *occasionally* and *at times* feel hostility toward us. This hardly constitutes serious "unconscious" rage on your part.

Therapy-instigated anger, therefore, rarely represents your true or basic feeling, only occasionally reveals your general resentment, frequently exaggerates how angry you feel—and *encourages* you to make yourself far angrier than you usually would. It provides a great boost to the therapist's silly ego—and, often, a distinct hindrance to you. If you come across any therapist who seems obsessed with your getting in touch with your angry feelings, rather than helping you acknowledge and *give them up*, you'd better suspect his or her own motivations and problems—and run to another, saner therapist as soon as possible!

Theodore Isaac Rubin holds that real anger leads to warmth and health and seems as necessary as eating or loving. He implies that if your anger takes the form of spontaneous, direct expression of feelings of displeasure, we can then call it "real" and look forward to cultivating rather than suppressing it.

This view has its dangers. To use a term like "real anger" amounts to using a term like "real love." All love, as I have said in *The American Sexual Tragedy* and other of my writings, emerges as "real" love—whether short or

enduring, mild or passionate, marital or nonmarital, con-
jugal or romantic. Because "real" mainly means
existent—and not ideal. So with anger. Virtually all anger
falls under the heading of "real," and it seems to consist
almost always of two fairly clear-cut elements: (1) sincere
and sometimes profound disappointment when someone
treats you unfairly or badly and (2) the irrational belief that
this unfair or bad treatment should not, must not exist,
and that its perpetrator amounts to a totally rotten individual. The more sincerely, directly, authentically, and
spontaneously you experience anger, the more it seems to
include both these elements.

Rubin means that when people treat you unfairly, you
can legitimately feel intense disappointment, sorrow, regret, and frustration and that *this element* of anger usually
has a healthy quality because it helps you go after what
you want and fight against the injustices of the world.
Rubin fails to define anger very accurately and also believes it abets love. I believe it often does just the opposite. The more you express your sincere disappointment
with people's poor behavior, the more they tend to feel
turned off, less loving. Sometimes, of course, they agree
that they have disappointed you in some ways, and they
change those ways, thus helping create a warm and
healthy relationship between the two of you. But often
nothing of the sort happens!

Moreover, when you express downright anger—no
matter how directly and spontaneously you give vent to
it—you imply, if not state, that others do not have the
right to disappoint you and that they thus rate very poorly
with you. This almost always turns them off and leads
them to return hatred rather than love. Occasionally, if
you express great hostility toward someone for whom you
truly care, you will make yourself so contrite about the
action you have taken that you will act much better after

having done so, and your love for them and theirs for you may therefore rise. Also, if they have sufficiently strong positive attitudes toward you to begin with, your anger may inspire them to go out of their way to make amends to you and to cement your relationship. Occasionally! But don't count on it, for the opposite appears much more likely to happen in most cases. In most cases love begets love, and hate begets hate.

Jay Kuten, along with Theodore Rubin and George Bach, also develops the thesis that rewarding sexual love requires a joint recognition of separateness and individual integrity, which you can provide by occasional adaptive exchanges of anger and hostility. The first part of his thesis makes good sense since you will not likely love anyone else too much if you do not first and foremost accept yourself and strive for a goodly degree of separateness and individual integrity. But normally, you would attain such integrity by assertiveness, not by hostility. If you show your sex-love mate that you want some degree of individuality and will, if necessary, break up the relationship if you don't get it and if you don't angrily whine when this mate blocks you from achieving the degree that you want, you will have a greater likelihood of ultimately forming a warm and lasting relationship with this individual than if you superimpose a Jehovian command on your wish and angrily insist that your mate not block you. Self-assertiveness and good love relationships correlate fairly highly; hostility and love do not!

You may wonder about rage reduction techniques, such as that of Dr. Robert Zaslow, where a therapist and a member of a therapeutic group deliberately tickle a person, hold him or her down, and throw taunts and invectives designed to enrage that person—until he or she feels relaxed and assertive rather than enraged. Almost any therapeutic technique will work—sometimes. Zaslow's method got highly touted several years ago, after he had invented it by first working with autistic children. Fight therapists, such as George Bach, enthusiastically endorsed it, and felt sure that Zaslow's own claims would prove valid. Said Zaslow: "I'm doing for rage what Freud did for sex. Today, rage is socially unacceptable, just as sex used to be. But rage is really esthetic. When the tiger goes for his food in the jungle, it's an esthetic expression. That's the only way he can survive, and he's beautiful at it. As Dante said, hell is a place waiting for heaven to shine through. Rage is hell, and rage reduction propels you into heaven."

Brave words! But the actual results don't always seem to bear them out. Several clients of therapists using rage reduction methods have reported feeling greatly harmed. Although some individuals have probably received some degree of help by these rigorous methods, I would doubt whether they more than temporarily overcame their feelings of deep-seated hostility and would guess that most of them ended up more hostile. Other unfortunate results of this kind of treatment seem common and sometimes fairly severe. Dr. Hyman Spotnitz has commented in this connection: "The new development of encouraging physical contact with patients, I am sorry to say, leads to violent outbursts, as my own experience of many years ago showed. Therefore, I do not encourage such actions. A study of the literature and case reports will show that where therapists unnecessarily touch their patients or struggle with them physically, the therapy is unsuccessful."

Fritz Perls claims that we have to give in to our aggression and express it directly toward others or toward the world because otherwise we will retroflect it and take it out on ourselves. I disagree. We can, of course, refuse to display our anger toward others and then condemn ourselves for failing to do so. In this case, this anger gets retroflected back onto ourselves. But we can also, and probably more likely, directly take out our anger on others—and then *also* condemn ourselves for doing this. The main point which many fail to realize in their anger theories and therapies, is that no hydraulic force exists which makes us angry here (i.e., against ourselves) if we stop expressing our anger there (i.e., against others). Our attitude *toward* our nonexpression may well make us feel depressed and self-downing. But the strain of nonexpression merely remains like the strain of any other kind of nondoing: a moderate strain that we can easily encompass and master. As a diabetic I strain myself to forgo eating sugar, which I really like to eat, but I merely tell myself, "Tough! Sugar does me much more harm than good; so I will force myself to give it up." So I feel only moderate strain, and no anger against the world, from my decision to forbear.

As a human I may strain myself to forgo expressing my feelings of anger toward my boss or my mate when I'd feel good—temporarily!—about letting them out. But I then may foolishly tell myself, "I *shouldn't* have to control my anger. In fact, I wouldn't feel angry at all if that louse didn't act the way he does. Why can't he change, and not make me angry or, at least, let me express my anger? And why can't I 'strongly' express it and take the consequences, thereby proving how I rise to noble heights?" Because of these irrational ideas, I may make a federal case out of not expressing my anger—and I *therefore* choose to turn it inward and take it out on myself. But I can *stop* this crazy kind of thinking if I choose!

12

More Ways of Overcoming Anger

The rational approach to anger involves a hardheaded, persistent, relentless effort to admit that you do feel enraged rather than merely annoyed; that you largely (though not exclusively) brought on these feelings yourself and have the responsibility for continuing to feel them or for giving them up; that you can distinctly control and reduce them, although probably never to absolute zero; that they mainly bring you and your associates considerably more harm than good; and that it would seem advisable, though hardly necessary, for you to ameliorate and often eliminate these angry feelings.

You may accomplish this through:

1. *Review of pragmatic results.* Albert Bandura's investigations of hostility and the operant conditioning theories of B. F. Skinner call to our attention three major facts. (1) Anger and violence rarely arise from "good" social interactions but generally follow from experiences that include—or that *appear* to include—serious frustrations and deprivations. (2) Once we react in certain hostile ways to frustrations and annoyances, we get reinforced and penalized by our reactions. Hostility either

reinforces us by helping us to remove the stimuli that we find obnoxious or it brings us other satisfactions (e.g., the pleasure of feeling superior to the people we fight). Or else hostility penalizes us (e.g., helps bring on counterattacks from those we hate and attack). (3) After getting reinforced or penalized for our aggressive feelings and moves, we finally can weigh the short-term and long-term advantages and disadvantages of the results we achieve and can, on a pragmatic basis, influence the establishment of frustrating and less frustrating conditions in the future and at least semirationally decide how we will react to inevitable frustrations that remain.

For example, I have promised to share an apartment with you and, after persuading you to go to great expense to fix it up, have refused to move in with you. I have thus set up a set of frustrating conditions for you to deal with. If you then choose to feel and act angrily toward me, you will get certain reinforcements and penalties. On the reinforcing side, you may remove yourself from my frustrating presence, influence me to make some monetary restitution, and feel vastly superior to me since you act "well" and I act "badly." On the penalizing side, you may encourage me to treat you still worse in the future, receive the disapproval of some of our mutual friends for your vindictiveness toward me, and consume much valuable time and energy futilely trying to get restitution from me. These reinforcements and penalties will tend, consciously or unconsciously, to make you feel more hostile or less hostile when similar frustrations and annoyances occur in your future life.

Finally, after feeling angry at me for quite a while and perhaps instituting some kind of a vindictive feud with me, you (as a human) have the ability to review the entire situation with me and put it in the context of your general life. You can decide, for example, that your anger has some advantages—but that it helps you get an ulcer or high blood pressure and therefore brings you more harm than good. You can decide that your hostility makes you feel superior to me—but that this kind of an ego game really doesn't prove very rewarding. You can decide that you can live successfully with your displeasure and your anger—but that you could live more happily if you arranged to stay away from people like me in the future and thus could "block" the frustrations that we would probably foist upon you.

If, in other words, you make yourself fully aware, in Bandura's terms, of how frustrations contribute to your anger, of what kinds of reinforcements and penalties immediately tend to accompany your angry feelings, and of what long-term consequences may result even from your "rewarding" angry "victories," you bring to your attention a full-scale analysis of the complex roots and maintainers of hostility. You then have a wide range of solutions available to you, including changing the frustrating stimuli or Activating Events that contribute to your angry feelings, arranging for different kinds of reinforcers and penalties that will tend to make you feel less angry when still faced with obnoxious stimuli, taking a long-range instead of a short-range hedonistic view of the advantages and disadvantages of hostility, and changing your philosophic outlook toward frustrating people and events, so that again you make them seem less frustrating and less penalizing.

Bandura, Skinner, and other advocates of social reinforcement theories of anger seem to repeat, in their own way, the ancient Greek adage: knowledge equals power. The more you understand the biological, social, cognitive, and other sources of your angry feelings and actions, the greater your chance of changing and controlling the several different kinds of influences on you and of looking for more pragmatic solutions.

2. *Frustration reduction.* Although frustration does

not seem to directly or invariably cause anger, it certainly significantly contributes! Most humans who suffer severe deprivation for considerable periods of time have a strong tendency to upset themselves about this—and finally to lash out angrily at frustrating people or conditions. Although, therefore, you had better work very hard to raise your frustration tolerance and to reduce your whining about the unniceties of the universe, you can also very wisely work to reduce these frustrations themselves.

You *don't have* to work at a boring job, stay with annoying friends, let your mate or children keep taking advantage of you, or remain with a sex partner who has insatiable demands or who requires two hours of steady sex play practically every day to come to orgasm. Temporarily you may do yourself a lot of good by deliberately remaining in these unpleasant kinds of conditions so as to work on your own low frustration tolerance and show yourself that you can stand what you don't like. Temporarily! But in the long run you almost always have better alternatives. Look for them. Work at instituting them. On the other hand, don't try to live with *zero* frustration (for you won't succeed!) or even at times with *minimal* frustration (for you may thereby lose out on enormous potential pleasures). But gratuitous and inordinate thwarting you really don't need. Do something to reduce some of it. If not immediately, at least ultimately. And often—soon!

3. *Frustration tolerance*. Anger and violence rarely stem from mere frustration but from low frustration tolerance. When you feel furious, your basic view consists of the idea that whatever frustrates you *should* and *ought* not exist, that it not only proves unfair, but this unfairness, again, *must* not prevail, that you *can't stand* frustration, and that those who unduly balk and block you amount to almost total vermin who, once again, *should* not act the way they indubitably do.

Obviously, you can find an antidote to this kind of thinking by teaching yourself higher frustration tolerance. How? By seeing that frustration *should* exist (because it does), as should unfairness and injustice. In this respect, you can heed the words of Erich Fromm:

> First of all, we might consider a basic fact of life: that nothing important is achieved without accepting frustration. The idea that one can learn without effort, i.e., without frustration, may be good as an advertising slogan, but is certainly not true in the acquisition of major skills. Without the capacity to accept frustration man would hardly have developed at all. And does not everyday observation show that many times people suffer frustration without having an aggressive response? What can, and often does, produce aggression is what the frustration *means* to the person, and the psychological meaning of frustration differs according to the total constellation in which the frustration occurs.

Fromm does not so indicate but "the total constellation in which the frustration occurs" also includes:

a. your basic tendency to demand that frustration must not exist

b. your full acknowledgment that you *have* such a demand or command

and then, it is hoped:

c. your realization that you will almost inevitably defeat yourself unless you ameliorate or surrender your demandingness

d. your firm decision to give that up and replace it with a desire but not an absolutistic insistence that you receive relatively little frustration, and

e. your determinedly working—cognitively, emotively, and behaviorially—to live up to that decision.

Your philosophy *about* frustration, then, seems the real issue, and even when you have little control over getting frustrated, you have lots of possibilities of modifying that philosophy.

4. *Counterattacking narcissism and grandiosity.* As Gregory Rochlin points out, narcissism or childish grandiosity has profound roots in human nature and tends to underlie much of our behavior. We don't merely want others to love and care for us; we utterly insist that they do, and we frequently feel completely shattered when they don't. Such shattering is self-induced since *we*, rather than they, down ourselves by our dire need for others' acceptance. We often foolishly claim that *they* destroy us by rejecting our "needs." This frequently leads to our feeling exceptionally angry and acting violently against those who presumably have "failed" us. Rochlin emphasizes how often hostility springs from wounded self-esteem and neglects its other important sources. But he does have a point: a good deal of our fury against others originally arises from the "hurt" they give us—the "hurt" to our narcissistic demands for approval.

Moral: you can give up your infantile narcissism if this truly constitutes one of the main sources of your anger. You don't *have to* run the universe. You don't *need* to feel good about yourself mainly because others acknowledge your outstandingness. No reason exists why you *must* have the center of the stage or why you *should* even receive minimum respect from others.

No, the world *doesn't* care too much for you and most likely never will. The more famous you get, moreover, the more enemies you will tend to make. The better you behave toward many people, the more they will often take advantage of you. Reality operates that way. The universe has no *special* interest in you. Nor ever will. Now, how can you fully face and accept that "cruel," "cold" fact and live happily in spite of it? If you can, one of the main sources of your hostility to others will come to a fairly abrupt halt.

As both Freud and Adler noted many years ago and as I have stated in my earliest writings on Rational-Emotive Therapy, almost all anger stems from childish grandiosity. As humans we believe that because the possibility exists that others *can* treat us very well—in fact, specially—and because we'd greatly benefit from this worshipful kind of treatment, they *should* bestow it on us. As H. Peters has noted:

> There have been philosophers, such as Bertrand Russell, who have held that jealousy is always inappropriate as an emotion, basically because it presupposes unjustifiable claims to a special relationship with another person. If psychologists could show that human beings were unable to avoid appraising situations in this way, that would be an important assertion to make. For there is a sense in which "ought" implies "can."

Peters somewhat overstates the case here. Humans *tend to* avoid appraising situations in this way, but they *can* avoid, at least to some extent, doing so. If, whenever you feel extremely angry at someone, you fully face the fact that you do state or imply a godlike command to the effect that this person *ought to* accord you special treatment and if you firmly rip up that *ought* many times and replace it with "I would find it very *preferable* if this person treated me specially, but the chances remain that he or she often won't," you will minimize your anger.

It seems significant that childish grandiosity and ego aggrandizement motivate anger, including extreme violence, on both sides of the intellectual dullness continuum. On the dullness side, Hans Toch found that a great many of the criminals whom he investigated, who in education and brightness clearly ranged on the dull half of the scale, could get classified as "self-image promoters" or "reputation defenders." They committed violent crimes largely because their social position, physical size, or group status seemed low and "obligated" them to compensate in a physically violent way—"a matter of 'noblesse oblige,' so to speak," as Toch notes.

At the other end of the continuum, highly educated and intellectual revolutionaries also overreact to "oppression" and to "ego insult" by behaving very angrily and violently. Black Muslims, as Lionel Tiger points out, may fight against social subjugation by whites because they feel deprived of their "manhood" and therefore require the "masculinization" involved in violence. Libertarian "crazies," Nat Hentoff indicates, no matter what they claim to stand for, may easily act authoritarianly and reveal that they truly swear by "anti-life, anti-individuality, anti-spontaneity. And anti-me." Theodore Gold, a twenty-three-year-old Weatherman killed in a dynamite-blasted town house in New York while assembling a bomb to fight for "liberty," told an old college friend before his death, "I've been doing a lot of exciting underground things, and I know I'm not afraid to die." One of his Weatherman friends defended his actions by stating, "We don't think in terms of being happy. We think in terms of being strong people."

Watch your own grandiosity and overrebelliousness. Certainly, the side you oppose may have many wrongnesses and injustices that it upholds. Surely, your own cause may seem much more correct and humane than "theirs." But you never know indisputably that your way will lead to much more good than harm and theirs to all kinds of holocausts. By all means defend your own views —and fight, verbally and even actively, to see if you can get them to prevail. But watch your grandiosity! Watch your dogmatism! The stronger you feel about a cause, the more you will likely ignore its limitations and disadvantages. Try to bring these incisively to mind, too. And see if you can determinedly go after what you want—without enraging yourself and insisting that because you find it right and proper, it *must* prevail.

5. *Liberalization of attitudes.* Attitudes toward others and how one "should" react to them when they treat one unfairly correlate significantly with one's general attitudes toward humans and the rules they "ought" to follow. Stuart Taylor and Jan Smith found that males with traditional beliefs reacted more hostilely to their opponents than did males with more liberal beliefs. If, therefore, you want to curb your tendencies toward making yourself angry at others and to interfere with the aggressive and violent actions you take toward them when they do the "wrong" thing, you might consider taking a distinctly more liberal general view of the world than the conservative, traditional, or reactionary view that you now may have.

6. *Knowledge of history.* History, as Daniel J. Boorstin points out, provides us with many striking illustrations of the consequences of hostility, ranging from the prolonged wars in ancient Israel and Greece, to Hitler's and Stalin's holocausts, and right up to the numerous religious, political, economic, and other bloodbaths still very much extant. Moreover, Boorstin reminds us, history also helps us scotch our utopianism and respect our possibilities for progress:

> "The voice of the intellect," observed Sigmund Freud (who did not underestimate the role of the irrational) in 1928, "is a soft one, but it does not rest until it has gained a hearing. Ultimately, after endlessly repeated rebuffs, it succeeds. This is one of the viewpoints in which one may be optimistic about the future of mankind." Beneath the strident voice of the present we must try to hear the insistent whisper of reason. It does not sound "with it." It speaks only to the attentive listener. It speaks a language always unfamiliar and often archaic. It speaks the language

of all past times and places, which is the language of history.

7. *Awareness of the harm of anger and violence.* You might think that anger and violence have obviously wreaked so much harm on individuals and communities that virtually everyone, including yourself, has full awareness of the harm caused and uses this awareness to keep himself or herself from reacting irately to others. What a wrong conclusion! You may indeed have a general awareness of some of the enormous disadvantages of rage, but how often do you bring this general awareness into specific focus and make yourself see exactly what harm you will most likely do yourself and others by making yourself enraged? Very seldom, I would wager!

Let me briefly review some of the distinct disadvantages of resentment and anger that authorities on the subject have pointed out for many centuries:

7a. *Focusing on reprisal.* Although you ostensibly make yourself angry at others in order to protect yourself from their predations and to correct their wrong thinking and behaving, once you enrage yourself at these "wrongdoers" you tend to lose sight of the real issues involved and to obsess yourself with futile and harm-inciting revenge. Milton Schwebel indicates that even firebrands with legitimate grievances and good motivation to remove these grievances often will "use any excuse or organization to stimulate confrontations, not in order to right wrongs or correct injustice but to provoke reprisal and repression in order to trap the great, uncommitted center to the side of revolution and anarchy."

7b. *Abuse of weaker individuals.* As I point out elsewhere in this book, anger and even righteous indignation spur you to abuse some of your subordinates who act poorly, including powerless children over whom you may, unfortunately, have control. In recent years an enormous amount of evidence has accumulated in regard to child abuse—up to and including the maiming and killing of children by thousands of irate parents. Most of our statistics in this regard come from highly "civilized" countries like the United States—as shown by such authorities as Vincent Fontana and his associates, Ray E. Helfer and C. Henry Kempe, Naomi F. Chase, and David G. Gil and by a large bibliography of "Selected References on the Abused and Battered Child" published by the National Institute of Mental Health Communication Center. But other countries do just as poorly in this respect, as indicated by the statement of a British psychiatrist, Dr. John Howells, who told a Royal Society of Health conference that more children get beaten to death at home by parents than ever died in the workhouses of Victorian England. Said Dr. Howells: "Two children die each day in the United Kingdom killed by their parents. . . . Many more are maimed in mind and body."

7c. *Political violence.* Although the nations of the United Nations have so far managed to ward off another major holocaust like World War I and World War II, almost innumerable international and intranational conflicts continue to exist. Guerrilla warfare, hijackings, political murders, kidnappings, open warfare between political factions, and all kinds of bloodshed remain rife in virtually every part of the civilized and less civilized world today.

7d. *Religious warfare.* Just as political warfare stems from hatred of and bigotry against other groups, so does religious warfare. Religious warfare reigns all over the world today, including various overt and covert wars between Catholics and Protestants, Jews and Christians, Jews and Moslems, Moslems and Christians, Hindus and non-Hindus, etc. Each group, as usual, tends to believe that its views have sacred rightness and that its opponent's views have demoniacal wrongness—and that therefore, the opposing group has to get denounced, downed, and preferably extirpated. Even members of peace-loving groups, such as Jews and Christians, turn to bloodshed and murder when they make themselves grandiosely angry against members of other religious groups.

7e. *Belief in the power of aversive harm.* Anger frequently includes the unwarranted belief that if you deal with others aversively and painfully when they disagree with you or oppose your actions, they will learn by this aversive experience and will change their ways. How seldom they will! Usually, as Adah Maurer and her associates point out, people who suffer aversive responses to their aversive behavior learn that the giving of hurt serves as an acceptable method of gaining power, and they tend to retaliate in kind rather than to stop their undesirable behavior. Love may well beget love, and hate frequently begets hate. Punishing others encourages them to punish back in return. A vicious circle of violence leading to more violence thus ensues.

7f. *Prejudice against self and others.* Hatred of others often leads you to view them as devils incarnate, and to magnify their possession of "evil" traits. Curiously enough, by attributing to them these traits and using them as an excuse for your own hatred, you frequently endow yourself with demoniacal characteristics as well so that you have a doubly magical and intensely negative view of humans. Then, since hating yourself amounts to just about the worst feeling you can have, you may drive yourself to having prejudices against others and to hating them even more. As Marie Jahoda notes, "Despising others becomes a way of trying to bolster one's own shaky self-esteem by making others seem more inferior or contemptible. In fact, the only way some people can salvage their own self-respect is to feel 'lucky' they are not a Negro, a Catholic, an Italian—or whoever is set up as the scapegoat for their own secret misery."

7g. *Taking on characteristics of those you hate.* Ironically, you tend to hate others for their poor characteristics—for their bullying, their prejudice, their violence, and their arrogance—and through hating them and justifying almost any action you can perpetrate to stop them, you frequently take on the very features that you may loathe. As I have pointed out for many years, if you thoroughly hate Hitler, you tend to turn into a Hitler—one who condemns others in their entirety because he dislikes some of their traits. William Irwin Thompson points out that "we become what we hate" and notes that "in watching the conflict of the Irish Troubles, the Dublin yogi, George William Russell, developed the maxim into a principle of political science: 'By intensity of hatred nations create in themselves the characters they imagine in their enemies. Hence it is that all passionate conflicts result in the interchange of characteristics.'"

7h. *Anger as a "pain in the gut."* Because we often feel highly pleased and self-righteous when we experience anger, we forget that we also experience it as a "pain in the gut"—and as a distracting, obsessive feeling that prevents us from doing many joyful things and that frequently leads to self-destruction.

Paul Hauck, in *Overcoming Frustration and Anger*, rightly notes that letting yourself get angry when someone tries to "get your goat" only does you double injury. He states:

> There are two statements I usually make to myself which help me keep my cool. The first is that I am not God and am neurotic to insist I have to have my way. This usually cools me off nicely. However, if that doesn't do the trick, I always throw in this next thought. "Hauck, be smart,

someone is trying to shaft you. That's bad enough, old boy. Surely you're not going to be dumb now and do to yourself what that fellow is trying to do. No, sir! Maybe he doesn't give a hoot about my feelings, but I sure do. Therefore, I'm going to forcibly talk myself out of the angry mood which is beginning to come over me." Having trouble is one thing, and it's often unavoidable. But making *double trouble* for myself is another matter entirely.

7i. *Interference with individuality within groups.* Alfred McClung Lee points out that group solidarity or group egotism may have certain advantages but has distinct disadvantages as well, that groups do *not* consist of individuals who act exactly like each other, who have the same tastes and preferences. One disadvantage of group solidarity is the enormous intragroup prejudice and hostility that it breeds. Says Lee: "Apologists for group-egotism praise its contribution to the participant individual's sense of identity with one specific part of a pluralistic society. But what of its cost in intergroup hostility, exploitation, and bloodshed. Think of the untold millions . . . who have died or lived in deprivation because of their group identity!"

Dr. Lee could well have added sex warfare to his list of group ego centeredness. Certainly women have for many centuries been kept at a certain level in our society and males have acted chauvinistically to keep them there— because of group egotism and neglect of societal individuality! Now some among the feminist women tend to go to the same extreme and fill themselves with overwhelming hostility against males, globally rating almost all men as bastards and carrying on what amounts to sex warfare. This prevents these women from seeing males as humans and in the long run probably makes for *greater* sex antagonism. Males, of course, who violently fight against feminism remain in the same defensive, hating boat. Both sets of extremists nicely "identify" with ideal or "total" males or females—none of whom ever seem to exist—and gain "strength," or what I call false integrity, by feeling and acting hostilely toward the other half of the human race.

7j. *Interference with activism.* Revolutionists usually insist that only through making ourselves exceptionally incensed at injustices and inequities can we propel ourselves into action and work to change poor social conditions. Partly true—and largely wrong! As Hannah Arendt has indicated, violent riots and rebellions give their participants a false sense of action, frequently consist of wrong moves on the part of the rebels, and often tend to impede the careful planning, constructive action, and long-term follow-up procedures that would result in effective social change. Dramatic outbursts may at times serve as a prelude to constructive reorganization, but they frequently do not. Outbursts of verbal anger, moreover, can continue for years or decades and, if anything, prevent people from *doing* something about the execrable conditions against which they keep violently protesting.

Determined (rather than hysterical) *rebellion* against society or its conditions, on the other hand, has its distinct advantages. First, it lets you take a stand for what you really care for: a different set of conditions that you personally approve, rather than the given or traditional set under which you live. Secondly, instead of letting yourself stew about the "horrors" of what exists, determined rebellion gives you something constructive to do: permits you to let off some legitimate steam through expressing your real feelings and gives you something to work for in a busy, concerted way, thereby distracting you from musterbation and insensate anger. Thirdly, constructive rebellion may well help change or ameliorate various kinds of frustrating conditions and thus remove some of the

obnoxious Activating Experiences which would commonly make you furious.

So don't think that lack of anger means merely turning
the other cheek or tolerating needless unpleasantnesses
and hassles. If you manufacture, instead of rage, a powerful determination to do what you can do to modify unfortunate arrangements, you will head off most of your
foolish angry responses and will devote yourself mainly to
ridding yourself of needless frustrations rather than child-
ishly whining about their existence.

7k. *Interference with the rights of others.* As Janet L.
Wolfe points out, assertiveness differs notably from aggressiveness in that the former consists of "the ability to
express feelings or legitimate rights straightforwardly,
without attacking others or violating their rights. Aggressive behavior, to the contrary, violates the rights of others, or puts them down." Anger, too, has an intrinsically
fascistic or elitist philosophy behind it, for it denies the
rights of others in favor of one's own "special" rights.

7l. *Deification of all aggressiveness.* When angry, you
tend to deify all forms of aggressiveness and rationalize
them as "good" or "healthy." Actually, we may call aggression "healthy" when it largely helps or abets some
basic human goals especially: the goals of remaining alive,
feeling relatively happy, living successfully in a social
group, relating intimately to some selected members of
that group, having a productive and enjoyable vocational
life, engaging in individually chosen and fairly satisfying
recreational pursuits, etc. But intense feelings of anger
help us to seek unhealthy as well as healthy goals. If we
unangrily looked at these unhealthy goals, we would tend
to see them as meretricious or of dubious value.

7m. *Overgeneralized and unfair discrimination.* When
we anger ourselves against a group of individuals, we tend
to overgeneralize so that we discriminate even against

those who act much differently from the others and whose behavior we might otherwise tend to favor.

7n. *Ignoring long-range values.* Anger helps you look only at short-range rather than at long-range values and gains. As Marshall Gilula and David N. Daniels have shown, one of the major obstacles to our removing violence from society consists of our slowness to recognize that a violent style of coping with problems will often soothe current feelings and lead to immediate satisfactions but that in the long run, it will help destroy us and ultimately, perhaps—in some final violent holocaust—the entire human race.

7o. *The perpetuation of disturbance.* Hostility usually constitutes some kind of temporary—or permanent—emotional disturbance. But when you indulge yourself in anger, you seem to deny that you feel disturbed and thus block your ability to deal with and possibly eliminate that disturbance. In extreme cases, we can identify the hostility factor as a neurotic or psychotic factor. In such instances, the more enraged individuals give in to their anger and act on it, the more they distract themselves from acknowledging their severe disturbances and from doing anything to ameliorate them. In fact, their overt and covert anger serves as a justification for their upset, provides them with a neurotic gain, and tends to keep them both angry and violent.

7p. *Interference with helping others to change.* The angrier you make yourself at others who hold opposing views to yours and the more you express that anger, the less you tend to help them change their views and come around to yours. On the contrary, they usually feel more justified in opposing you and claiming that your rage *proves* you wrong.

7q. *Encouraging feelings of depression.* Anger may sometimes help you cover up or avoid feelings of depression, and, if so, it seems an advantageous reaction. But it can also lead to depressed feelings. For if you merely feel frustrated about something, you rarely make yourself depressed. But if you feel frustrated and dogmatically insist, to yourself or others, that this frustration *should* not, *must* not exist and that you find it awful that it does, you will not only anger yourself, but often depress yourself as well. For if things must not exist badly, and they indubitably do, you can easily conclude that you have no power whatever over such things, that they will always exist, and that you can't stand them. If, instead of ranting and raving about frustrations, you focus on doing something to cope with them and think about how your angry behavior may well add to them, you may help yourself feel neither angry nor depressed.

7r. *Psychosomatic reactions.* Anger, both suppressed and overt, can easily result in psychosomatic reactions, including high blood pressure, heart problems, ulcers, and various other physical conditions. Although we often dramatize the effect of unexpressed anger in these respects, evidence seems to show that expressed rage also encourages physical pain and dysfunction.

7s. *Genocide.* As noted above, anger-inspired wars have existed since time immemorial and still do! A most vicious aspect of war includes genocide, the deliberate conquering of an enemy group and the complete extirpation, if possible, of that group. Naturally, we think of Hitler in this respect and of his plans to exterminate the entire Jewish and Gypsy population of Germany—and, eventually, of the world. Examples of actual or attempted extirpation of an entire group of people exist in ancient and modern times. And almost invariably these genocidal attempts stem from intense anger against a whole group when, at worst, only some of its members have acted badly in the eyes of the exterminators.

These, then, represent some of the distinct disadvantages of resentment and anger and our awareness of them will help to eliminate anger. As will picking up with our list again:

8. *Understanding attribution theory.* When someone treats us in a certain way, particularly a frustrating or unfair way, we tend to attribute various motives to this person's treatment, and we make ourselves more or less angry depending on the motives that we choose to attribute to them. In recent years a number of social psychologists have pointed out the importance of attribution theory in understanding human feelings and actions. Russell Geen and David Stonner, for example, set up an experiment whereby male college students—after having seen a violent movie—could presumably punish someone who had verbally attacked them. Under one set of experimental conditions the other subjects learned that the fighting stemmed from professional or altruistic motives and under another set of conditions that it stemmed from revenge motives. The results showed that those led by the experimenters to attribute the fighting to revenge motives acted significantly more angrily and punitively toward the people whom they subsequently punished than did those who believed that the fighting stemmed from altruistic motives.

If you have a tendency—as you probably do—to attribute highly negative, vindictive motives to people who frustrate or attack you, *force yourself to stop and question your attributions* and try to see *other* possible reasons for the frustration or the attack. In our usual illustration, I renege on my promise to share an apartment with you, and you assume that:

1. I truly want to do you in.
2. I knew all along that I would never share the apartment with you and deliberately misled you.

3. I now have no good reasons for pulling out of our deal, but I still viciously insist on pulling out of it.
4. I have no intention of compensating you in any way for the trouble I have caused you.

Stop and review the probability that I really do have such vindictive motives. Consider my possible other reasons for backing out on our deal, such as:

1. I had an honest change of heart after first thinking about the advantages of my living with you.
2. I cannot afford to go through with our deal, though I would really like to do so.
3. I think that you have somehow treated me unfairly, and therefore, I don't want to share an apartment with you.
4. The conditions of my life have radically changed, so that I really would find it quite handicapping if I went through with my original plans for you.

Look for and check your attributions! Others frequently frustrate, annoy, and treat you unfairly. But only rarely do they do so because they thoroughly and personally hate you; only rarely do they *intend* to act vindictively toward you; only rarely do they have no good reasons for treating you the way they do, do they fully admit the iniquity of their ways and still persist in pursuing them. In many instances they have such severe disturbances that they cannot easily help treating you badly, or they have very little awareness of their injustices to you, or they believe that they cannot possibly solve some of their own basic problems unless they deal with you unfairly. Seek, if you possibly can, their true motives and attitudes. And watch your exaggerated or invented attributions!

9. *Combating romanticism and unrealism.* Romanticism and utopian fantasizing have their assets: they give

you something to look forward to in life, and while you feel romantically obsessed with a person or thing, you have some wonderfully exhilarating experiences. Your problem, as usual, consists of escalating romantic wishes and preferences into rigorous demands and commands. If you want Ms. Jones or Mr. Smith to love you devotedly and to have a continuing romantic involvement with you, fine! But if you absolutely, dogmatically must have that kind of attachment, and have it practically forever, beware!

Ingrid Bengis, author of *Combat in the Erogenous Zone* and a self-confessed man-hater, sagely notes: "When I was sixteen I commented to an adult that in my opinion all cynics were disappointed idealists. What I would add today is that most man-haters are probably disappointed romantics. Or at the very least, I would say, that is what I am."

So foster your own romanticism if you will. Look for high-level, imaginative, long-lasting involvements. But don't command; don't insist! You do not *need* the romantic attachments that you want. And if you believe this, really believe this, you will stop hating those who don't want to get into or maintain a rip-roaring romantic relationship with you.

10. *Overcoming feelings of inadequacy.* Many authorities correctly point out that feelings of hostility can compensate for feelings of inferiority since hating others seems hugely better than downing oneself. Writers on crime and violence, such as Marvin Wolfgang and Franco Ferracuti and Hans Toch, show how certain subcultures in our society encourage their members to think that hostility and the use of force has fine, "manly" qualities, and consequently certain immature personalities in this subculture tend to employ violence as a compensatory tool, to cover up their basic feelings of inadequacy. If this thesis has a good deal to it—and it would seem that it

probably has—then one solution to the problem of anger and violence would consist of helping basically immature individuals to act more maturely. This, of course, brings us right back to RET and to some of the points on anger we made in the first few chapters.

If you want to get rid of anger that stems from feelings of insecurity and inadequacy, read over this early material and learn to stop downing yourself. Your traits, deeds, and performances may indeed fall far below the level of desirability. For personal reasons or because you come from a certain "lower" socioeconomic class, you may have many cards stacked against you and may do decidedly worse than many other people. Too bad! Most unfortunate! Abysmally unfair! But if you really do have inferior traits or easily and prejudicedly get downed for what your social group wrongly defines as "inferiorities," *you* still do not have to rate yourself as a lowly person and deem yourself unworthy of joy.

The more you accept yourself unconditionally—because you *choose* to remain alive and to strive for happiness, and for no other reason—the less tendency you will have to cover up your "inadequacy" with compensatory anger. This does not mean that you cannot rightly fight against social injustice or act as a rebel *with* a cause. You can! But try to do so because you want to right real wrongs and want to better your own life—and not to prove your "strength" or "manliness" or "nobility." Who needs that kind of self-justification? Answer: people who first foolishly put themselves down.

11. *Familiarity and ritualistic behavior.* Peter Marler, in studying the behavior of animals and humans, has observed that "perhaps the most subtle and difficult to understand, and yet perhaps ultimately the most important, factor in reducing the probability of aggression is familiarity." He notes that strangeness seems to stimulate

conflict and fighting, while habitual companionship leads to more peaceful coexistence. He feels that some animals have the involved ritual of prancing and preening before one another in order to gain familiarity.

Konrad Lorenz notes that the promotion of personal friendships between members of different ideologies and nations often goes a long way toward reducing hostility. Yehuda Amir, in reviewing the literature on contact in ethnic relations, observes that "there is increasing evidence . . . to support the view that contact between members of ethnic groups tends to produce change in attitude between these groups" and that prejudice gets minimized as this kind of social contact and mutual acceptance increases. Morton Deutsch indicates that a cooperative and friendly process in human affairs will likely lead to productive conflict resolution because it encourages the recognition of the legitimacy of each person's interests and of the desirability of searching for a solution responsive to the wishes of both sides. It also leads to a trusting attitude which increases sensitivity to similarities and common interests, while minimizing the salience of differences and limiting hostility.

You can sometimes reduce anger between yourself and others by making yourself more thoroughly familiar with them, and they with you. The more acquainted you become with strangers, the less danger you will tend to feel from them—and the less they will tend to feel from you. This does not necessarily relate to close ties since when you have a close friend, mate, or relative, you sometimes make yourself more angry and violent at him or her than you would feel toward others, as you irrationally *demand* considerate and fair behavior from this person while you merely *prefer* it from others. As Marvin Wolfgang and several other students of crime have reported, homicides and serious assaults generally occur among people who have a fairly close relationship with each other. But if you will teach yourself to expect your close associates to act humanly and fallibly, your intimacy with them may encourage you not to hate them unduly.

12. *Fair fighting.* In *Creative Aggression*, Bach and Goldberg present a nine-step program by which you may engage in a "fair fight" with one of your intimates. As they note, "fair fighting is not a verbal free-for-all but a controlled technique for assertive communication." It largely consists of formally requesting your opponent for a fight, having an open huddle and rehearsal, stating your beef and explaining how it negatively affects you, getting your opponent to state your beefs back to you and at the same time making sure that you accurately report back his or her gripes, asking your partner to change, hearing his or her objections to changing, continuing to express your view after you listen to and carefully repeat your partner's view, agreeing on change or on no changes, and discussing, at a future meeting, the success or failure of your and your partner's agreement.

The distinguishing features of fair fighting include: agreeing on a limited kind of fight, listening carefully to your opponent, restating this opponent's views before trying to answer them, agreeing on whether or not you both desire a change, and restating this agreement. Essentially, then, in fair fighting you agree *not* to fight in the usual nonlistening, pure bellyaching, disruptive manner, but to do so in a civilized way, largely using the listening and restating methods developed by Thomas Gordon, Ted Crawford, and other proponents of creative listening.

This does not mean that fair fighting will solve everything. With some people, it will merely bring out into the open their simmering differences, and they will ultimately either go on interminably or agree to part. But it does, at least implicitly, get rid of the musts that lead to anger. For when you agree on fair fights, you agree that you do not *have* to get your way, that you *can* listen carefully to your partner, that you *may* legitimately compromise, and that you finally *do* feel able to stop your overdemandingness and to give your partner the right to control his or her own destiny.

In analyzing a fair fight, according to the Bach and Goldberg method, you also look at your and your partner's style of blaming and damning and get some understanding of how each of you illegitimately resorts to this kind of self-defeating rage, and you thereby do manage to get some insight into your anger-creating philosophies. So even though the technique seems mainly active, it has a distinct antimusturbational element in it and may lead to the knowledge and the feeling that the bad blood between you and your partner does not *have* to exist. As Bach and Goldberg note, "fair fighting is designed to avoid a win-lose approach and provide a procedure that results in a mutually comfortable resolution and learning experience."

13. *Avoidance of drugs and alcohol.* Abusers of drugs and alcohol frequently turn up as very angry people, even after they have given up drugs or gone on the wagon for a number of years. In all probability, part of their drinking and drug abuse stems from their undue upsettability. Alcoholics, for example, may either drink heavily to control and mask their anger, or they may only feel able to express themselves angrily when under the influence of liquor. So their open or masked hostility tends to drive them to drink.

At the same time, both drugs and alcohol also enhance anger in a good many instances. Sedative drugs, like marijuana or phenobarbital, may tend to make some people less enraged than they would normally feel, but they may also lead to irritability if the sleep or relaxation that the drugs normally produce get interfered with and do not actually occur. Amphetamines also tend to increase irritability and nastiness, and some people act very hostilely whenever they get high on these kinds of substances. Alcohol frequently helps create or exacerbate irritability and nastiness. Even the *belief* that you have consumed alcohol may result in more aggressive behavior, regardless of the actual alcoholic content of the drinks you may have had—as an experiment by Alan R. Lang, Daniel J. Goeckness, Vincent J. Adesso, and G. Alan Marlatt showed.

If you have any serious problem with hostility, watch what drugs and drinks you take. This doesn't mean that you necessarily have to remain a teetotaler, but monitor your own drug-taking and alcohol-imbibing behavior.

14. *Lack of reinforcement.* Aleksandr I. Solzhenitsyn has pointed out that if we keep reinforcing outbursts of violence, by doing nothing to penalize them and letting their perpetrators get away with almost any assaultive behavior they desire, we encourage their perpetuation and exacerbation: "Both hijackings and all other forms of terrorism have been spreading tenfold precisely because everyone is ready to capitulate before them. But as soon as some firmness is shown, terrorism can be smashed. Just remember that."

This also tends to hold true for self-angering. If you let yourself get away with outbursts of temper and assaultive behavior toward others, especially if you reinforce yourself by falsely letting yourself "know" how strong and nobly you behave for letting yourself act violently, you will tend to increase your anger-inciting tendencies. But if you very firmly insist that you'd better stop this kind of nonsense, and swiftly and drastically penalize yourself in some way almost every time you do indulge in an outburst of fury, you will tend to condition yourself to feel much less angry. You do harm yourself by inward and outward raging, and the penalties you impose on yourself for this kind of childishness may well show you that rage does *not* pay off very well and that you'd better do something to discourage it.

15. *A philosophy of fallibility.* I can hardly overemphasize the point that all humans remain incredibly fallible and that this seems their basic and almost invariant nature. Naturally, they can change and do better. But only within limits! They have just about no chance of acting invariably or perennially fair, just, ethical, right, or proper.

A concomitant point that often gets lost in the shuffle: humans have an unusually fine ability sadly to accept the fallibility of others and to forgive them for their enormous crimes. An excellent case in point consists of the incident that John M. Gullo and I included in our book *Murder and Assassination.* When a young man in the city of Philadelphia sexually attacked and killed a three-and-a-half-year-old girl some years ago, her father, Professor Anatol Hold of the University of Pennsylvania, wrote a remarkable letter to the Philadelphia *Bulletin,* in which he said he hoped that the murderer would get brought to justice, psychologically treated, but *not* made to suffer the death penalty. For as much as he missed and grieved over his dead child, this father wrote, he could not help acknowledging that the slayer seemed an exceptionally disturbed individual, driven to his deed by enormous feelings of inadequacy and worthlessness, and he could not, in all conscience, desire the death of such a disordered person. Wrote Professor Hold: "My final word has to do with the operation of the machinery of justice. Had I caught the boy in the act, I would have wished to kill him. Now that there is no undoing of what has been done, I only wish to help him. Let no feelings of caveman vengeance influence us. Let us rather help him who did so human a thing."

In a remarkably similar case, Joseph Sturek, a mental

health therapy aide at Central Islip State Hospital in New York, felt exceptionally sad when his sixteen-year-old son and several of his friends found Sturek's twelve-year-old daughter, Jennifer, who had been brutally murdered a few days before. But when evidence clearly seemed to show that a fifteen-year-old boy, a neighbor of the Stureks, had committed the murder, Sturek said, "We must forgive the boy. He is very sick. Jennifer would have wanted us to forgive him. . . . The fifteen-year-old's father should have known that there was something wrong, and should have done something about it, perhaps through psychiatry," said Sturek, adding, "I feel so sorry for the boy's parents, because whether they are good or bad, they're going through their own hell now."

Sturek's hinting that the boy's parents might *be* good or bad—ratable as whole people for various of their traits—does not fall within rational-emotive views. People clearly have good and bad traits—meaning characteristics that help and that harm themselves and others—but we'd better not designate them, holistically, as good or bad people. Obviously, however, Sturek accepted the possibility of forgiving the alleged murderer of his daughter, even though he could not condone his wrong acts.

Can you do anything to aid this kind of compassion in yourself and others? Yes—if you acknowledge your philosophy of revenge and retribution and substitute for it one of accepting human fallibility, if you see what harm revenge and retribution frequently do to you and to your associates and therein realize that they mainly confirm your naturally acquired and self-conditioned tendencies to carry on rather than to drop unfortunate conflicts and altercations. Dr. Harry Harlow has pointed out that although humans and primates have the innate tendency both to love and to hate, they will tend to feel and behave less angrily in their later life if they have had early experiences—either with their siblings or their adult caretakers—which bring out their love and friendliness.

Even though human propensities toward aggression have a strong biological underpinning, that does not mean that they *have* to flower "beautifully." For your own children or pupils, you can see that they interact more socially with their peers; you can provide something of a head start to their accepting and forgiving behaviors and inhibit the development of their aggressiveness. Don't expect miracles in these respects since strong innate predispositions toward combativeness and vindictiveness don't easily disappear. But if we can train "naturally" antagonistic animals, such as dogs and cats or cats and mice, to live together peacefully—which we definitely can—we can also encourage "naturally" antagonistic humans to behave much less assaultively. Why not try?

Michael Efran and J. Allan Cheyne, in commenting on an experiment, note that seemingly trivial social encounters may appear as potential interpersonal disputes and that "the mundane encounters which we all experience each day constitute unpleasant, even stressful, events. The ubiquity of these events may make them more potent contributors to the 'stress of modern life' than has previously been assumed." You could try to reduce the number of ordinary social encounters of a "stressful" nature that you experience on a day-to-day basis. This solution, however, has its distinct limitations since it involves a great deal of social withdrawal. You reduce stress but possibly also reduce many socially satisfying experiences.

Another solution involves changing your attitude *toward* social stress. If you work on yourself so that you do not *have to* do well in social encounters and do not *need to* have minimal social frustration, you can make yourself more accepting (though not necessarily approving) of the unpleasantness of everyday living, and you will thereby tend to react less agonistically when these common stresses occur. As we have consistently noted throughout this book, full acknowledgment of your right to deal *badly* with social encounters and of the rights of others to frustrate you in such encounters will probably go a long way toward helping you take such encounters much less seriously and self-provokingly.

16. *Countering abuse of children and subordinates.* We have given increasing attention in recent years to the abuse of children, to parents or parent-surrogates who not only strictly discipline their offspring, but physically abuse them and sometimes even beat them literally to death. In studies made of such parents, including one of the cases that John M. Gullo and I presented in *Murder and Assassination,* it appears that they frequently have unusual frustrations and feelings of inadequacy in their own lives and that they sometimes take these out on their young victims. As Linda Charlton has noted, "above all, there is the abuse that is the product of stress, of parents striking at children because of unbearable pressure."

While we rightfully tend to dramatize incidents of child abuse, we fail to observe that the ill-treatment of older individuals frequently occurs, too. Professors, for example, can unfairly treat college and graduate students. Bosses, union officials, supervisors, and police and military officers can abuse their subordinates. Public inspectors and other officials can tyrannize those over whom they have some power. Mates who know that their partners neurotically need them can act as little Hitlers over such partners. Physically or intellectually strong adolescents often savagely abuse those they find weaker or less capable.

The main causes of this almost ubiquitous phenomenon of the "strong" victimizing their less powerful subordinates? Again, feelings of great inferiority on the part of the former, which they avoid facing or compensate for by hopping on the backs of those they can command, and continual stresses and frustrations experienced by the victimizers which make them more than willing to seek out distracting and often enjoyable combative or abusive pursuits.

If those with inferiorities and socioeconomic disadvantages have their positions in life raised, so that they no longer look down on themselves, they may no longer have the temptation of resorting to violence as a cover-up for their own inordinate—while, to some degree, legitimate—feelings of extreme frustration. Such social solutions appear long past due, and unless we somehow increasingly arrange them, the abuse of the "weak" by the "strong" will almost certainly continue. And pandemically! What to do *until* that time? In countries like the United States and Sweden social injustice has in many ways enormously decreased as prosperity has improved and various forms of protective legislation (for example, minimum wages, social security, and public assistance for the poor) have passed into law. And in countries like the Soviet Union and China economic equality has increased notably during the past century. But the millennium has hardly arrived in these respects, and considerable injustice and inequality still exist.

What then? Clearly, as Epictetus showed two thousand years ago and as the philosophy of RET shows today, we'd better feel highly frustrated and regretful about the remaining inequities, motivate ourselves to do as much as we can to ameliorate them, but stop whining about what still exists and continue our determined—and not hostile!—efforts to change what we can change as we accept what we cannot.

17. *Dealing with counteraggression.* When someone deals with you angrily or seems angrily to make an inordinate, unreasonable demand of you, counteraggression

commonly arises. The history of humanity shows that with such instances, innumerable arguments, feuds, and even national and international wars ensue. Let us list some rules that you can use to put a stop to your own counteraggression:

17a. Assume that the aggressors have something to their point of view. Yours may have more "rightness" than theirs; it seems unlikely that they have no point whatever. Try to look for and, in your own mind, emphasize their point of view.

17b. Even if you conclude—rightly or wrongly—that your opponents have no good arguments or reasons, assume that they definitely *think* they do. They rarely fight for what they call "right" when they know perfectly well that they have no justification whatever. However deluded, they just about always believe, and often devoutly believe, in their point of view. Acknowledge to yourself that they do believe in it, and even let them know, if possible, that you see that they have this ("wrong") view.

17c. Often use a creative listening attitude, such as Ted Crawford's technique, Revolving Discussion Sequence (RDS). You may *think* you really know the other's outlook, but to make sure that you do and to show him or her that you really *want* to see the other side of the argument, repeat back to an aggressor your own interpretation of that person's presentation, and then check with him or her whether you have heard it correctly. Keep checking and repeating the other's view until it seems almost certain that you have understood it. You can use this procedure with your friends, with your co-workers, with your family members, and even with your pronounced enemies. At least *know* what their opposing views consist of, show them that you do know, and keep arguing with them out of real conviction, not because you don't really see their viewpoint.

17d. Sometimes use RET methods with your opponents. If a male friend, for example, severely castigates you for your lateness when you, according to your understanding, came to an appointment on time, you can often say something like: "Well, naturally, I don't see it just the way that you do—or else I don't think I would have arrived at ten o'clock instead of, as you say I agreed, at nine. But let's assume you acted rightly and I behaved wrongly. I knew, let us say, that we made the appointment for nine, and I deliberately or carelessly came at ten, thereby really inconveniencing you. Okay. In that case, I clearly behaved badly. But even so, why do you have to upset yourself about my poor behavior and make yourself needlessly incensed at me? If I do wrong, I do wrong, and I certainly have a problem. But don't you keep telling yourself, 'He *shouldn't* come late! He has *no right* to make a mistake! He amounts to a *total worm* for acting that wormy way!' If so, don't you *also* have a problem? And before you waste your time going on incessantly about how poorly *I* behaved and about what a louse *I* amount to for behaving that way, wouldn't it seem good for you to do a little work on your own problem—on your own needless feelings of anger?" Watch it, for with many of your friends and acquaintances, this kind of RET argument may well backfire! But at times it may prove very useful.

17e. Remember that when someone aggresses against you, even most unfairly in your eyes, you don't *have to* show this person the error of his or her ways and you don't *have to* make a "strong" counterpresentation. Usually, you will *want to* present your own view and continue the argument on the merits of your and your opponent's presentations. But don't think this *necessary*! Real strength very often consists of your letting your opponent "win" the argument, in spite of the unfairness of this outcome, and then, pretty much ignoring this "win," going on to more constructive and useful things. Don't forget: your goal had better not involve showing your opponent, and the world at large, your correctness or virtue. Let it, instead, consist of your ultimately trying to get more of what you want and less of what you don't want out of life. And letting others, at least temporarily, "win" arguments with you may well lead to the fulfillment of *this* kind of goal.

17f. Beware of your vindictiveness! When you have lost an argument or even won it after an expensive hassle, don't focus on getting even with your opponents at all costs. Revenge or vindictiveness normally keeps you emotionally involved with your opponents practically forever, consumes enormous amounts of time and energy, distracts you from more constructive goals, gives you needless pain in your own gut, encourages counter-revenge and prolonged feuds, rarely convinces your opponents of your strength but usually makes them feel that you have inordinate weakness and nastiness, and results in harm to many innocent bystanders who would rather have no part of your quarrel but who easily get affected by it. Revenge and vindictiveness may help you have a less boring life. But at what a cost!

17g. Most of the time you do not have to incense yourself, or even too seriously to frustrate yourself, when your opponents seem to have overweening and ridiculous demands. If you *look* carefully at these demands, you will usually see more reasonable aspects of them. For one thing, your opponents may have deliberately overstated them, knowing that you would not accede, but hoping for a more reasonable compromise. For another thing, they may have little knowledge of your attitudes and your wishes. Or they may not see the impracticality of what they keep asking for. Just because they have a great emotional stake in their requests and frequently feel that they simply *have to* achieve them, they may not easily see the consequences of what they demand and may even defeat themselves by some of the things they put in their ultimatums.

In dealing with the "demands" and the "unnegotiable" requests of some of the student protest groups at the University of Illinois, David D. Henry, president of the university, discovered that such terms often do not carry the harshness of their surface meaning. "While the word 'demand' normally offends me," Henry said to reporters, "I translate it to mean 'proposal.'" He then felt much better able to cope with these "demands" and to negotiate "unnegotiable" requests of the students.

If, similarly, you really try to see your opponent's point of view, the negotiability of his or her "demands" on you, and the possibility of your reacting to them without hostility and with reasonable consideration, you will tend to act much less angrily toward that person—and probably encourage him or her to aggress less against you. Remember in this connection that just as almost all of us seem to have easy, probably innate tendencies to fight vehemently against another's "demands," so do we have natural tendencies to fight much less and to compromise more when we see that other people give our "demands" due consideration. While, on the one hand, we natively tend to fight, we also natively tend to compromise. So give your opponents' compromising proclivities a more than even chance to assert themselves!

18. *Nonviolence as a philosophy.* Violence as a philosophy has tended to rule the human kingdom. Only in a few notable cases has nonviolence risen to the fore as a planned, practical method of getting your way without open warfare between you and your opponents. Gandhi's prolonged fight to get the British to abdicate as the political ruler of India represents one such case, and notwithstanding that the nonviolent approach might well *not* work with certain other kinds of opponents than Gandhi had—

with, for example, the Nazis—it seems important to recognize that it has great advantages.

As C. Lasch points out, the Indian doctrine of nonviolence, or satyagraha, assumes decency as latent in all people, as part of their very humanity: "To decide in advance that certain adversaries are incapable of decency is therefore to accuse them of inhumanity and to fall into precisely that arrogant moralizing from which Satyagraha proposes to deliver us in the first place."

Erik Erikson has nicely portrayed Gandhi's nonviolent approach. He points out that Gandhi's truth consists of the acceptance of the idea that violence against your adversary really amounts to the same as violence against yourself. Martin Luther King subscribed to this same truth and wrote that "for practical as well as moral reasons, nonviolence offers the only road to freedom for my people. In violent warfare, one must be prepared to face ruthlessly the fact that there will be casualties by the thousands."

Barbara Deming also indicates the practical, hardheaded results of the difficult path of nonviolence:

> [When noncooperation] is nonviolent, I believe it is immensely more powerful in the long run, because one has, as it were, two hands on the adversary; with one hand, one shakes up his life drastically—makes it impossible for him simply to continue as he *has been;* with the other hand we calm him, we control his response to us, because we respect his rights as well as ours, his real, his human rights, because we assure him that it is not his destruction we want, merely justice. We keep him from responding to our actions as men respond to violence, just mechanically, blindly. We force him to think, to ask all kinds of questions of himself about the nature of our actions and our grievances, about the real issues involved, about what others watching the struggle will think, about where his own real, long-term interests lie, whether they don't lie in adjusting himself to change.

In your own life, you probably do not have to practice passive resistance or complete nonviolence against any barbaric horde either for political or other motives. But you can, if you wish, show your subordinates, your peers, and your supervisors that you firmly believe in nonviolence and that although you may sometimes or often resist doing what they want you to do, you will do so in a physically unassaultive manner. Just as libertarians, such as Walter Block, will promulgate the view that we can legitimately call no act immoral unless it involves some amount of physical coercion of one human by another, so can you promulgate the doctrine that you will virtually never oppose others' enmity with counterforce, but that you will passively resist their trespasses on your liberty.

Personally, I don't advocate taking this view to extremes. If a thug attacks me and I feel convinced that he would most probably harm me physically if I didn't resist him, I think that I would choose either (1) to run like hell or, if that didn't prove feasible, (2) to return his assault to protect myself. I would try to do so efficiently—and unangrily.

Joan Baez notes in her nonviolent way: "If all recourse to violence is taken away, you're forced to really use your mind to search for alternatives. And you're forced to acknowledge—and this is what *I* mean by revolution— that no man has the right to do injury to another person or to be an accomplice in the doing of injury. This means you have to recognize that everybody is equal and there's no such thing as an enemy."

When questioned by Nat Hentoff, "Wouldn't you have considered Adolf Hitler an enemy?" she replied:

No, he was a human being, too. But recognizing his humanity didn't mean you had to like him and it certainly didn't mean you had to carry out his orders. In a civilized society, people wouldn't have followed him. They would have seen that he was a wreck, a very sick man; and seeing that, they would have gotten him some help. The term enemy just gets in the way of understanding that we are all human beings. Admittedly, it takes an awful lot of un-brainwashing to come to that point. To be this kind of revolutionary requires the right-winger to throw away his flag and the left-winger to forget all those posters about power coming out of the barrel of a gun.

I agree with Joan Baez. To live without designating those who seriously disagree with you as *enemies* means to take an unusually revolutionary point of view. But if you can work on yourself to adopt some such view as this one, you will make yourself immensely less hostile—yet, as she indicates, by no means a nonactivist.

Some empirical confirmation of this point of view comes from the experiments of Harry Kaufmann and Seymour Feshbach. They found that disruptive behaviors were substantially reduced by prior exposure to constructive but not to punitive communication.

This would tend to show that if you deal with the Hitlers of the world in a nondamning, constructive manner, you may actually help them modify their behavior more than if you view them in a castigating, hostile way.

In any event, you can, if you wish, adopt a philosophy of nonviolence. Those who choose to live by it, even at great risk of personal suffering and annihilation, may sanely do so not only to decrease their own feelings of hostility, but also in order to set a fine human example for others to follow.

Does this seem senseless—to sacrifice yourself for the sake of other humans? Not entirely—since one of your personal goals, usually, consists of living in a social group and helping the other members of that group, including your intimate associates, survive happily. So some amount of self-sacrifice can come under that kind of basic goal or value.

19. *Recognizing the irony of hatred.* Hatred can consume you more than almost any other feeling and, like jealousy and a few other passions, can literally obsess you and run your life. It usually goes far beyond feelings of deprivation and bothersomeness associated with mere frustration and brings with it an illusion of self-interest. On the surface, you seem absorbed in your own situation and *ostensibly* strive—through the feeling of anger—to get what you want and to get rid of what you don't want. But what an illusion!

Just as feelings of anxiety—spurred by the irrational belief "I must do well and win others' approval and would see it as horrible if I didn't!"—make you other-directed rather than self-directed, feelings of hatred have a similar effect. You can make yourself so beset about people who have treated you unfairly that you thereby make *them* the center of your attention and normally lose yourself in the process. You *seem* to want greater satisfaction for your own life, but you really obsess about changing *them,* doing *them* in, gloating over possible or actual injury that may come to *them.*

If you will force yourself to realize how other-directed this kind of thinking makes you, you can become aware of how you defeat yourself by hating while deluding yourself that your hatred helps. You can then more easily go back to your main interest: "What, in view of the disadvantages of their treatment of me, can *I* do to make *my* life happier?" As Ken Olsen notes, "Hate is a means by which we punish and destroy ourselves for the actions of others." How ironic! See that you sink that irony into your brain many, many times—until you replace most of your hostility with self-interest.

20. *Humanistic values.* If you see yourself as an integral part of the human race, if you see that all humans have a right to live and achieve happiness (and freedom from needless pain) merely because they exist, and if you see

222 HOW TO LIVE WITH—AND WITHOUT—ANGER

that your own right to live and enjoy will most likely be
fulfilled if you act humanely to others, you will tend to feel
much less angry and punishing against others even when
they treat you shabbily, especially when they have done
you no direct wrong. This does not mean that you have to
go completely out of your way to help or sacrifice yourself
for others. But it does mean that the more you acquire a
humanistic set of values the less cruelly you will tend to
treat others even when given approval for acting sadistically.

To acquire a more humanistic philosophy, try to remember that you abhor needless mistreatment, that most
people feel the same way you do in this respect, that
concern for others tends to bring about the kind of conditions that you would like; that treating others well in spite
of their unfairness has challenging, self-growth elements,
and that just as you can, alas, enjoy hurting others, you
can also enjoy helping them. Without living as a Florence
Nightingale or St. Francis, you can find real satisfaction in
trying to make the world a little better a place in which to
live.

Bernard J. Siegel points out that some tribal groups
(such as the Taos American Indians) and international
groups (such as the Jews) form "defensive groups," which
make a conscious attempt to maintain comparatively strict
controls among the members and to instill peaceful values
"by requiring constant exercise of control over behavior
potentially destructive to the group in relation to external
threats." Such groups maintain inner peace in order to
mobilize themselves more effectively to survive in what
they deem a hostile world. At the same time, this kind of
defensive nonaggression has its disadvantages. Intratribal
peace may encourage external paranoia and combativeness. But it at least shows the feasibility of rearing groups
of humans so that they deliberately inhibit their angry

feelings and actions toward each other, albeit at the expense of alienating themselves from other groups.

21. *Focusing on the pain of the victim.* When angry, we tend to enjoy our own emotional outburst and to assume that somehow the victim of our anger will take our fury well and will ultimately benefit from it. Nothing of the sort may occur! This individual may take it very badly; feel acute physical or emotional pain, depending on whether we assault him or her verbally or bodily; and, if our attacks include verbal invective, may internalize our criticism and feel affected by it forever. Don't, especially, delude yourself into thinking that your victims have no feelings or that they only benefit from your hostility. Call to mind vividly some of the negative results that can and do accrue to them because of your overt expressions of anger, and use these to inhibit further expressions.

Don't, of course, go to the other irrational extreme and down yourself for displaying anger. However mistaken and "rotten" your deed, you don't turn into a rotten *person* for performing it. But your anger does have consequences—and, often, very inhumane consequences to others who have great vulnerability. Keep that vulnerability in mind; try to see that even if their behavior has its unniceties, they do not really "deserve" to keep suffering—through your anger—because of it; try to realize that their suffering will not necessarily eliminate the behavior.

22. *Focusing on relating to others.* An obvious advantage of your not making yourself incensed at others includes your getting along much better with them under unangry conditions. Amazingly, however, you easily tend to forget this—and you concentrate on other goals, most of them specious. As a parent, for example, you focus on teaching your children to do the right thing and insist to yourself that they *have to do* this. Consequently, when

they do the wrong thing, you incense yourself at them—
and scream that they'd better change. Result: you have
poor relations with them and they do change—usually for
the worse!

Haim Ginott, in this connection, notes the case of a boy
of seven who broke a toy gun given to him and, frightened
by his own ineptness, hid the gun. In finding parts of the
gun, the father tried to get him to say where he had put
the rest of it, and the boy replied that he didn't know. The
father said, "You broke the gun! If there's one thing I hate,
it's a liar!" And he gave the boy a good spanking. But as
Dr. Ginott notes:

> Instead of playing detective and prosecutor, the father
> would have been more helpful to his son by saying:
>   "I see your new gun is broken."
>   "It didn't last long."
>   "It's a pity. It was expensive."
> The child might have learned some valuable lesson:
>   "Father understands. I can tell him my troubles. I must
> take better care of gifts."

So remind yourself: "If I make myself angry and express
my anger to others, I will usually antagonize them and
encourage them to keep acting badly. If I accept them
with their poor behavior and do not demand that they stop
behaving that way, I will get along much better with them
and also frequently serve as a much more effective teacher
for the points of conduct I want to make. The less angry I
feel and act, the more effective a teacher of the 'right way'
I shall probably prove."

23. *Discriminate the constructive aspects of anger.*
Anger, as many authorities have pointed out, has its constructive aspects: without feeling some considerable degree of irritation, frustration, and annoyance we would
hardly remove obnoxious stimuli that impinge upon us,
and in a sense, all human progress might well stop. H. H.

Wolff has pointed out that we can employ aggression against others "constructively in many fields, including self-preservation, and defense of basic physical needs, sexual conquest and experience, as well as for other predominantly psychological purposes such as competition, the defense of one's rights as an individual or those of one's family or the group one belongs to, the struggle for the development of one's identity, the maintenance of value systems and ideals and especially for creative purposes of all kinds, an area which is most highly developed, if not confined to the human species."

Paula Heimann and Arthur Valenstein also note that "normally every child has a thrust towards activity, towards asserting himself and towards mastery; it need not necessarily become an overweening urge towards destructiveness, which in itself suggests a possible neurotic quality."

Albert Rothenberg separates anger from hostility and notes that anger has strong communication aspects for humans and, therefore, great constructive potential despite its dangers and its frequent linkage with feelings of anxiety. If we can rid ourselves of the anxiety, Rothenberg hypothesizes, we can constructively use our feelings of anger.

Albert E. Trieschman shows that children often use temper tantrums as a problem-solving device since they cannot easily devise better means of coping with an emotional crisis. The wild threats and insults of these children "represent a primitive effort to feel some sense of competence. Robbed of his sense of bodily control, the youngster proposes alternatives as if he had some control of options. He tries to compensate for his lack of control by acting as if he could manipulate his environment, which includes [his parents'] feelings."

Usually, when you feel angry, you very much want to get your own way, to remove unpleasant stimuli, to control others, and to preserve your own physical and emotional health. Good! Why shouldn't you want what you want, try to rid yourself of what you don't like? At the same time, you would do well to recognize fully that most *other* humans want exactly what you do: their own way. They have just as much a right to their preferences as you have to yours. Obviously both you and they frequently cannot get what you want—especially when your and their desires seem incompatible. So you would also do well to separate the constructive from the destructive aspects of your own hostile or aggressive feelings.

If you give yourself the full right to want and give them a similar right and if you don't demand that they *have to* acknowledge your right while you blithely ignore theirs, you will much better accept the constructive while minimizing the self-defeating aspects of your ardent wishes.

24. *Cooperative outlook.* RET does not teach that competition has enormous evils and that you should therefore, at all costs, avoid it. On the contrary, it assumes that as a human you will often want to get what you want, to acquire more than others acquire, and to obtain things at others' expense.

Although we usually think of competition in regard to professional and business affairs, it also applies to ventures like gaining someone else's approval or love. You want to establish an intimate relationship with, let us say, a member of the other sex, and some other person wants to establish an equally intimate relationship with him or her. The person you choose has only the time or inclination for a monogamous intimacy, so either you or your competitor will lose out. Shall you withdraw from competition? Angrily fight with your competitor for the single "prize"? Obsessively plot and scheme to win the competition? What?

The usual RET answer: try, as strongly as you can, to get what you want and to win the competition, but don't insist that you *must* win it or that you will amount to a total slob, and your opponent will turn into a villain, if you lose. Feel fairly determined—but not absolutely insistent—on gaining what you want. At the same time, consider the advantage of a more cooperative outlook. Sometimes both you and your opponent can "win," though neither of you completely, and you may even find it enjoyable to help him or her to achieve partial satisfaction. The goal you seek—whether another's love, money, professional success, or what you will—need not constitute your *only* preference. Sharing with others; cooperatively planning so that both of you or all of you may partially gain what you want; feeling friendly toward your opponents—these aims may also motivate you, and in a less than utterly competitive way.

Competition, remember, has both short-range and long-range disadvantages as well as gains. It takes time and effort. It encourages enmity from others. It overemphasizes winning. It has distinct social consequences for third parties—as when a union and management compete for industrial spoils and other members of the public suffer from the consequences of ensuing strikes and lockouts. In a wider social context, extreme competition can easily lead to intranational and international conflict and war.

In RET terms, the more you train yourself to *want* but not to *need* interpersonal bonding on a highly selective, monogamous basis and the more you get yourself to accept the virtues of cooperating with many individuals in your community rather than a small selected group of family members, the less competitive and hostile you may feel.

You may not, of course, crave the satisfactions of

cooperativeness over competitiveness and may therefore not work for them. But you do have at least two viable options here, and the mere fact that you naturally and as a result of your upbringing have tended to favor one of them—competition—doesn't mean that you have to favor it forever.

25. *Diversionary methods of overcoming anger.* RET views hostility and other forms of emotional disturbance as mainly stemming from your thoughts, ideas, beliefs, and philosophies, and it therefore tries to help you *change* them. However, it also realizes that you can temporarily shunt aside or divert yourself from your own upsetting ideas by a variety of methods, such as relaxation, meditation, games, emotional attachments, physical exercises, and a host of other pleasure-seeking distractions. Even anger itself, as several writers have shown, can divert you from certain other forms of hostility, as when the people of one nation make themselves incensed at the people of another nation and thereby lose a great deal of their hostility toward each other.

Some diversionary pastimes can also lead to some measure of cure, and not merely the sidetracking or palliation, of anger. If you feel unassertive, hate yourself for your unassertiveness, and thus feel anger, you can engage in games like chess or football or in selling others on your political ideas to overcome your unassertiveness and thereby to rid yourself of much of your "reason" for self-downing and self-hatred. This doesn't constitute a truly elegant cure since you could also choose to remain unassertive and, therefore, go on downing yourself, and because of this self-downing finally wind up feeling very angry at others who "suppress" you. But it could represent at least a partial cure.

Hans Toch, who has particularly studied violent individuals who cover up their self-deprecation with deprecation against others, notes that diversionary activity may sometimes help in cases like these:

> It might be possible to offer such an individual the alternative of joining extracurricularly an activity or club involving contemporaries who have shown themselves similarly troublesome. In this setting, group discussions of violence could occur, violence-related games could be played, skits or plays could be produced, and behavior patterns could be generated that could meet the boy's requirements for self-affirmation, without its destructive consequences.

If you feel prone to hostility and violence, you may consider the possibilities of diverting or sublimating some of your urges in these more constructive ways. You can sometimes arrange for limited or playacting forms of competition that will give you some amount of satisfaction and self-expression and thereby more easily refrain from more global or intense forms of violence that will "satisfy" you all right, but at the expense of other values and to the creation of certain dangers. Again, diversions of this kind will probably not completely solve your problems of hostility. But in some respects they may help.

26. *Antidepressive methods.* The psychological literature probably exaggerates the extent to which anger may cover up depression and depression may cover up anger. These kinds of cover-ups do at times occur, but not *all* anger consists of depression turned outward, nor does all depression consist of anger turned inward. Nonetheless, times do exist when you may severely anger yourself for taking on a self-pitying (depressed) attitude, and you may then go on to lash out at the world and at others in it who presumably have "caused" the "horrible" events that you think you can't stand.

You can deal with the depressed feelings that underlie your feelings of anger by way of the usual rational-emotive method. First determine the Activating Event. Generally, you will have failed at something at *A* or perhaps been rejected by someone whose approval you would definitely want to have. But feelings of failing and rejection do not in themselves equal depression. In order to reach a state of depression, you probably would have downed yourself for failing or pitied yourself enormously. And then you might have put the world down for having rejected you.

In the RET formulation you would have, at *B*, told yourself a set of sensible or rational Beliefs (*rB*s), such as "I don't like failing. I wish that I had succeeded and got accepted by this person. How unfortunate for me to fail and get rejected!" This set of rational Beliefs would lead you to feeling sorry, sad, and frustrated about what happened to you at point *A*.

At point *iB*, however, your set of irrational Beliefs would tend to take over: "How awful for me to fail and get rejected. I'll never really get what I want! This reveals me as a rotten person. How hopeless! I'll go on forever, never really getting what I most desire!"

At this point, you will begin to feel the undesirable Emotional Consequence (*C*)—your depression. Which you would then Dispute (*D*) with the usual rational-emotive questions: "What makes it awful for me to fail and get rejected? What evidence exists that I'll never get what I want? Even if I continue failing and being rejected, how does that make me a rotten person who will hopelessly go on forever, never really getting what I most desire?"

The cognitive Effect (*cE*) of disputing would include answers along these lines: "Nothing makes it awful for me to fail and be rejected. Only inconvenience and annoyance result. Just because I fail *now* hardly means that I have to keep doing so *in the future*. In fact, the more I try, the more I'll most probably succeed. But even if I never get exactly what I want and keep going on to many more rejections, it will prove, at the worst, that I have certain undesirable traits, not at all that I rate as a totally rotten human."

If you keep doing your ABCDEs in this manner, you will wind up, in practically all cases, feeling sorry, concerned, frustrated, and displeased, but not depressed; you will have no particular incentive to rationalize away or otherwise cover up your depression with anger or fury; and since you won't, in your own eyes, amount to a worm or a no-goodnik for having failed and got rejected, you will not have to put down the person who rejected you.

27. *General undisturbability.* Under general feelings of disturbance, I cannot too strongly emphasize overcoming your feelings of self-downing, vulnerability, and inadequacy since these arise so frequently and intensely. And they have pronounced connections with anger. If you use your own temper flare-ups as indications of the fact that you probably have a generally commanding attitude toward yourself and others and if you acknowledge that this commandingness means that you have *chosen* this way of life, you will almost always have the ability to reevaluate your choice and to change it.

In the RET framework all these kinds of feelings of inadequacy amount largely to your convincing yourself, at point *B*, that you have some weakness, inferiority, or inadequacy, at point *A*, and that you have to find this awful and down yourself as a human for having it. The solution in RET terms: to convince yourself that you may well have this failing but that you cannot legitimately rate yourself as a rotten person for having it. *It* seems unfortunate, but *you* have the ability to live reasonably happily in spite of this misfortune. Using RET in this fashion, you can surmount your feelings of self-deprecation and undermine the angry emotions to which they may easily lead.

28. *Training courses and workshops.* You can learn

how to deal with others, including your intimates, more effectively by taking certain kinds of training courses and workshops. Many individuals and organizations now give fight training courses, usually along the lines devised by George Bach. These have their value, when presented by nonangry leaders, but they also have their limitations. They may help you feel and act more hostilely, under the guise of having you assert yourself. Assertiveness training along rational and behavioral lines will prove more helpful, usually, than any course or workshop which includes the word "fight" in its title.

Human relations courses, such as those pioneered by Norman Kagan, can also help you considerably with your social skills and thereby decrease your tendency to interact combatively with others. Child management procedures, such as those outlined by W. Becker, Don Dinkmeyer, and Thomas Gordon, also show you how to relate more effectively to your children. They have, as well, abuse prevention potential. Some organizations, such as the Institute for Rational Living in New York and other American cities, specialize in teaching people how to relate more permissively and less angrily. Look for these kinds of seminars and workshops. But again: watch out for "growth centers" that specialize in psychomotor, bioenergetic, primal, and Reichian methods of "creative expression" because in my opinion they will sometimes teach you have to augment your "assertiveness" in a highly angry way.

If you find that courses and workshops, as well as the other techniques suggested in this book, don't help you very much—if you still often break out into self-defeating rages—you might well consider intensive individual or group therapy. Rational-Emotive Therapy, cognitive-behavior therapy, Adlerian individual psychology, George Kelly's fixed role playing—therapies such as these which contain a highly cognitive element and that help you understand and significantly change your basic philosophic assumptions that create anger (and other disturbed feelings) may help considerably. Organizations like the Institute for Advanced Study in Rational Psychotherapy in New York City, the Institute for Rational Living in several American cities, and the Society for Adlerian Psychology in various parts of the United States can help you find a suitable therapist in this respect.

13

Accepting Yourself
with Your Anger

Hopefully this book has clearly shown you how you can rid yourself of your anger and other irrational and inappropriate feelings that plague our everyday lives. Because you remain a fallible human, however, you will in all probability find yourself slipping back, from time to time, into these self-defeating attitudes. So we'd better look at how you can best deal with yourself and others when these occasions arise.

Let us say that with skill and success you have practiced the various techniques introduced in this book. Yet just the other day your boss acted so nastily and stupidly toward you, that you felt like really letting him have it. Fortunately, he had to leave the office before you had a chance to blow up in his presence, but even after he had gone, it took you more than half an hour to cool down. Now let's see how you could have dealt with your anger a little better under those conditions.

Firstly—and importantly—you could have acknowledged fully to yourself that you did have enraged feelings against your boss rather than denying them or rationalizing them away, and you could have fully acknowledged that *you* brought them on and that *you* behaved foolishly in that respect. You made yourself angry—your boss didn't. And you did so wrongly, stupidly. You rightly felt annoyed and irritated at his presumably nasty and foolish behavior. Why should you like it when it went against your own desires and interests? But you then angered yourself *about* his nastiness and his foolishness. You didn't have to do so.

Secondly, and perhaps even more important, you can accept yourself *with* these feelings. You would then acknowledge the wrongness of the feelings but not the badness of you. Humans not only act badly, but see that they do, and they frequently take their poor behavior and make it into a new Activating Experience and then belabor themselves mightily for acting that way. As a fallible human person you have a right to do wrong, to make yourself inappropriately angry. You don't rate as a louse or a worm for doing so. You merely amount to a person who has acted stupidly—not a stupid *person.*

Say to yourself something like "I really behaved badly or self-defeatingly in incensing myself at my boss, but I can easily do so and have a right, as a human, to act that silly way. My acts clearly prove wrong, but I can't legitimately see myself as a really rotten person." In other words, accept yourself while *not* accepting your behavior. Fully acknowledge its mistakenness: that it most likely brings you more harm than good. Review your anger and see why it does you harm. It gives you a "pain in the gut"; it doesn't help you solve your problem with your boss; it easily may communicate itself to him and make your relationship much worse; it may lead to poor physical reactions on your part (high blood pressure, etc.); it makes you preoccupied with your boss and his apparent irrationality, instead of focusing on how to do your job better and please him more, etc.; it sabotages your efficiency in many ways. If you feel determined to accept you, your humanity, in spite of your anger, you will have little trouble in fully acknowleding it as bad or self-sabotaging, whereas, if you insist on downing you, your totality, for your anger, then you will tend to deny, repress, and excuse your anger. And you will find yourself dealing unsatisfactorily with it. Look at it as bad but correctable!

Review what you mistakenly told yourself to make yourself angry. Resolve to tell yourself something different in the future—and practice doing so in your head. Perhaps you'll see that you *demanded* that your boss act nicely and intelligently with you and that when he didn't fulfill this demand, you told yourself, "How awful! He has no right to act the way I don't want him to! I can't stand his stupidity! I hope he drops dead!"

Now you ask yourself—at *D* for Disputing—what makes it *awful* for your boss to act nastily and stupidly? Why has he no right to act that way? Prove that you really can't stand his stupidity. And does he really amount to a total villain who should drop dead to please you?

You might answer thus: "Nothing makes it awful for my boss to act nastily and stupidly. It's only annoying and inconvenient! He does have the right to act any way that he acts. Even though he acts wrongly and I don't like this behavior, I can definitely stand his stupidity. I certainly don't amount to a villain when I wrongly displease him. So he doesn't either!"

Note that by approaching the situation in the ABCDE manner, you have not chosen to feel irresponsible about your fury at your boss, thereby encouraging future fury. You have honestly acknowledged your anger—but acknowledged *its* wrongness. You have made an attempt really to understand what you did to make yourself angry and what you can do in the future to stop making yourself enraged again. That seems the main point. You live most successfully with your anger *by understanding* it; by realistically seeing that humans easily and naturally make themselves angry, just as they easily and naturally over-eat and avoid going to the dentist; *by accepting* yourself for creating it; and *by showing yourself how to Dispute it.*

Israel Charny states, "The key to the psychotherapist's contributions, I believe, is that he teach an awareness and acceptance of the universality of *angry feelings* and inner wishes to destroy another human being, but that *overt acts* of such violence at another's person are never to be condoned except in clear self-defense against physical attacks." I agree. Then Charny goes on: "However, to feel like hitting is not wrong. Even to feel like killing is human." I agree that to feel like hitting your boss or even killing him when he acts badly to you constitutes a human, natural position. But I still think it wrong since your feeling goes with the overgeneralization that he has no right to act badly to you and deserves physical assault or death for acting that way. He does have the right. So no matter how human your anger, you'd better acknowledge it as foolish and mistaken while still fully accepting yourself with this idiotic behavior!

You can follow certain practical procedures that will let you get some of your steam off relatively harmlessly and also, perhaps, help those at whom you feel angry to reconsider their own behavior and perhaps modify it. For example:

1. Try to assert yourself to the people at whom you feel angry in I-statements rather than in you-statements. If you hate your boss for making you work overtime and not compensating you, don't say to him or her, "You keep treating me unfairly by making me work overtime! I don't understand how you can do that!" Such a statement distinctly accuses the other of rotten behavior and assumes

that he or she has full responsibility for that behavior and therefore shouldn't do it.

Instead, you can give the same message in the following kind of I-statement: "I feel that I keep getting asked to work overtime without additional compensation, and I don't like that. I wonder whether this kind of thing proves fair. And assuming that from my point of view it has an unfair element, I wonder how you see it from your point of view." This kind of I-statement shows your feelings and shows that you think of something as wrong, but it does so diplomatically and objectively. It reveals your displeasure, but not your immense anger—even if you happen to feel angry while stating it.

2. When you feel angry at people whom you think have acted badly and don't seem aware of the poor way they have acted, try to speak authoritatively rather than authoritarianly. If, for example, you have an employee who keeps coming in late, you don't have to say, "How can you do that all the time? You know goddamned well that we don't tolerate any lateness here!" You can say, instead, "I don't know whether anyone pointed it out to you clearly when you joined this firm, but the firm has a very strict policy about lateness. Anyone who comes even a few minutes late several times gets talked to by his or her supervisor and strictly penalized if he or she does not thereafter start coming on time. The company has had this rule for a long time and finds it advisable to stick to it; I therefore have called you in to talk about the problem of your lateness."

Of if you notice that someone in your class keeps asking to borrow your homework in order to copy it and you feel angry about this, you can say something like: "Maybe you don't agree with the homework rule and think it silly. But I have personally found that I really don't understand what goes on in class unless I regularly do my homework.

It seems to me that the only real way to learn this subject, or almost any other subject, consists of practicing it on one's own. So I feel that lending you my homework to copy won't really do you much good and that you'd do yourself a disservice by copying it. Therefore, I don't think I will lend it to you." This kind of response seems much better than your authoritarianly telling the attempted borrower, "Look, dear! One just does not borrow homework to copy in this class. That won't do at all!"

3. Usually you will get along much better in life if, when someone puts you down and you feel angry about it, you refrain from following suit and putting him or her down in turn. Such a revengeful retort will often make you feel better—but not get better. It will tend to make you feel more angry, and you will win the other's enmity. So your best retort frequently consists of seeming to agree with the put-down; ignoring it; agreeing with it in part; or showing the other person that you do not take it too seriously, do not agree with it, and can firmly but unangrily render it invalid.

If an acquaintance of yours, for example, laughs at you for dressing in a certain manner, you can make these kinds of retorts: (a) "Yes, my jacket does seem on the loud side"; (b) "I see that you really don't like the way I dress"; (c) "I guess my jacket does seem on the loud side but I find it exciting and attractive"; (d) "I can see what you mean and that others might agree with you, but I don't consider things like this that important"; (e) "Apparently we just don't agree on what constitutes loudness"; (f) "You may think it loud, but almost everyone seems to wear this kind of color these days, and you therefore may constitute a minority of one."

With these kinds of retorts, you hold your ground but do not display hostility to and put down others. Even when you feel angry as you respond in this way, your responses tend to calm you down and make you feel less rather than more irate. You never lose integrity by acting this way, for even if your "put-downer" thinks that you act weakly, that remains his or her problem, and you need never feel in any way truly put down.

4. As Herbert Fensterheim and Jean Baer rightly point out, this does not mean that you had better give an apologetic or self-downing retort when someone puts you down and you feel angry. If someone criticizes your taste in a jacket, you do not, in order to avoid a confrontation, reply, "Yes, I guess people do think less of me when I wear loud colors like this," or "Oh, I thought everyone was wearing this color this year, and that led me to buy this jacket." Acting weakly frequently encourages the other person to keep trying to put you down further and sets a bad example for still others, who may similarly try to take advantage of you. As I have stated in *How to Live with a "Neurotic,"* I normally advocate an attitude of firm kindness. Not unfirm kindness; not firm unkindness. Simply firm kindness—and the maintaining of your own integrity no matter what others may think of you.

5. Occasionally, you will find it best to retort to put-downs in a sarcastic, mean, or very critical manner, just as you will sometimes, though seldom, find it the better part of valor to fight physically with an opponent rather than to run away from him or her. For in certain groups—such as tough street-corner groups—if you don't combatively stand up for yourself and return unkindness in kind, the members of the group will view you as weak and prone to serving as a victim and will plague you practically forever.

Fensterheim and Baer give some good examples of how to respond in such circumstances, including (a) forcing yourself to answer instead of running away from the situation; (b) taking time to think of a good retort; (c) using you-statements instead of I-statements; (d) not asking the other to elaborate on what he or she finds wrong with you;

(e) learning some stock phrases, such as "What do you find so damned wrong with my behavior?" or "How come you seem so critical today?" However, I still would say: make this the exception rather than the rule, even when others have clearly tried to down you and you feel angry about this.

6. Don't think perfectionistically about your dealing with your own anger and replying to people when you feel angry at them. Inevitably, you will at times retort badly, weakly, and ineffectually, or you will make yourself so incensed that you will reply to them in an extremely bottled up, chokingly furious, perhaps unduly excoriating manner. So you will! It would prove lovely if you always handled yourself beautifully when angry and did not act like a horse's ass. But you *will* act that way at times; you darned well will!

If so, learn to accept yourself with your weakness—as well as with your anger. Your stupidity merely shows your humanity. (Leonardo da Vinci, Isaac Newton, and Albert Einstein frequently acted idiotically. And so do you.)

7. Acknowledge the possibility of your changing and of making yourself less angry. Perfect lack of hostility you will never achieve, but you can make yourself much less frequently and less intently irate. Try and don't give up too easily. Give yourself practice at talking yourself out of your rage, and try, at the same time, to talk some of your close friends and associates out of a good deal of their rage. If you can show some of them how to feel much less hostile, they will then tend to act as good examples for the becalming and eradicating of your own hostility.

8. When you do feel angry, try to acknowledge this to both yourself and others. Not always, of course! If you feel terribly angry at your school principal or at one of your students, perhaps you'd better pretend that you don't. But with your friends and associates—with whom you can act fairly honestly—by all means do so. Admit to them

how angry you feel—and also to yourself that *you* made yourself angry and that you sabotage your own happiness in the process. In so admitting, you will avoid the necessity of squelching your anger, keeping it under strong wraps (thereby consuming time and energy which you could much better spend in facing it and doing something to reduce it).

If you want to live successfully with your anger, you'd better do some of the very same things that you would do if you wanted to get rid of it. Rational processes—or what I and my associates would tend to call rational-emotive processes—work in much the same way whether you want to eliminate an emotional disturbance or live more happily while you, to some degree, still experience this disturbance. You can see this, for example, in Paul A. Hauck's book, *Overcoming Frustration and Anger*, one of the few treatises ever written on this subject from a rational-emotive viewpoint. Dr. Hauck gives several good rules for avoiding the buildup of hostile feelings and actions, but some of these rules also can serve you usefully if you still make yourself angry on a good many occasions and want to survive happily while you try to lessen your anger-creating experiences.

He points out, for example, that righteous indignation gives you no good excuse to remain angry, for all anger tends to include righteousness: "In fact, anger wouldn't arise in the first place if you didn't think you were completely right in your opinion and that the other person was completely wrong. That even applies to things and nature. When you give your flat tire an angry kick you really are trying to tell the world that that tire had no right to go flat on you, that it has done a mean and dirty trick, and that it deserves a kick for being such a lousy tire."

Recognizing your "righteous indignation" and fully facing its foolishness will help you stop kicking the tire—and also help you angrily kick it while humorously acknowledging your own anger and accepting it as part of your very fallible all-too-human condition.

Dr. Hauck shows that when you feel angry at a person or object, you frequently note real failings and can legitimately make yourself problem-oriented (to remove those failings), instead of blame-oriented (condemning the person or object for having deficiencies). Here he brings out the RET view that you'd better make yourself problem-centered rather than self-centered about virtually everything that happens wrongly in your life, whether caused by you or anyone else. But he goes a little beyond this to point out that when you feel angry, you can legitimately find yourself fault-oriented. "If you don't know what's at fault, you can't very well change the trouble. So being fault-oriented is good and not at all the same as blame-oriented."

Your anger, when you experience it, can help you see that something probably has serious faults and that you can note and try to remove or minimize these faults. In this sense, you can constructively use and live with your anger—if you employ it to help you detect your own, others', and the world's deficiencies, and to give serious thought, in a problem-oriented manner, to doing something to ameliorate these deficiencies.

Along the same lines, Dr. Hauck notes that "the trick is to *forgive everything*, and *forget nothing*." Nicely stated! For by forgiving me for promising to share an apartment with you and then reneging on my promise, by accepting me as a human *with* my crummy behavior, you can size up the problem of dealing with other incidents of this sort and perhaps you can prevent them from happening or deal more effectively with them if and when they do occur. Again, if you do this, you can live more successfully

with your feelings of anger by using them to assess my
failings, to figure out what to do about them, and thereby
to feel less angry and more problem-solving.

Paul Hauck also recommends the diversion technique
of counting to ten to help you deal with your anger: "As
corny as this may sound, the method nevertheless has
merit. It will not of course prevent you from thinking
angrily (only challenging the idea that you must have your
way can do that). But it will aid you in controlling your
anger long enough to prevent you from putting your foot
into your mouth and will give you time to collect your
thoughts."

Quite so. And similarly, you can use many of the other
diversion techniques mentioned in our chapter on behavioral methods not only to give yourself time to become
less angry but also to live more successfully with your
feelings of rage. As long as you see that these methods
temporarily interrupt but do not really cure your anger, as
long as you acknowledge that you still wrongly enrage
yourself, and as long as you use diversion to calm yourself
so that you can continue to work at eliminating your
anger, you can almost happily live with feelings of rage
and resentment while you count ten, take a walk, turn on
the TV set, or otherwise give yourself a breathing period
that interrupts your hostility-inspired tendencies to act
foolishly.

In conclusion, let me say that just about all the anger-
reducing methods outlined in this book can also help you
live much better and suffer much less while you still feel
enraged. In the course of your wrathful experiences you
can recognize that you basically create your own feelings,
that you can eventually think your way into unangry
channels, that you can divert yourself temporarily into
pathways that will reduce the intensity of the anger, that
you can focus on solving your problems with people and

things rather than on mainly upsetting yourself about them, that you can train yourself to feel and act less angrily, and that although rage seems to control you, you really have remarkable, albeit often unused, powers to control and change it. These very recognitions will help you live much better, with far less penalizing results, with your mild or severe hostile feelings.

You may find behaving in this manner sufficiently satisfying to stop right there. You don't *have to* make yourself unangry almost every time your anger rises. You can accept yourself with your resentful feelings and do yourself a lot of good by this very acceptance. I think you will often find, however, that when you consistently start to reach this stage, when you stubbornly refuse to down yourself when you feel angry and when you look more at the problem-solving aspects of obnoxious life situations and less at their "horrible" unfairness, you will probably want to go on to the next and more elegant step: surrendering your anger for a more forgiving, less damning attitude toward the world and the people in it. Not that you have to. But why not try it and see?

Appendix 1

SAMPLE RATIONAL-EMOTIVE THERAPY
HOMEWORK REPORT

SAMPLE HOMEWORK REPORT

Institute for Advanced Study in Rational Psychotherapy / 45 East 65th Street / New York, N.Y. 10021

(A) ACTIVATING EXPERIENCES (OR EVENTS)

I went for a job interview and I failed to get the job.

(B) BELIEFS ABOUT YOUR ACTIVATING EXPERIENCES

(rB) rational Beliefs (your wants or desires)

How unfortunate to get rejected!
I don't like getting rejected.
I wish I had gotten accepted.
How annoying!
Looks like I'll have difficulty getting the job I want.

(iB) Irrational Beliefs (your demands or commands)

1. How awful to get rejected!
2. I can't stand this rejection!
3. I should have given a better interview and got accepted.
4. This rejection makes me a rotten person.
5. I'll never get the kind of a job I want!
6. I'll always do poorly on job interviews.

(C) CONSEQUENCES OF YOUR BELIEFS ABOUT ACTIVATING EXPERIENCES

(deC) desirable emotional Consequences (appropriate bad feelings)

Sorrow and regret
Frustration and irritation
Determination to keep trying

(dbC) desirable behavioral Consequences (desirable behaviors)

Continued search for a job
Attempt to upgrade my skills

(ueC) undesirable emotional Consequences (inappropriate feelings)

I felt depressed.   I felt worthless.
I felt anxious.   I felt angry.

(ubC) undesirable behavioral Consequences (undesirable behaviors)

I refused to go for other job interviews.
I felt so anxious I functioned badly on other interviews.

(D) DISPUTING OR DEBATING YOUR IRRATIONAL BELIEFS

(State this in form of questions)

1. Why is it awful to get rejected for a job?
2. Why can't I stand this rejection?
3. What evidence exists that I should have acted better on the interview and got accepted?
4. How does this rejection make me a rotten person?
5. In what way will I find it impossible ever to get the kind of job I want?
6. Why must I always do poorly on job interviews?

(E) EFFECTS OF DISPUTING OR DEBATING YOUR IRRATIONAL BELIEFS

(cE) cognitive Effects of disputing (similar to rational beliefs)

1. Nothing makes it awful to get rejected, even though I find it highly inconvenient.
2. I can stand rejection, though I'll never like it.
3. I can find no reason why I should or must have given a better interview, though it would have proved nice if I had.
4. Rejection never makes me a rotten person—but a person with some unfortunate traits.
5. I won't find it impossible to get a good job, though I may find it difficult to do so.
6. I don't have to do poorly on job interviews always, especially if I try to learn from my errors.

(eE) emotional Effects (appropriate feelings)

I felt sorrowful but not depressed.
I felt concerned but not anxious.
I felt self-accepting.
I felt frustrated but not angry.

(bE) behavioral Effects (desirable behaviors)

I went for some more job interviews.
I started to look into getting some additional training.
I registered with an employment agency.
I sent out more letters applying for jobs.

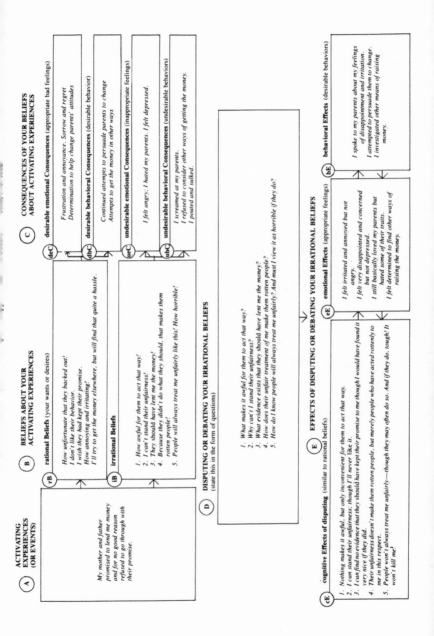

(A) ACTIVATING EXPERIENCES (OR EVENTS)

My mother and father promised to lend me money and for no good reason refused to go through with their promise.

(B) BELIEFS ABOUT YOUR ACTIVATING EXPERIENCES

(rB) rational Beliefs (your wants or desires)

How unfortunate that they backed out!
I don't like their behavior.
I wish they had kept their promise.
How annoying and irritating!
I'll try to get the money elsewhere, but will find that quite a hassle.

(iB) Irrational Beliefs

1. How awful for them to act that way!
2. I can't stand their unfairness!
3. They should have lent me the money!
4. Because they didn't do what they should, that makes them rotten people!
5. People will always treat me unfairly like this! How horrible!

(C) CONSEQUENCES OF YOUR BELIEFS ABOUT ACTIVATING EXPERIENCES

(deC) desirable emotional Consequences (appropriate bad feelings)

Frustration and annoyance. Sorrow and regret
Determination to help change parents' attitudes

(dbC) desirable behavioral Consequences (desirable behavior)

Continued attempts to persuade parents to change
Attempts to get the money in other ways

(ueC) undesirable emotional Consequences (inappropriate feelings)

I felt angry; I hated my parents.
I felt depressed.

(ubC) undesirable behavioral Consequences (undesirable behavior)

I screamed at my parents.
I refused to consider other ways of getting the money.
I pouted and sulked.

(D) DISPUTING OR DEBATING YOUR IRRATIONAL BELIEFS (state this in the form of questions)

1. What makes it awful for them to act that way?
2. Why can't I stand their unfairness?
3. What evidence exists that they should have lent me the money?
4. How does their unfair treatment of me make them rotten people?
5. How do I know people will always treat me unfairly? And must I view it as horrible if they do?

(E) EFFECTS OF DISPUTING OR DEBATING YOUR IRRATIONAL BELIEFS

(cE) cognitive Effects of disputing (similar to rational beliefs)

1. Nothing makes it awful, but only inconvenient for them to act that way.
2. I can stand their unfairness; though I'll never like it.
3. I can find no evidence that they should have kept their promise to me though I would have found it very nice if they did.
4. Their unfairness doesn't make them rotten people, but merely people who have acted rottenly to me in this respect.
5. People won't always treat me unfairly—though they may often do so. And if they do, tough! It won't kill me!

(eE) emotional Effects (appropriate feelings)

I felt irritated and annoyed but not angry.
I felt very disappointed and concerned but not depressed.
I still basically loved my parents but hated some of their traits.
I felt determined to find other ways of raising the money.

(bE) behavioral Effects (desirable behaviors)

I spoke to my parents about my feelings of disappointment and irritation.
I attempted to persuade them to change.
I investigated other means of raising money.

HOMEWORK REPORT

Institute for Advanced Study in Rational Psychotherapy / 45 East 65th Street / New York, N.Y. 10021

INSTRUCTIONS: Please fill out the **ueC** section (undesirable emotional Consequences) and the **ubC** section (undesirable behavioral Consequences) **first.**
Then fill out all the A-B-C-D-E's. PLEASE PRINT LEGIBLY. BE BRIEF!

(A) ACTIVATING EXPERIENCES (OR EVENTS)

(B) BELIEFS ABOUT YOUR ACTIVATING EXPERIENCES

(rB) rational Beliefs (your wants or desires)

(iB) irrational Beliefs (your demands or commands)

(C) CONSEQUENCES OF YOUR BELIEFS ABOUT ACTIVATING EXPERIENCES

(deC) desirable emotional Consequences (appropriate bad feelings)

(dbC) desirable behavioral Consequences (desirable behaviors)

(ueC) undesirable emotional Consequences (inappropriate feelings)

(ubC) undesirable behavioral Consequences (undesirable behaviors)

(D) DISPUTING OR DEBATING YOUR IRRATIONAL BELIEFS
(State this in the form of questions)

(E) EFFECTS OF DISPUTING OR DEBATING YOUR IRRATIONAL BELIEFS

(cE) cognitive Effects of disputing (similar to rational beliefs)

(eE) emotional Effects (appropriate feelings)

(bE) behavioral Effects (desirable behaviors)

W-UP. What new GOALS would I now like to work on? ....

....

....

....

c ACTIONS would I now like to take?..

....

....

on after feeling or noting your undesirable emotional CONSEQUENCES (ueC's) or your undesirable behavorial
NCES (ubC's) of your irrational BELIEFS (iB's) did you look for these iB's and DISPUTE them?................

....

....

usly did you dispute them? ....

....

t dispute them, why did you not do so?..

....

HOMEWORK ASSIGNMENT(S) given you by your therapist, your group or yourself: ....

....

....

d you actually do to carry out the assignment(s)? ....

....

any times have you actually worked at your homework assignments during the past week?..........................

....

any times have you actually worked at DISPUTING your irrational BELIEFS during the past week?................

....

you would now like to discuss with your therapist or group ....

....

....

by the Institute for Rational Living, Inc., 45 East 65th Street, New York, N.Y. 10021

Appendix 2

RATIONAL-EMOTIVE PSYCHOTHERAPISTS IN THE UNITED STATES, CANADA, AND ABROAD

A good many accredited RET practitioners exist in various parts of the United States and abroad. The Institute for Rational Living, 45 East 65th Street, New York, New York 10021, has a complete list of them and will send it to anyone who asks for it and encloses a stamped, self-addressed envelope. Some of the main centers and individuals that specialize in the practice of RET (some of whom also offer various professional or public education programs in RET) include the following:

ALABAMA

Ruth P. Thomas, M.S.W., 70 Heritage Hill, Tuscaloosa, Alabama 35401. (205) 345-2241.

ARIZONA

Scottsdale Guidance Center, 2923 North 67th Place, Scottsdale, Arizona 85251. (602) 945-3431. John Hudson, Ph.D., Director.

CALIFORNIA

Los Angeles Institute for Rational Living, 2100 North Sepulveda Boulevard, Manhattan Beach (near Los Angeles), California 90266. (213) 546-2711. John Minor, Ph.D., Director.

Institute for Rational Living, San Francisco Branch, 2435 Ocean Avenue, San Francisco, California 94127. (415) 334-3450. Virginia Anne Church, Ph.D., Director.

CANADA

Behavior Therapy Clinic, Lakeshore Psychiatric Hospital, 3131 Lakeshore Boulevard W., Toronto, M8V 1K9, Canada. (416) 239-0525. Stephen Neiger, Ph.D., Director.

Dr. Donald Meichenbaum, Psychology Department, University of Waterloo, Waterloo, H2L 3G1 Canada.

Jack Goldner, P.S.W., Student Counseling Services, Concordia University of Sir George Williams University, 1455 Quest Boulevard de Maisonneuve, Montreal, Canada. (514) 879-4028.

CONNECTICUT

Lee M. Silverstein, M.S.W., Erdoni Road, Columbia, Connecticut. (203) 524-2710.

FLORIDA

Institute for Rational Living, Clearwater Branch, 1409 Court Street, Clearwater, Florida 33516. (813) 441-3825. Erik Thoreson, Director.

Psychological Associates, 326 NE 26th Street, Miami, Florida 33137. (305) 573-7373. Leonard Haber, Ph.D., Director.

GEORGIA

Family Guidance Center and Institute for Personal Growth, 951 Edgewood Avenue, NE, Atlanta, Georgia 30307. (404) 688-0050. Robert Stein, Ph.D., Director.

ILLINOIS

Institute for Rational Living, Chicago Branch, 4747 West Peterson Avenue, Chicago, Illinois 60646. (312) 283-4111. Kenneth Peiser, Ph.D., Director.

Institute for Rational Guidance, 1511 South Fifth, Maywood, Illinois 60153 (near Chicago). (312) 344-0645.

Paul A. Hauck, Ph.D., 3425 53rd Street, Moline, Illinois 61265. (309) 764-3161.

John M. Gullo, Ph.D., 629 North Rutledge, Springfield, Illinois 62703. (217) 523-8131.

INDIANA

William C. Lucas, 109-C Knoll Court, Noblesville, Indiana 46060 (near Indianapolis). (317) 264-7557 or (317) 264-8013.

IOWA

Allan F. Demorest, M.A., 413 Snell Building, Fort Dodge, Iowa 50501. (515) 576-1221.

Mid-Eastern Iowa Community Mental Health Center, 302 South Gilbert, Iowa City, Iowa 52240. (319) 338-7884.

KANSAS

Department of Psychology and Counseling Services, Kansas State College, Pittsburg, Kansas 66762 (near Joplin). (316) 231-7000, Ext. 344. Dr. C. H. Merrifield, Director.

KENTUCKY

Rational Behavior Therapy Department, University of Kentucky Medical Center, Lexington, Kentucky 40506. (606) 233-6009. Maxie C. Maultsby, Jr., M.D., Director.

MAINE

Bangor Mental Health Institute, Box 926, Bangor, Maine 04401. (207) 947-3326.

MARYLAND

Irvin Greenberg, Ph.D., 1190 West Northern Parkway, Baltimore, Maryland 21210. (301) 433-7161.

Morris Roseman, Ph.D., 222 St. Paul Street, Baltimore, Maryland 21202. (301) 837-0830.

MASSACHUSETTS

Barbara Sansone, M.S.S.W., 43 Williams Street, Rehoboth, Massachusetts 02769 (near Boston). (617) 252-3898.

Richard Seaman, M.A., 140 Mt. Vernon Street, Newton, Massachusetts 02160 (near Boston). (617) 261-8585.

George J. Breen, M.Ed., 30 Commons Drive Court, Shrewsbury, Massachusetts 01545. (617) 844-9909.

MICHIGAN

Michigan Institute for Rational Living, Charles H. Baty, Ph.D., 30161 Southfield Road, Southfield, Michigan 48076 (near Detroit). (313) 642-1115.

W. Alan Canty, Ph.D., 906 Fisher Building, Detroit, Michigan 48202. (313) TR 5-0140.

Ned Papania, Ph.D. 16040 West McNichols, Detroit, Michigan 48235. (313) 273-8100.

William E. Carlson, Ed.D., Western Michigan University, 3109 Sangren Hall, Kalamazoo, Michigan 49001.

Delores B. Storey, Ph.D., 6161 Evanston Avenue, Muskegon, Michigan 49442. (616) 788-4696.

Peter Rettich, Ph.D., 2433 Fort Street, Wyandotte, Michigan 41892. (313) 283-4440.

MINNESOTA

Dana Lehman-Olson, Ph.D., 200 Nicollet Boulevard, E. Burnsville, Minnesota 55337. (612) 435-8195.

Meadowbrook Treatment Center, 6490 Excelsior Boulevard, Minneapolis, Minnesota 55426. (612) 788-1229.

Fairview Hospitals, Paul D. Arnold, Ph.D., 2312 South Sixth Street, Minneapolis, Minnesota 55406. (612) 332-0282, Ext. 323.

D. N. Weiner, Ph.D., 1920 South First Street, Minneapolis, Minnesota 55404. (612) 335-4400.

Ralph Underwager, Ph.D., 122 W. Franklin Avenue, Minneapolis, Minnesota 55404. (612) 871-2332.

MISSOURI

Dennis Doughterty, Ph.D., and Robert Costello, Ph.D., Rockhurst College, 5225 Troost Avenue, Kansas City, Missouri 64108. (816) 363-4010.

Patricia Lacks, Ph.D., 7345 Westmoreland, St. Louis, Missouri 63130. (314) 727-4617.

Jeanine Owen, Ph.D., 3 Pitman Place, St. Louis, Missouri 63122. (314) 965-3590.

NEW HAMPSHIRE

Peter Fernald, Ph.D., Conant Hall, University of New Hampshire, Durham, New Hampshire 03824. (603) 862-2360.

NEW JERSEY

Jefferson House, North Camden County Psychiatric Hospital, 589 Stevens Street, Camden, New Jersey 08103. (609) 964-0897.

Ft. Lee Consultation Center, 2015 Venter Avenue, Fort Lee, New Jersey 07024. (201) 944-5889.

Bernard Waltzer, Ed., D., 141 Madison Court, Livingston, New Jersey 07039. (201) 992-1431.

Murray O. Gegner, M.S., 210 N. Rumson Avenue, Margate, New Jersey 08402 (near Atlantic City). (609) 822-6571.

Arnold Lazarus, Ph.D., 56 Herrontown Circle, Princeton, New Jersey 08540. (609) 924-8450.

Liane Werts, M.S., 3413 Wells Drive, Parlin, New Jersey 08859. (201) 727-2653.

Maxim Young, Ph.D., 44 Niagara Lane, Willingboro, New Jersey 07046 (near Camden). (609) 871-0857.

NEW YORK

Robert Athanasiou, Ph.D., 13 Lawnridge Avenue, Albany, New York 12208. (518) 489-6971.

John Tucker, Ph.D., University Counseling Center, State University of New York at Albany, Albany, New York 12206. (518) 457-8038.

Solomon Goldstein, Ph.D., 110 Oak Street, Binghamton, New York 13905. (607) 724-8038.

Maria Moulton-Barrett, M.D., 42 Johnson Avenue, Binghamton, New York 13905.

Carmel Kussman, M.A., 19 Girard Street, Brooklyn, New York 11235. (212) 332-7685.

Dr. William Naigles and Heather Rieger, P.O. Box 323, Latham, New York 12110.

Joel Block, Ph.D., Island Professional Center, 100 Manetto Hill Road, Plainview, Long Island, New York 11803. (516) 822-6809.

Marvin Goldfried, Ph.D., and Gerald Davison, Ph.D., Department of Psychology, State University of New York at Stony Brook, Stony Brook, New York 11790.

Howard Kassinove, Ph.D., 3684 Crest Road, Wantagh, Long Island, New York 11793. (516) 785-5188.

Institute for Rational Living and Institute for Advanced Study in Rational Psychotherapy, 45 East 65th Street, New York, New York 10021. (212) 535-0822. Albert Ellis, Ph.D., Director.

Sol Gordon, Ph.D., 760 Ostrom Avenue, Syracuse, New York 13210. (315) 476-5541.

Leonard Hersher, Ph.D., Department of Pediatrics, State University
     of New York, 750 East Adams Street, Syracuse, New York 13210
     (315) 476-5541.
Richard Wessler, Ph.D., 90 Grandview Avenue, Pleasantville, New
     York 10570. (914) 769-3200 Ext. 286.
W. S. Applegate, Ph.D., 125 Eldridge Drive, Vestal, New York 13850
     (near Binghamton).

NORTH CAROLINA

William Reevy, Ph.D., Psychology Services Federal Correctional In-
     stitute, Old North Carolina Highway 75, Butner, North Carolina
     27509. (919) 575-4541.
John Reckless, M.D., John Reckless Clinic, 5504 Durham-Chapel Hill
     Boulevard, Durham, North Carolina 27707. (919) 489-1661.
Rowan County Mental Health Center, Salisbury, North Carolina
     28144. (704) 633-3616.

OHIO

Edwin E. Wagner, Ph.D., 76 North Revere Road, Akron, Ohio 44313.
     (216) 836-2816.
Cleveland Institute for Rational Living, 3659 Green Road, Cleveland,
     Ohio 44122. (216) 464-1144. James Bard, Ph.D., Director.
Dayton Area Psychological Service, 4130 Linden Avenue, Dayton,
     Ohio. (513) 256-5874.

OREGON

Wallowa County Mental Health Center, Wallowa Memorial Hospital,
     Enterprise, Oregon 97828. (503) 426-3111.
Joseph Matarazzo, Ph.D., Department of Medical Psychology, Uni-
     versity of Oregon Medical School, 3181 S.W. Sam Jackson, Port-
     land, Oregon 97201. (508) 225-8644.

PENNSYLVANIA

John Lembo, Ph.D., 117 Victoria Road, Millersville State College,
     Millersville, Pennsylvania 17551. (717) 872-5411, Ext. 241.
Maxim Young, Ph.D. Eastern Psychiatric Institute, Henry Avenue &
     Abbortsford Road, Philadelphia, Pennsylvania 19129. (215) 842-
     4494.
Edward Silverman, Ed.D., Governor Mifflin Apartments 117 D Colo-
     nial Drive, Shillingeon, Pennsylvania 19607 (near Reading). (215)
     355-0490.

Joseph G. Rosenfeld, Ph.D., 43 Springwood Drive, Southampton, Pennsylvania 18966 (near Philadelphia). (215) 355-5232.

Aaron T. Beck, M.D., 406 Wynmere Road, Wynnewood, Pennsylvania 19096 (near Philadelphia). (215) MI 9-2191.

RHODE ISLAND

Barbara Sansone, M.S.S.W., 43 Williams Street, Rehoboth, Massachusetts 02769. (401) 722-7855.

SOUTH CAROLINA

Jane Higbee, M.D., 1000 Rockwood Road, Columbia, South Carolina 29209.

TENNESSEE

Ruth Gat, M.S., 403 Tulsa Road, Oakridge, Tennessee 37830. (615) 483-7422.

TEXAS

G. Fred Cromes, M.D., Department of Physical Medicine and Rehabilitation, 5323 Harry Hines Boulevard, Dallas, Texas 75235. (214) 631-3220, Ext. 2288.

Donald A. Pool, Ph.D., Health Science Center, University of Texas, 5323 Harry Hines Boulevard, Dallas, Texas 75235. (214) 350-6723.

Barry Brown, M.D., 1417 Memorial Professional Building, Houston, Texas 77002. (713) 224-9287.

James L. McCary, Ph.D., Psychology Department, University of Houston, 3801 Cullen Street, Houston, Texas 77004. (713) 748-6600. Ext. 1841.

Mary Ruth Wright, M.A., 508 Hermann Professional Building, Houston, Texas 77030. (713) 797-9934.

VIRGINIA

Russell Grieger, Ph.D., 2319 Tarleton Drive, Charlottesville, Virginia 22901. (804) 973-3848.

Student Counseling Service, University of Virginia, Charlottesville, Virginia 22903. (804) 294-3633.

E. Lakin Phillips, Ph.D., Route 2, Box 275-E, Oakton, Virginia 22124 (near Washington, D.C.). (703) NO 7-2226.

Hearst and Fischer Psychological Associates, Pembroke 4, Suite 231, Virginia Beach, Virginia 23462.

WASHINGTON

Northwest Branch, Institute for Rational Living, 1214 Boylston Avenue, Seattle, Washington 98101. (206) 323-8181. John Williams, M.A., Director.

WASHINGTON, D.C.

Robert A. Harper, Ph.D., 4830 V St., N.W., Washington, D.C. 20007. (202) 377-4978.

WEST VIRGINIA

Hibbard Clinic, 615 Sixth Avenue, Huntington, West Virginia 25701. (304) 697-4752. Robert Hibbard, M.D., Director.

WISCONSIN

Louis W. Stamps, Ph.D., 2854 Scenic Drive, LaCrosse, Wisconsin 54601. (608) 784-7825.

Juliette Martin, Ph.D., Department of Psychology, University of Wisconsin, Milwaukee, Wisconsin 53201.

Eunice B. Thielen, M.S., 2303 North 49th Street, #9, Milwaukee, Wisconsin 53208. (404) 444-4340.

ENGLAND

Stephen Flett, Darenth Park Hospital, Dartford, Kent DA2 6LZ, Darmouth, England.

Institute for Rational Therapy, Kelsale Court, Kelsale, Suffolk, England. John Drummond, Director.

FRANCE

Emanuel Petrakis, 18 rue Boulegon, Aix-en-Provence 13100 France. 27-63-08.

GUATEMALA

Guillero A. Forno, M.D. Instituteo de Ciencias de la Conducta. 3a Calle Final, Zona 10, Guatemala City, Guatemala.

INDIA

P. M. Mathew, Mental Health Centre, Christian Medical College and Hospital. Vellore 2, India.

K. M. Phadke, K.M., Sir Sorabji Pochkanawala, Bankers Training College Juhu Vile Parle, Development Scheme, Ville-Parle (West), Bombay 400 056, India.

ISRAEL

Marilyn P. Safir, Ph.D., Psychology Department, University of Haifa, Mt. Carmel, Haifa, Israel.

MEXICO

Psicologos Asociados, Santa Monica 20, Mexico City, D.F., Mexico. 523-90-26; 536-50-48.

PUERTO RICO

Aracelis M. Nazario, M.A., Francisco M. Quinones Street 28, Sabana Grande, Puerto Rico 00747. (809) 873-5482.

NETHERLANDS

Instituut voor Rationele Therapie, Lombokstraat 22, Nijmegen, Netherlands. 080-232436. Rene Diekstra, Ph.D., Director.

Bibliography

In the following list of references you may find items preceded by an asterisk (*) of particular help if you want additional reading material in the general area of rational living or the specific area of living with and without anger. The Institute for Rational Living, Inc., 45 East 65th Street, New York, New York 10021, publishes or distributes the items in this list preceded by a check (√). The Institute will continue to make available these and other materials, as well as to present talks, seminars, workshops, and other presentations in the area of human growth and rational living. If interested, send for its current list of publications, events, and recordings.

Adler, Alfred. *Superiority and Social Interest.* H. L. and R. R. Ansbacher, eds. New York: Viking, 1973.

*———. *Understanding Human Nature.* Greenwich, Conn.: Fawcett, 1968.

Adler, Nathan. "Paris Had Its Hippies in the 1830s: They Drove the Establishment Mad." *California's Health,* 27(2) (1969), 7–11.

√*Alberti, Robert E., and Michael E. Emmons. *Your Perfect Right: A Guide to Assertive Behavior.* San Luis Obispo, Calif.: Impact, 1974.

———. "Assertion Training in Marital Counseling." *Journal of Marriage and the Family,* 2(1) (1976), 49–54.

Alvy, Kerby T. "Preventing Child Abuse." *American Psychologist,* 30 (1975), 921–28.

Amir, Yehuda. "Contact Hypothesis in Ethnic Relations." *Psychological Bulletin*, 71 (1969), 319–42.

Ansbacher, Heinz L. "Love and Violence in the View of Adler." *Humanitas*, 2 (1966), 109–27.

*Ansbacher, H. L., and R. R. Ansbacher. *The Individual Psychology of Alfred Adler*. New York: Harper & Row, 1970.

*Ard, Ben N., Jr. *Counseling and Psychotherapy*. Palo Alto, Calif.: Science and Behavior Books, 1976.

Ardrey, Robert. *Territorial Imperative*. New York: Delta, 1967.

Arendt, Hannah. "Reflections on Violence." *New York Review* (February 27, 1969), 19–32.

Aristotle. *Basic Works*. New York: Random House, 1941.

Arnold, Arnold. *Violence and Your Child*. Chicago: Regnery, 1969.

Bacon, Francis. *Essayes or Counsels*. New York: British Book Center, 1974.

Bach, George R. "A Theory of Intimate Aggression." *Psychological Reports*, 12 (1963), 449–50.

Bach, George R., and Herb Goldberg. *Creative Aggression*. New York: Avon, 1975.

*Bach, George R., and Peter Wyden. *The Intimate Enemy*. New York: Avon, 1971.

Bach, Richard. *Jonathan Livingston Seagull*. New York: Avon, 1973.

Baez, Joan. "Playboy Interview." *Playboy* (July 1970), 53–64, 136, 152–57.

*Bandura, Albert. *Aggression: A Social Learning Analysis*. Englewood Cliffs, N.J.: Prentice-Hall, 1973.

Bandura, Albert, and Clarissa Wittenberg. "The Impact of Visual Media on Personality." In Segal, J., ed., *Mental Health of the Child*. Washington: National Institute for Mental Health, 1971, 247–66.

Baraheni, Reza. "Torture in Iran: 'It Is a Hell Made by One Man for Another Man.'" *New York Times* (April 21, 1976), 37.

*Barksdale, L. S. *Building Self-esteem*. Los Angeles: Barksdale Foundation, 1974.

Barnett, S. A. "The Biology of Aggression." *Lancet* 2, No. 7363 (1964), 803–07.

Barton, Robert A. "Aggression as a Function of Magnitude of Victims' Pain Cues, Level of Prior Anger Arousal, and Aggressor-Victim Similarity." *Journal of Personality and Social Psychology*, 18 (1971), 48–54.

———. "Reducing the Influence of an Aggressive Model: The Restraining Effects of Peer Censure." *Journal of Experimental and Social Psychology,* 8 (1972), 266–75.

———. "Sexual Arousal and Physical Aggression." *Bulletin of the Psychonomic Society,* 3(5-A) (1974), 337–39.

———, and Paul A. Bell. *Effects of Heightened Sexual Arousal on Physical Aggression. Proceedings 81st Annual Convention of the American Psychological Association,* 1971.

———. "Aggression and Heat: The Influence of Ambient Temperature, Negative Affect, and a Cooling Drink on Physical Aggression." *Journal of Personality and Social Psychology,* 33 (1976) 245–53.

Baudhin, R. Scott, "Rational-Emotive Therapy and General Semantitherapy: A Review and Comparison." *ETC: A Review of General Semantics* 32 (1975), 107–113.

Baumrind, Diana. "Discussion of Symposium, Adolescents and Their Parents: Sources of Generational Conflict." Paper presented at the American Psychological Association Convention, San Francisco, 1968.

√*Beck, Aaron T. *Cognitive Therapy and the Emotional Disorders.* New York: International Universities Press, 1976.

√*Bedford, Stewart. *Instant Replay.* New York: Institute for Rational Living, 1974.

Bem, Daryl. "Self-perception." *Psychological Review,* 74 (1967), 183–200.

Bengis, Ingrid. *Combat in the Erogenous Zone.* New York: Knopf, 1972.

Berkowitz, Leonard. "The Effects of Observing Violence." *Scientific American,* 210(2) (1964), 2–8.

———. "On Not Being Able to Aggress." *Journal of Social and Clinical Psychology,* 5(2) (1966), 130–39.

*———. "Experimental Investigations of Hostility Catharsis." *Journal of Consulting and Clinical Psychology,* 35, (1970), 1–7.

———, James A. Green, and Jacqueline R. Macaulay. "Hostility Catharsis as the Reduction of Emotional Tension." *Psychiatry,* 25 (1962), 221–31.

———, John P. Lepinski, and Eddy J. Angulo. "Awareness of Own Anger Level and Subsequent Aggression." *Journal of Personality and Social Psychology,* 11 (1969), 293–300.

———, and Edna Rawlings. "Effects of Film Violence on Inhibitions Against Subsequent Aggression." *Journal of Abnormal and Social Psychology,* 66 (1963), 405–12.

Berlin, Irving N. "From Confrontation to Collaboration." *American Journal of Orthopsychiatry*, 40 (1970), 473–80.

Betts, Robert. "Religious Bigotry Compounds Woes of North Ireland." San Diego *Union* (April 28, 1969), A-6.

Bird, Lois. *How to Make Your Wife Your Mistress*. New York: Doubleday, 1972.

Blackburn, Ronald. "Personality in Relation to Extreme Aggression in Psychiatric Offenders." *British Journal of Psychiatry*, 19 (1968), 144, 821–25.

———. "Dimensions of Hostility and Aggression in Abnormal Offenders." *Journal of Consulting and Clinical Psychology*, 38 (1972), 20–26.

Block, Walter. *Defending the Undefendable*. New York: Fleet Press, 1976.

Boelkins, R. Charles, Jon F. Heiser. "Biological Bases of Aggression." In Daniels, D., ed., *Violence and the Struggle for Existence*. Boston: Little, Brown, 1970, 15–52.

Bolton, Ralph. Quoted in *Human Behavior* (August 1973), 62.

Boorstin, Daniel J. "A Case of Hypochondria." *Newsweek* (July 6, 1970), 27–29.

*Bourland, D. David, Jr. "A Linguistic Note: Writing in E-Prime." *General Semantics Bulletin*, 32–33 (1965–1966), 111–14.

———. "The Semantics of a Non-Aristotelian Language." *General Semantics Bulletin*, 35 (1968), 60–63.

Branden, Nathan. *The Psychology of Self-Esteem*. Los Angeles: Nash, 1969.

Brill, Henry, "Drugs and Aggression." *Medical Counterpoint*, 1(6) (1969), 33–38.

Brown, Paul, and Rogers Elliott. "Control of Aggression in a Nursery School Class." *Journal of Experimental Child Psychology*, 2 (1965), 103–07.

Buss, Arnold H. *The Psychology of Aggression*. New York: Wiley, 1961.

Casriel, Daniel. *A Scream Away from Happiness*. New York: Grosset & Dunlap, 1974.

Cavell, Edith. In George Seldes, *Great Quotations*. New York: Dell, 1967.

Charlton, Linda. "A Satisfying Job: Helping End the Abuse of Children." New York *Times* (August 24, 1975), E 9.

Charny, Israel W. "The Psychotherapist as Teacher of an Ethic of Nonviolence." *Voices*, 3(4) (1968), 57–66.

————. "Normal Man as Genocider." *Voices*, 7(2) (1971), 68–79.

Cline, Victor B. Quoted in "L Tracks That Violence Leaves." *Life* (January 1, 1970), 57–59.

Cline-Naffziger, Claudeen. "Women's Lives and Frustration, Oppression and Anger." *Journal of Counseling Psychology*, 21 (1974), 51–56.

Cogley, John. "Dorothy Day, Comforter." New York *Times* (November 11, 1972), 47.

Crawford, Ted, et al. R.D.S. (Revolving Discussion Sequence). Los Angeles, Calif. (P.O. Box 91725): R.D.S. Core Group, 1970.

Danto, Arthur. "Student Morality." *Columbia Forum*, 12(3) (1969), 34–38.

*Danysh, Joseph. *Stop Without Quitting*. San Francisco: International Society for General Semantics, 1974.

Daugherty, Robert I. Quoted in Seymour Shubin, "Coping with the Angry Patient." *Practical Psychology for Physicians*, 2(3) (March 1975), 28–38.

Davis, Robert G. "Rimbaud and Stavrogin in the Harvard Yard." *New York Times Book Review* (June 28, 1970), 2, 38.

Day, Dorothy. Quoted in John Cogley, "Dorothy Day, Comforter." New York *Times* (November 8, 1972), 47.

Delgado, Dr. Jose M. R. Quoted in Albert Rosenfeld, "The Psycho-Biology of Violence." *Life* (June 21, 1968), 67–71.

Deming, Barbara. "Nonviolent Battle." *Direct Action*, No. 90 (June 1968), 8.

Denenberg, Victor H., and M. J. Zarrow. "Rat Pax." *Psychology Today*, 3(12) (1970), 45–47, 66–67.

De Rivera, Joseph. *A Structural Theory of the Emotions*. New York: International Universities Press, 1977.

Deutsch, Morton. "Conflicts: Productive and Destructive." *Journal of Social Issues*, 25 (1969), 7–41.

————. *The Resolution of Conflict: Constructive and Destructive Processes*. New Haven: Yale University Press, 1972.

————. Review of Erich Fromm, *The Anatomy of Human Destructiveness*. *Contemporary Psychology*, 20 (1975), 106–07.

Dewey, John. *Human Nature and Conduct*. New York: Modern Library, 1930.

Dinkmeyer, Don, and Gary D. McKay. *Raising a Responsible Child*. New York: Simon & Schuster, 1973.

Dollard, John, Leonard W. Doob, Neal E. Miller, O. H. Mowrer, and

Robert R. Sears. *Frustration and Aggression*. New Haven: Yale University Press, 1939.

Donaldson, F. J. "On the Physiological Interpretation of Anger." *Central African Journal of Medicine*, 15 (1969), 79–82.

Donnerstein, Edward, Marcia Donnerstein, and Ronald Evans. "Erotic Stimuli and Aggression." *Journal of Personality and Social Psychology*, 32 (1975), 237–44.

Dorsey, John M. "A Psychotherapeutic Approach to the Problem of Hostility." *Social Forces*, 29 (1950), 198–206.

Drabman, Ronald S., and Margaret H. Thomas. "Does Media Violence Increase Children's Toleration of Real-life Aggression?" *Developmental Psychology*, 10 (1974), 418–21.

*Dreikurs, Rudolf. *Psychodynamics, Psychotherapy and Counseling*. Chicago: Alfred Adler Institute, 1974.

Dunlap, Knight. *Personal Adjustment*. New York: McGraw-Hill, 1946.

Efran, Michael G., and J. Allan Cheyne. "Affective Concomitants of the Invasion of Shared Space." *Journal of Personality and Social Psychology*, 29 (1974), 219–26.

Ekkers, C. L. "Catcholamine Excretion, Conscious Function and Aggressive Behavior." *Biological Psychology*, 3 (1975), 15–30.

Elizur, Abraham. Quoted in Anne Kaufman, "Coping with Anger." *New Outlook*, 23(6) (1969), 1–4.

√*Ellis, Albert. *Reason and Emotion in Psychotherapy*. New York: Lyle Stuart, 1962.

———. *The American Sexual Tragedy*. New York: Lyle Stuart and Grove Press, 1962.

√*———. *Executive Leadership: A Rational Approach*. New York: Citadel Press, 1972.

√*———. *Growth Through Reason*. Palo Alto, Calif: Science and Behavior Books; and Hollywood: Wilshire Books, 1973.

√*———. "The No Cop-out Therapy." *Psychology Today*, 7(2) (1973), 56–62. Reprinted: New York: Institute for Rational Living, 1973.

√*———. "Psychotherapy and the Value of a Human Being." In J. W. Davis, ed., *Value and Valuation: Essays in Honor of Robert S. Harman*. Knoxville: University of Tennessee Press, 1972. Reprinted: New York: Institute for Rational Living, 1973.

√*———. "Healthy and Unhealthy Aggression." Paper presented at the American Psychological Association 81st Annual Convention, Montreal, August 27, 1973. New York: Institute for Rational Living, 1973.

√*———. *The Sensuous Person: Critique and Corrections.* New York: Lyle Stuart and New American Library, 1974.

√*———. *Humanistic Psychotherapy: The Rational-Emotive Approach.* New York: Julian Press and McGraw-Hill Paperbacks, 1974.

√*———. *How to Live with a "Neurotic."* New York: Crown, 1975.

√*———. On the Disvalue of "Mature" Anger. Rational Living, 1975, 10(1), 24–27.

√*———. *Sex and the Liberated Man.* New York: Lyle Stuart, 1976.

√*———. "Fun as Psychotherapy." Paper presented at the American Psychological Association Convention, Washington, D.C., September 3, 1976. Tape recording: New York: Institute for Rational Living, 1977.

√*———. "The Biological Basis of Human Irrationality." *Journal of Individual Psychology,* 32 (1976), 145–68.

√*———. "Techniques of Handling Anger in Marriage," *Journal of Marriage and Family Counseling,* 2 (1976), 305–16. Reprinted: New York: Institute for Rational Living, 1977.

√*———. *A Garland of Rational Songs.* New York: Institute for Rational Living, 1977. Also: Tape recording.

√*———, and Russell Grieger. *Rational-Emotive Therapy: Handbook of Theory and Practice. New York: Springer, 1977.*

√*———, and John M. Gullo. *Murder and Assassination.* New York: Lyle Stuart, 1972.

√*———, and Robert A. Harper. *A Guide to Successful Marriage.* Hollywood: Wilshire Books, 1973.

√*———, and Robert A. Harper. *A New Guide to Rational Living.* Englewood Cliffs, N.J.: Prentice-Hall; and Hollywood: Wilshire Books, 1975.

√*———, Paul Krasner, and Robert Anton Wilson. "Impolite Interview with Dr. Albert Ellis." *Realist,* No. 16 (1960), 9–11; No. 17 (1960), 7–12. Reprinted: New York: Institute for Rational Living, 1970.

√*———, Janet L. Wolfe, and Sandra Moseley. *How to Raise an Emotionally Healthy, Happy Child.* Hollywood: Wilshire Books. 1972.

*Epictetus. *The Works of Epictetus.* Boston: Little, Brown, 1899. Also see Hadas, Moses.

*Erikson, Erik H. *Gandhi's Truth, or the Origins of Militant Nonviolence.* New York: Norton, 1969.

Eron, Leonard D. "Relationship of TV Viewing Habits and Aggressive Behavior in Children." *Journal of Abnormal Social Psychology,* 67 (1963), 193–96.

Etzioni, Amitai. "The Kennedy Experiment." *Western Political Quarterly,* 20 (1967), 361–80.

Evans, David R. "Specific Aggression, Arousal and Reciprocal Inhibition Therapy." *Western Psychologist,* 1 (1970), 125–30.

Falck, Hans S. "Thinking Styles and Individualism." *Bulletin of the Menninger Clinic,* 33 (1969), 133–45.

Farrelly, Frank, and Jeffrey Brandsma. *Provocative Therapy.* San Francisco: Shields Publishing Company, 1974.

*Fensterheim, Herbert, and Jean Baer. *Don't Say Yes When You Want to Say No.* New York: Dell, 1975.

Feshbach, Seymour. "The Function of Aggression and the Regulation of Aggressive Drive." *Psychological Review,* 71 (1964) 257–72.

*———. "Dynamics and Morality of Violence and Aggression." *American Psychologist,* 26 (1971), 281–92.

Fischer, Donald G., Harold Kelm, and Ann Rose. "Knives as Aggression-Eliciting Stimuli." *Psychological Reports,* 24 (1969), 755–60.

Fontana, Vincent J., Denis Donovan, and Raymond J. Wong. "The 'Maltreatment Syndrome' in Children." *New England Journal of Medicine,* 269 (1963), 1389–94.

Frank, Jerome D. "Control of Conflict and the Sense of Community. *International Understanding,*" 6 (1968) 5–10.

Frankl, Viktor E. *Man's Search for Meaning.* New York: Washington Square Press, 1966.

Freud, Sigmund. *Collected Papers.* New York: Collier Books, 1963.
———. *Civilization and Its Discontents.* London: Hogarth, 1949.

*Fromm, Erich. *The Anatomy of Human Destructiveness.* Greenwich, Conn.: Fawcett, 1974.

Gambaro, Salvatore, and Albert I. Rabin. "Diastolic Blood Pressure Responses Following Direct and Displaced Aggression After Anger Arousal in High- and Low-Guilt Subjects." *Journal of Personality and Social Psychology,* 12 (1969), 87–94.

√*Garcia, Edward, and Nina Pellegrini. *Homer the Homely Hound Dog.* New York: Institute for Rational Living, 1974.

Gardner, Richard A. "The Mutual Storytelling Technique in the

Treatment of Anger Inhibition Problems." *International Journal of Child Psychotherapy*, 1 (1972) 34–64.

Gautama Buddha. "Food for Thought." *Encounter*, 2(3) (1972), 2.

Geen, Russell S. "Effects of Frustration, Attack, and Prior Training in Aggressiveness Upon Aggressive Behavior." *Journal of Personality and Social Psychology*, 9 (1968), 316–21.

―――. "Perceived Suffering of the Victim as an Inhibitor of Attack-Induced Aggression." *Journal of Social Psychology*, 81 (1970), 209–15.

―――, and David Stonner. "The Meaning of Observed Violence." *Journal of Research in Personality*, 8 (1974), 55–63.

―――, David Stonner, and Gary L. Hope. "The Facilitation of Aggression: Evidence Against the Catharsis Hypotheses." *Journal of Personality and Social Psychology*, 31 (1975), 721–26.

Gendlin, Eugene. *Experiencing and the Creation of Meaning*. New York: Free Press, 1962.

*Gershberg, Jack M. "Psychotherapy and Problems of Hostility." *Pennsylvania Psychiatric Quarterly*, 5 (1965) 3–8.

Gil, David G. *Violence Against Children*. Cambridge: Harvard University Press, 1974.

Gilula, Marshall F., and David N. Daniels. "Violence and Man's Struggle to Adapt." *Science*, 164 (1969), 396–405.

*Ginott, Haim. *Between Parent and Child*. New York: Macmillan, 1965.

Glasser, William. *Reality Therapy*. New York: Harper, 1964.

Gold, Theodore. Quoted in Michael T. Kaufman, "Underground 'Exciting' to Gold." New York *Times* (March 3, 1970), 27.

Goldberg, Louis C. "Ghetto Riots and Others: American Civil Disorders in 1967." Paper given at American Sociological Association Convention, 1968.

*Goldfried, Marvin, and Gerald Davison. *Clinical Behavior Therapy*. New York: Holt, Rinehart and Winston, 1976.

*Goldfried, Marvin, and Michael Merbaum, eds. *Behavior Change Through Self-Control*. New York: Holt, Rinehart and Winston, 1973.

Goldman, Morton, John G. Kretschmann, and Nelle Westergard. "Feelings Toward a Frustrating Agent as Affected by Replies to Correction." *Journal of Social Psychology*, 88 (1972), 301–02.

√*Goodman, David, and Maxie C. Maultsby, Jr. *Emotional Well-Being Through Rational Behavior Training*. Springfield, Ill.: Thomas, 1974.

Gordon, Thomas. *Parent Effectiveness Training*. New York: Peter Wyden, 1971.

Gorney, Roderic. "Interpersonal Intensity, Competition, and Synergy Determinants of Achievement, Aggression, and Mental Illness." *American Journal of Psychiatry*, 21 128 (1971), 436–45.

Gornick, V., and M. Moran, eds. *Women in Sexist Society*. New York: New American Library, 1971.

Gottschalk, L. A., S. M. Kaplan, Goldine C. Gleser, and Carolyn M. Winet. "Variations in Magnitude of Emotion: A Method Applied to Anxiety and Hostility of the Menstrual Cycle." *Psychosomatic Medicine*, 24 (1962), 300–10.

*Graham, H. D., and T. R. Gurr. *Violence in America*. New York: New American Library, 1969.

*Greenwald, Harold. *Decision Therapy*. San Diego: Edits, 1977.

Grier, Williams, and Price Cobbs. *Black Rage*. Basic Books: New York, 1968.

Gunn, John and John Bonn. "Criminality and Violence in Epileptic Prisoners." *British Journal of Psychiatry*, 118 (1971), 337–43.

*Hadas, Moses, ed. *Essential Works of Stoicism*. New York: Bantam, 1962.

Hague, Patti. "Accepting Anger." *Radical Therapist*, 3(4) (1975), 11.

Haley, Jay. "The Amiable Hippie." *Voices*, 4(2), 1020 (1968), 102–10.
———. *Strategies of Psychotherapy*. New York: Grune and Stratton, 1963.

Hanratty, Margaret A., Edgard O'Neal, and Jefferson L. Sulzer. "Effect of Frustration upon Imitation of Aggression." *Journal of Personality and Social Psychology*, 21 (1972), 30–34.

Harlow, Harry F. Quoted in *Science News* (January 15, 1972), 43.
———. "Harlow's Lecture on Love in Relation Aggression." *APA Monitor* (December 1975), 3.

*Harper, Robert A. *The New Psychotherapies*. Englewood Cliffs, N.J.: Prentice-Hall, 1975.

Harris, Mary B., and George Samerott. "The Effects of Aggressive and Altruistic Modeling on Subsequent Behavior." *Journal of Social Psychology*, 95 (1975), 173–82.

√*Hauck, Paul A. *Overcoming Depression*. Philadelphia: Westminster Press, 1973.

√*———. *Overcoming Frustration and Anger*. Philadelphia: Westminster Press, 1974.

√*———. *Overcoming Worry and Fear*. Philadelphia: Westminster Press, 1975.

Hearn, Margaret T., and David R. Evans. "Anger and Reciprocal Inhibition Therapy." *Psychological Reports*, 30 (1972), 943–48.

Hebda, Mary E., Rolf A. Peterson, and Leon K. Miller. "Aggression Anxiety, Perception of Aggressive Cues, and Expected Retaliation." *Developmental Psychology*, 7 (1972), 85.

Heidigger, Martin. *Being and Time*. London: SCM Press, 1962.

Heimann, Paula, and Arthur F. Valenstein. "The Psychoanalytical Concept of Aggression: An Integrated Summary." *International Journal of Psychoanalysis*, 53 (1972), 31–35.

Helfer, Ray E., and C. Henry Kempe, eds. *The Battered Child*. Chicago: University of Chicago Press, 1968.

Henry, Andrew F., and James F. Short. *Suicide and Homicide: Some Economic, Sociological, and Psychological Aspects of Aggression*. New York: Free Press, 1954.

Henry, David D. Quoted in "How to Deal with Student Dissent." *Newsweek* (March 10, 1969), 66–71.

Hentoff, Nat. "On Basic Self-Defense at Public Meetings." *Evergreen Review* (July 1969), 69–71.

Herrell, James M. "Use of Systematic Desensitization to Eliminate Inappropriate Anger." *Proceedings 79th Annual Convention, American Psychological Convention*, 1971.

Hewes, David D. "On Effective Assertive Behavior: A Brief Note." *Behavior Therapy*, 6 (1975), 269–71.

Hinde, R. A. "Aggression in Animals." *Proceedings of the Royal Society of Medicine*, 63 (1970), 162–63.

Hokanson, Jack E. "Physiological Evaluation of the Catharsis Hypothesis." In Edwin I. Megargee and Jack E. Hokanson, eds., *The Dynamics of Aggression*. New York: Harper & Row, 1970, 74–86.

Hold, Anatol. Letter to *The Philadelphia Bulletin*. Quoted in Albert Ellis and John M. Gullo, *Murder and Assassination*. New York: Lyle Stuart, 1972.

Homme, Lloyd. *How to Use Contingency Contracting in the Classroom*. Champaign, Ill.: Research Press, 1969.

Hopper, A. E., E. O. Timmons, and J. R. Rawls. "Conditioning and Generalization of Hostile Verbalization." *Psychological Reports*, 25 (1969), 255–59.

*Horney, Karen. *Collected Writings*. New York: Norton, 1972.

Hovland, Carl I., and Robert R. Sears. "Minor Studies of Aggression: Correlation of Lynchings with Economic Indices." *Journal of Psychology*, 9 (1940), 301–10.

Howells, John. Quoted in "Deadly Parents." New York *Post* (April 24, 1975), 3.

Ilfeld, Frederick W., Jr. "Overview of the Causes and Prevention of Violence." *Archives of General Psychiatry*, 20 (1969), 675–89.

Jaffe, Yoram, Neil Malamuth, Joan Feingold, and Seymour Feshbach. "Sexual Arousal and Behavioral Aggression." *Journal of Personality and Social Psychology*, 30 (1974), 759–64.

Jahoda, Marie. "What Is Prejudice?" *World Mental Health*, 13 (1961), 38–45.

James, William. *Essays in Radical Empiricism*. New York: Longmans Green, 1922.

Janov, Arthur. *The Primal Scream*. New York: Dell, 1970.

Johnson, Roger S. Quoted in "Possible Cure for Violence." *Los Angeles Times News Service* (November 4, 1968).

Joseph, Edward D. "Aggression Redefined—Its Adaptational Aspects." *Psychoanalytic Quarterly*, 42 (1973), 197–213.

Jung, C. G. *The Practice of Psychotherapy*. New York: Pantheon, 1954.

Kaczkowski, Henry, and Katherine Owen. "Anxiety and Anger in Adolescent Girls." *Psychological Reports*, 31 (1972), 281–82.

Kahn, Marvin W., and William E. Kirk. "The Concepts of Aggression: A Review and Reformulation." *Psychological Record*, 18 (1968), 559–73.

Kanin, Eugene J. "Male Sex Aggression and Three Psychiatric Hypotheses." *Journal of Sex Research*, 1 (1965), 221–31.

Kaufman, Michael. "Underground 'Exciting' to Gold." New York *Times* (March 13, 1970), 27.

Kaufmann, Harry, and Seymour Feshbach. "The Influence of Antiaggressive Communications upon Responses to Provocation." *American Psychologist*, 18 (1963), 387–88.

Kelley, H. H. "Interpersonal Accommodation." *American Psychologist*, 23 (1968), 399–410.

*Kelly, George. *The Psychology of Personal Constructs*. New York: Norton, 1955.

Kelly, John. "Aggression in Children: Could It Be an Allergy?" *Practical Psychology for Physicians*, 2(12) (1975), 55–58.

Kennedy, Florynce. Quoted in Claudeen Cline-Naffziger, "Women's

Lives and Frustration, Oppression, and Anger: Some Alternatives." *Journal of Counseling Psychology,* 21 (1974), 51–56.

Kermani, E. J. "Aggression, Biophysiological Aspects." *Diseases of the Nervous System,* 30 (1969), 407–14.

King, Martin Luther. "Nonviolence: The Only Road to Freedom." *Ebony,* (October 1966), 27–34.

√*Knaus, William J. *Rational-Emotive Education: A Manual for Elementary School Teachers.* New York: Institute for Rational Living, 1974.

*Korzybski, Alfred. *Science and Sanity.* Lancaster, Pa.: Lancaster Press, 1933.

√*Kranzler, Gerald. *You Can Change How You Feel.* Eugene, Oreg.: Author, 1974.

Kuehn, John L., and John Burton. "Management of the College Student with Homicidal Impulses—The 'Whitman Syndrome.'" *American Journal of Psychiatry,* 125 (1969), 148–53.

Kurtz, Paul. "Notes from the Editor." *Humanist* (May–June 1969), 1.

Lang, Alan R., Daniel J. Goeckner, Vincent J. Adesso, and G. Alan Marlatt. "Effects of Alcohol on Aggression in Male Social Drinkers." *Journal of Abnormal Psychology,* 84, 5080 (1975), 508–18.

*Lange, Arthur, and Patricia Jakubowski. *Responsible Assertive Training.* Champaign, Ill: Research Press, 1976.

Lasch, C. Review of Erik Erikson, *Gandhi's Truth. New York Times Book Review* (July 13, 1969), 1, 22–23.

*Lazarus, Arnold. *Behavior Therapy and Beyond.* New York: McGraw-Hill, 1971.

√*———. *Multimodel Therapy.* New York: Springer, 1976.

√*———, and Allen Fay. *I Can If I Want To.* New York: William Morrow, 1975.

Lee, Alfred McClung. *Toward Humanist Sociology.* Englewood Cliffs, N.J.: Prentice-Hall, 1972.

Leland, Tom W. "Violence: Aggression Out of Control." *Voices,* 4(2), (1968), 56–57.

√*Lembo, John M. *Help Yourself.* Niles, Ill.: Argus Communications, 1974.

√*———. *The Counseling Process: A Rational Behavioral Approach.* New York: Libra, 1976.

Lévi-Strauss, Claude. Quoted in John L. Hess, "French Anthropologist, at Onset of 70's, Deplores the 20th Century." New York *Times* (December 31, 1969), 9.

Leyens, Jacques-Philippe, Leoncio Camino, Ross D. Parke, and Leonard Berkowitz. "Effects of Movie Violence on Aggression as a Function of Group Dominance and Cohesion." *Journal of Personality and Social Psychology*, 32 (1975), 346–60.

Lieberson, Stanley, and Arnold R. Silverman. "The Precipitants and Underlying Conditions of Race Riots." *American Sociological Review*, 30 (1965), 887–98.

Liebert, Robert M., and Robert A. Baron. "Some Immediate Effects of Televised Violence on Children's Behavior." *Developmental Psychology*, 6 (1972), 100–21.

Lion, J. R. "The Role of Depression in the Treatment of Aggressive Personality Disorders." *American Journal of Psychiatry*, 129 (1972), 347–49.

———, G. Bach-y-Rita, and F. R. Ervin. "Enigmas of Violence." *Science* (June 27, 1969), 1465.

Loew, Clemens A. "Acquisition of a Hostile Attitude and Its Relationship to Aggressive Behavior." *Journal of Personality and Social Psychology*, 5 (1967), 335–41.

Lorenz, Konrad. *On Aggression.* New York: Harcourt, Brace and World and Bantam Books, 1968.

———. Quoted in Walter Sullivan, "The Family to Lorenz Is All." New York *Times* (January 22, 1970), 39.

*Low, Abraham. *Mental Health Through Will-Training.* Boston: Christopher, 1950.

Lowen, Alexander. *The Betrayal of the Body.* New York: Macmillan, 1966.

Lunde, Donald T., and David A. Hamburg. "Techniques for Assessing the Effects of Sex Hormones on Affect, Arousal, and Aggression in Humans." *Recent Progress in Hormone Research*, 28 (1972), 627.

Lynn, John G. "Preliminary Report of Two Cases of Psychopathic Personality with Chronic Alcoholism Treated by the Korzybski Method." In *General Semantics.* New York: Arrow Editions, 1938. Reprinted Lakeville, Conn.: Institute of General Semantics, 1970.

*Mace, David. "Marital Intimacy and the Deadly Love-Anger Cycle." *Journal of Marriage and Family Counseling*, 2 (1976), 131–37.

*Marcus Aurelius. *The Thoughts of the Emperor Marcus Aurelius Antonius.* Boston: Little, Brown, 1900. Also see Hadas, Moses.

Marlatt, G. Alan, Carole F. Kosturn, and Alan R. Lang. "Provocation to Anger and Opportunity for Retaliation as Determinants of Alcohol Consumption in Social Drinkers." *Journal of Abnormal Psychology*, 84 (1975), 652–59.

Marler, Peter. "On Animal Aggression." *American Psychologist*, 31 (1976), 239–46.

*Maslow, A. H. *Toward a Psychology of Being*. Princeton: Van Nostrand, 1962.

———. "Toward a Humanistic Biology." *American Psychologist*, 24 (1969), 724–35.

√*Maultsby, Maxie C., Jr. *More Personal Happiness Through Rational Self-Counseling*. Lexington, Ky.: Author, 1971.

√*———. *How and Why You Can Naturally Control Your Emotions*. Lexington, Ky.: Author, 1974.

√*———. *Help Yourself to Happiness*. New York: Institute for Rational Living, 1975.

√*———, and Albert Ellis. *Technique for Using Rational-Emotive Imagery*. New York: Institute for Rational Living, 1974.

√*———, and Allie Hendricks. *You and Your Emotions*. Lexington, Ky.: University of Kentucky Medical Center, 1974.

Maurer, Adah, (chair). "The Real Roots of Violence." *Proceedings 80th Annual Convention American Psychological Association* (1972), 923.

May, Rollo. *Power and Innocence: A Search for the Sources of Violence*. New York: Norton, 1972.

McCord, William, Joan McCord, and Alan Howard. "Familial Correlates of Aggression in Nondelinquent Male Children." *Journal of Abnormal and Social Psychology*, 62 (1961), 79–93.

McNeil, Elton B. "Violence Today." *Pastoral Psychology*, 21 (1971), 216–30.

Meadows, Chris M. "Constructive View of Anger, Aggression, and Violence." *Pastoral Psychology*, 21 (1971), 9–20.

*Megargee, Edwin I., and Jack E. Hokanson, eds. *The Dynamics of Aggression*. New York: Harper & Row, 1970.

Meehl, Paul E., and others. "Violent Man." *Psychology Today*, 3(1) (1969), 52–63.

*Meichenbaum, Donald H. *Cognitive Behavior Modification*. New York: Plenum, 1977.

Meissner, W. W. "Toward a Theology of Human Aggression." *Journal of Religion and Health* (1972), 324–32.

Melden, A. "The Conceptual Dimensions of Emotion." In T. Mischel, ed., *Human Action*. New York: Academic Press, 1969.

Montagu, Ashley. "Original Sin Revised: A Reply to Recent Popular Theories on Aggression." *Vista* (January–February 1967), 2-9, 47–48.

————. "Social Interest and Aggression as Potentialities." *Journal of Individual Psychology*, 26 (1970), 17–31.

Mooney, Frank, and Michael Patterson. "'Must Forgive Boy,' Says Jennifer's Dad." New York *Daily News* (November 12, 1974).

Morris, Desmond. *The Naked Ape*. New York: McGraw-Hill, 1967.

√*Morris, Kenneth T., and H. Mike Kanitz. *Rational-Emotive Therapy*. Boston: Houghton Mifflin, 1975.

Moyer, K. E. "The Physiology of Violence: Allergy and Aggression." *Psychology Today* (July 1975), 77–79.

————. *The Psychology of Aggression*. New York: Harper & Row, 1975.

Murdoch, B. D. "Electroencephalograms, Aggression and Emotional Maturity in Psychopathic and Non-Psychopathic Prisoners." *Psychologia Africana*, 14 (1972), 216–31.

Murphy, Gardner. "A Note on the Locust of Aggression." *International Journal of Group Tensions*, 1 (1971), 55–58.

National Commission on the Causes and Prevention of Violence. "Statement on Campus Disorders. New York *Times* (June 10, 1959), 30.

National Commission on the Causes and Prevention of Violence. "TV and Violence." *U.S. News and World Report* (October 6, 1969), 55–56.

National Institute of Mental Health. *Selected References on the Abused and Battered Child*. Washington: U.S. Government Printing Office, 1972.

Nelson, Janice D., Donna M. Gelfand, and Donald P. Hartmann. "Children's Aggression Following Competition and Exposure to an Aggressive Model." *Child Development*, 40 (1969), 1085–97.

Novaco, R. *A Treatment Program for the Management of Anger Through Cognitive and Relaxation Controls*. Ph.D. Thesis, Indiana University, 1974. Also published as *Anger Control*. Lexington, Mass.: Lexington Books, 1975.

Olsen, Ken. *The Art of Hanging Loose*. Greenwich, Conn.: Fawcett, 1975.

Papanek, Helene. "Expression of Hostility: Its Value in the Psychotherapy Group." *Journal of Individual Psychology*, 18 (1962), 62–67.

Parker, Rolland S. *The Emotional Stress of War, Violence and Peace*. New York: Stanwix House, 1972.

Pearl, Mike. "Parents Voice a Plea for Son's Killer." *New York Post* (February 26, 1976), 2.

Perls, Frederick C. *Gestalt Therapy Verbatim*. Lafayette, Calif.: Real People Press, 1969.

———. *Ego, Hunger and Aggression*. New York: Random House, 1969.

Peters, H. "The Education of the Emotions." In Magda Arnold, ed., *Feelings and Emotions*. New York: Academic Press, 1970, 187–203.

Pierce, Chester M. "Violence and Counterviolence: The Need for a Children's Domestic Exchange." *American Journal of Ortho-Psychiatry*, 39 (1969), 553–68.

Pinderhughes, Charles A. "Understanding Black Power: Processes and Proposals." *American Journal of Psychiatry*, 125 (1969), 106–11.

Pisano, Richard, and Stuart P. Taylor. "Reduction of Physical Aggression: The Effects of Four Strategies." *Journal of Personality and Social Psychology*, 19 (1971), 237–42.

Plato. *Dialogues of Plato*. New York: Random House, 1937.

Polk, Kenneth. "Class, Strain and Rebellion Among Adolescents." *Social Problems*, 17 (1969), 214–24.

Premack, David. "Reinforcement Theory." In D. Levine, ed., *Nebraska Symposium on Motivation*. Lincoln, Nebraska: University of Nebraska Press, 1965.

Rader, Dotson. "The Sexual Nature of Violence." New York *Times* (October 22, 1973), 32.

Radomisli, Michel. "Special Book Review: Love, Friendship and Aim-Inhibited Aggression." *Psychoanalytic Review*, 55 (1968) 57–61.

*Raimy, Victor. *Misunderstandings of Self*. San Francisco: Jossey-Bass, 1975.

Ramsay, R. W. "Emotional Training." *Behavioral Engineering*, 1 (1974), 24–26.

Ransford, H. Edward. "Isolation, Powerlessness, and Violence: A Study of Attitudes and Participation in the Watts Riot." *American Journal of Sociology*, 73 (1968), 581–91.

Reich, Wilhelm. *Character Analysis*. New York: Orgone Institute Press, 1949.

*Rimm, David C., and John C. Masters. *Behavior Therapy*. New York: Academic Press, 1974.

———, Joanne C. DeGroot, Parthena Boord, Julia Heiman, and Paul V. Dillow. "Systematic Desensitization of an Anger Response." *Behavior Research and Therapy*, 9 (1971), 273–80.

Robbins, Paul R., and Roland H. Tanck. "Community Violence and Aggression in Dreams: An Observation." *Perceptual and Motor Skills*, 29 (1969), 41–42.

Rochlin, Gregory. *Man's Aggression: The Defense of the Self.* Boston: Houghton Mifflin, 1973.

Roether, Hermann, and Joseph J. Peters. "Cohesiveness and Hostility in Group Psychotherapy." *American Journal of Psychiatry*, 128 (1972), 1014–17.

Rogers, Carl R. *On Becoming a Person.* Boston: Houghton Mifflin, 1961.
———. *Becoming Partners.* New York: Delta, 1973.

Rogers, Martin, and Barbara Bryant. Quoted in "Gay Activists and Mental Health." *Human Behavior* (August 1973), 44.

Rokeach, Milton. *The Nature of Human Values.* New York: Free Press, 1973.

Rosenthal, David. Quoted in "Inherited Criminality Supported by Rosenthal." *American Psychological Association Monitor*, 4(3) (1973), 6–7.

Roth, Martin. "Human Violence as Viewed from the Psychiatric Clinic." *American Journal of Psychiatry*, 128 (1972), 1043–56.

Rothenberg, Albert. "On Anger." *American Journal of Psychiatry*, 128 (1971), 454–60.

Rotter, Julian. *Clinical Psychology.* Englewood Cliffs, N.J.: Prentice-Hall, 1964.

Rubin, Theodore I. *The Angry Book.* New York: Macmillan, 1969.

Russell, Bertrand. *Marriage and Morals.* New York: Liveright, 1929.
———. *The Conquest of Happiness.* New York: Bantam, 1968.

Ryle, Gilbert. *The Concept of Mind.* London: Hutchinson House, 1949.

Ryterband, Edward C. "The Naked Ape." *Psychology Today*, 2(3) (1968), 10.

Sagarin, Edward, "On the Positive Function of Hatewa Hatewhite." *Salmagundi*, 1(1) (1965), 56–64.

Sampson, Ronald. "Prime Minister Without Portfolio." *Nation*, 209 (1969), 509–10.

Sanford, Nevitt. Quoted in "Violence and Psychological Sources of Aggression." *Wright Institute Report* (Winter-Spring 1976), 4.

Sartre, Jean Paul. *Existentialism and Human Emotion.* New York: Philosophical Library, 1957.

Schacter, Stanley. *Emotion, Obesity and Crime.* New York: Academic Press, 1971.

Schwebel, Milton. "Confrontation." *American Journal of Orthopsychiatry,* 40 (1970), 183–87.

Schwitzgebel, Ralph K. Quoted in John H. Fenton, "Psychologists Test Electronic Monitoring to Control Parolees." New York *Times* (September 7, 1969), 85.

Shepard, Richard F. "1915 Genocide Is Still Vivid to Armenians Here." New York *Times* (April 24, 1975), 37, 59.

Sherif, Muzafer and Carolyn W. Sherif, *Groups in Harmony and Tension.* New York: Harper & Row, 1953.

*Shibles, Warren. *Emotion.* Whitewater, Wis.: Language Press, 1974.

Shortell, James R., and Henry B. Biller. "Aggression in Children as a Function of Sex of Subject and Sex of Opponent." Extended version of a Brief Report in *Developmental Psychology* (1970), 43–56.

*Siegel, Bernard J. "Defensive Cultural Adaptation." In H. D. Graham and T. R. Gurr, eds., *Violence in America.* New York: New American Library, 1969.

Silverman, Lloyd H. "A Technique for the Study of Psychodynamic Relationships." *Journal of Consulting Psychology,* 30 (1966), 103–11.

"Six Youths Burn Woman to Death in Boston Attack." New York *Times* (October 4, 1973), 1, 34.

Skinner, B. F. *Beyond Freedom and Dignity.* New York: Knopf, 1971.

Smaby, Marlowe H., and Armas W. Tamminen. "Counselors Can Be Assertive." *Personnel and Guidance Journal,* 54 (1976), 421–24.

*Smith, Manuel J. *When I Say No, I Feel Guilty,* New York: Bantam, 1975.

Solnit, Albert J. "Aggression: A View of Theory Building in Psychoanalysis." *Journal of the American Psychoanalytic Association,* 20 (1972), 435–40.

Solomon, Philip, and Susan T. Kleeman. "Medical Aspects of Violence." *California Medicine,* 114 (1971), 19–24.

Solzhenitsyn, Aleksandr I. "Peace and Violence." New York *Times* (September 15, 1973), 31.

Spiegel, John P. "The Dynamics of Violent Confrontation." *International Journal of Psychiatry,* 10 (1972), 93–130.

Spinoza, Baruch. *Improvement of the Understanding, Ethics, and Correspondence.* New York: Dunne, 1901.

Spock, Benjamin. *Decent and Indecent.* New York: McCall's, 1970.

280 HOW TO LIVE WITH—AND WITHOUT—ANGER

Spotnitz, Hyman. Quoted in "Handling Violent Feelings in Group Psychotherapy." *Frontiers of Psychiatry*, 1(18) (1971), 2.

*Storr, Anthony. *Human Aggression*. New York: Atheneum, 1968.

Surgeon General's Scientific Advisory Committee on Television and Social Behavior, United States Public Health Services. *Television and Growing Up: The Impact of Televised Violence*. Rockville, Md.: U.S. Department of Health, Education and Welfare, 1971.

Taylor, Stuart P., and Charles B. Gammon. "Effects of Type and Dose of Alcohol on Human Physical Aggression." *Journal of Personality and Social Psychology*, 32 (1975), 169–75.

———, and Ian Smith. "Aggression as a Function of Sex of Victim and Male Subject's Attitude Toward Women." *Psychological Reports*, 35 (1974), 1095–98.

Thompson, William I. "We Become What We Hate." New York *Times* (July 25, 1971), E 11.

Tiger, Lionel. *Men in Groups*. New York: Random House, 1969.

Tinbergen, N. "On War and Peace in Animals and Man." *Science*, 160 (1968), 1411–18.

———. Quoted in Walter Sullivan, "Behaviorist Thinks Aggression Is Both Instinctive and Learned." New York *Times* (October 28, 1968), 6.

*Toch, Hans H. *Violent Men: An Inquiry into the Psychology of Violence*. Chicago: Aldine, 1969.

√*Tosi, Donald J. *Youth: Toward Personal Growth, A Rational-Emotive Approach*. Columbus, Ohio: Merrill, 1974.

Trieschman, Albert E. "Temper, Temper, Temper, Temper, Temper!" *New York Times Magazine* (April 12, 1970), 101–11.

Trotter, Robert J. "Aggression: A Way of Life for the Qolla." *Science News* (February 3, 1973), 76–77.

Truax, Charles, and Robert Carkhuff. *Toward Effective Counseling and Psychotherapy*. Chicago: Aldine, 1967.

Ulrich, Roger, and Marshall Wolfe. "Research and Theory on Aggression and Violence." *Science Teacher*, 36 (1969), 12–18.

Usdine, Gene L. "Civil Disobedience and Urban Revolt." *American Journal of Psychiatry*, 125 (1969), 1537–43.

Vandenberg, Steven G. Quoted in "Research on Twins Suggests Hostility May Be Inherited." New York *Times* (August 24, 1968), 22.

Van den Berghe, Pierre L. "Bringing Beasts Back In: Toward a Biosocial Theory of Aggression." *American Sociological Review*, 39 (1974), 777–88.

Van der Veen, Marjorie. "Family Journal." *Voices*, 7(4) (1972), 49.

Wachtel, Andrew S., and Martha Penn Davis. "Riots: Psychologic Techniques of Prevention and Control." *Journal of the Tennessee Medical Association*, 62 (1969), 1129–31.

Waddington, C. H., and others. "Why Is Man Aggressive?" *Impact of Science on Society*, 18 (1968), 85–95.

Wagner, Mervyn K. "Reinforcement of the Expression of Anger Through Role-Playing." *Behavior Research and Therapy*, 6 (1968), 91–95.

Walters, Richard H. "Implications of Laboratory Studies of Aggression for the Control and Regulation of Violence." *The Annals*, 364 (1966), 60–72.

Watzlawack, Paul, John Weakland, and Richard Fisch. *Change*. New York: Norton, 1974.

Wertham, Frederic. Quoted in "Nazi Killing of Mental Patients Held Related to Violence Today." *Frontiers of Hospital Psychiatry* (April 1, 1969), 3.

Williams, Denis. "Neural Factors Related to Habitual Aggression." *Brain*, 92 (1969), 503–20.

Windholz, George. "Discrepancy of Self and Ideal-Self and Frequency of Hero, Sexual and Hostile Daydreams Reported by Males." *Psychological Reports*, 25 (1969), 136–38.

Wittgenstein, Ludwig. *Philosophical Investigations*. New York: Macmillan, 1958.

Wolfe, Janet L. "Aggression vs. Assertiveness." *Practical Psychology for Physicians*, 2(1) (1975), 44.

*———, and Iris G. Fodor. "A Cognitive-Behavioral Approach to Modifying Assertive Behavior in Women." *Counseling Psychologist*, 5(4), (1976), 45–52.

Wolff, H. H. "The Role of Aggression in the Psychopathology of Illness." *Journal of Psychosomatic Research*, 13 (1969), 315–20.

Wolfgang, Marvin, and Franco Ferracuti, *The Subculture of Violence*. London: Tavistock Publications, 1967.

Wolpe, Joseph. *Psychotherapy by Reciprocal Inhibition*. Stanford: Stanford University Press, 1958.

———, and Lazarus, Arnold. *Behavior Therapy Techniques*. New York: Pergamon Press, 1966.

Woods, Sherwyn. "Violence: Psychotherapy of Pseudohomosexual Panic." *Archives of General Psychiatry*, 27 (1972), 255–58.

Yalom, Irving. *The Theory and Practice of Group Psychotherapy*. New York: Basic Books, 1975.

√*Young, Howard S. *A Rational Counseling Primer*. New York: Institute for Rational Living, 1974.

Zaslow, Robert. "Rage Reduction." *Explorations*, No. 17 (1969–1970), 17–20.

Zinberg, Norman H., and G. A. Fellman. "Violence: Biological Need and Social Control." *Social Forces*, 45 (1967), 533–41.

Index